Ozark Vernacular Houses

A Study of Rural Homeplaces in the Arkansas Ozarks 1830–1930

Ozark Vernacular Houses

A Study of Rural Homeplaces in the Arkansas Ozarks 1830–1930

Jean Sizemore

The University of Arkansas Press
Fayetteville • 1994

Manufactured in the United States of America

98 97 96 95 5 4 3 2

Designed by Ellen Beeler

The paper used in this publication meets the minimum requirements of the American National Standard for Permanence of Paper for Printed Library Materials Z39.48-1984. ♾

Library of Congress Cataloging-in-Publication Data

Sizemore, Jean.
Ozark vernacular houses: a study of rural homeplaces in the Arkansas Ozarks, 1830–1930 / Jean Sizemore.
p. cm.
Based on a thesis (doctoral)—University of Iowa, 1989.
Includes bibliographical references (p.).
ISBN 1-55728-310-9
1. Vernacular architecture—Arkansas—History—19th century. 2. Vernacular architecture—Arkansas—History—20th century. 3. Vernacular architecture—Ozark Mountains Region—History—19th century. 4. Vernacular architecture—Ozark Mountains region—History—20th century. I. Title.
NA730.A5S59 1994
728'.37'09767109034—dc20 94-18052
CIP

To all the Ozark people, who,

with their unfailing generosity of spirit,

answered my questions and entrusted me

with their memories

Contents

Preface

For several decades the Arkansas Ozarks region has proven to be fertile ground for students of traditional culture. Folklorists, geographers, historians, archaeologists, and musicologists have documented the customs, folk music, folk tales, agricultural practices, and Native American archaeological sites of the region. Strangely, traditional architecture has been largely ignored. This book is based upon a more voluminous and detailed study intended to rectify this omission, "Ozark Vernacular: A Study of Rural Houses in the Arkansas Ozarks, 1830–1930" (Ph.D. diss., University of Iowa), completed by this author in 1989. It is hoped that persons desiring to see additional photographs, to have more detailed information and to have more scholarly documentation will refer to the dissertation.

The material presented in this book is based upon months of extensive fieldwork conducted in preparation for the dissertation. This fieldwork was conducted using standard fieldwork techniques for comprehensive architectural inventories adopted by state historic preservation programs throughout the United States. By consulting quadrant maps of the United States Geological Survey for a given area, the researcher documented each house judged to be fifty years old or older with photographs, measurements, and field sketches. Both house plans and site plans were drawn and outbuildings were included in the documentation. For those houses selected for inclusion in the book, supporting documentation included personal interviews, early survey maps, old tax records, census and agricultural records, files and publications of county historical societies, old photograph collections, and archives of the special collections at both the University of Arkansas at Fayetteville and the University of Arkansas at Little Rock. Extensive use was made of both the architectural survey files and the files of the National Register of Historic Places at the Arkansas Historic Preservation Program. As a former architectural historian with the Arkansas Historic Preservation Program, the author helped conduct the comprehensive architectural survey of Stone County. Later the author independently conducted further fieldwork in Washington County and in selected areas of Madison County with funding from a research and travel grant from the Samuel Kress Foundation awarded by the School of Art and Art History of the University of Iowa.

A key issue that arises in any study of rural houses is the difficulty of precisely determining their construction dates. There are no building permits in rural areas; deeds often omit mention of structures on the land in question. Tax records have been assumed to be the most reliable indicators of construction dates. If an individual's tax records appeared to rise an appreciable amount in a given year that seems compatible with the estimated age of the house, then it is customarily assumed that the house was constructed around this time. Two difficulties with this procedure are that a small log structure might not represent an appreciable interest in tax assessment, and, secondly, it is well known that among the early settlers many Ozarkians were squatters. Despite these problems, early tax records were consulted to help date the older houses chosen for inclusion in this study. In the case of twentieth-century houses, generally an older member of the family could recall the construction date of the house or could date it from an old photograph and from the ages of the family members appearing in it. In such cases, this oral history construction date was accepted.

The faculty of the School of Art and Art History at the University of Iowa must be acknowledged for awarding me a generous grant through the Kress Foundation, making possible the fieldwork for the dissertation upon which this book is based. My advisor, Dr. Robert Alexander, over long distances, provided excellent direction, and my committee, Professors Wallace Tomasini, Robert Rorex, Wayne Begley, and Malcolm Rohrbaugh, made helpful suggestions.

Prof. Cyrus Sutherland of the University of Arkansas at Fayetteville was generous in sharing his extensive knowledge of Arkansas's vernacular architecture and in supporting the publication of this book. Several of my colleagues at the University of Arkansas at Little Rock deserve recognition: Donald Van Horn, chair of the art department, provided financial support for the graphics in the book; Dr. Gerald Hanson of the geography department drew maps; Dr. Byrd Gibbens of the English department helped with editing and gave her ever-warm encouragement; and my colleague in art history, Dr. Floyd Martin, deserves thanks on many levels, both personal and professional.

Throughout, I have depended upon my long-time friend, Dr. Sarah Brown, as a sounding board for ideas and as an unfailing source of knowledge about Arkansas architecture on both a scholarly and practical level. Another friend, Stephen Phillips, at a critical juncture, drew dozens of floor plans.

My appreciation is also extended to several archivists and historians whose cooperation was unfailing: Mary Parsons of the Shiloh Museum of Ozark History; Dr. Ethel Simpson of the University of Arkansas Special Collections; Shelley Wold and Linda Pine at the UALR library; and Ken Story at the Arkansas Historic Preservation Program.

In Stone County, local historian Edwin Luther untiringly shared with me his old photographs and encyclopedic knowledge of the county and the region.

As the dedication of this book indicates, I count myself fortunate to have spent many hours with members of an older generation of Ozark people, who have managed to retain an endearing hospitality, a solid integrity of character, and a simple lifestyle. On front porches and around kitchen tables, they have given me great gifts of spirit. Because this book would have taken a very different shape without them, I must single out the following: Novelle Blair Baumert and Jimmie and Cleda Driftwood of Stone County and Caswell Wilson and the late Rollans Wilson of Washington County. Mrs. Baumert and the Wilson brothers enabled me to draw the furnishings plans for the houses in which they grew up and to obtain much information about how Ozark families lived in these traditional spaces. In addition, I would like to mention several more who were also especially generous in sharing their time and their old photographs with me: In Stone County, Dorothy and Jimmie Ford and Mrs. Essie Ford, all of St. James; Lloyd Richardson of Timbo; Guy Lancaster and Thurlow Williams of Herpel; and Harmon Avey and the late Lonnie Avey of Big Spring. In Washington County, Ernest Bodine of Maguiretown; Sally O'Reilly of Evansville; Mrs. Agnes Pierce and Clara and Renzo Hurst of Cove Creek; Lloyd McConnell and Sylvia and Tom Howard of Fayetteville; and May and Charlie Stokenbury of Elkins. In Madison County, Geraldine and Pat Hamilton of Old Alabam; Clara and Lester Neal of Huntsville; Remmel Lawson of Drake's Creek; and Millard Johnson of Wesley.

At the University of Arkansas Press, my warmest thanks extend to my editor, Scot Danforth, for his great qualities as a human being and for his making the chore of preparing the manuscript as pleasant as possible. Thanks also to Ellen Beeler for her talent in layout and production and for her caring about the book.

Finally, at the place where it is customary for authors to thank their families, I look back to my unlikely beginnings of graduate school and a career in art history in mid-life, and I realize anew how much loving support I have received from my family. I would like to publicly thank my oldest sons, Chip and Chris, for helping financially in the hard times; my daughter, Deborah, for being my stalwart comforter and for assuming child-care responsibilities beyond her years; my youngest son, Ben, for being a cheerful latchkey child and for forgiving me for missing years of soccer games; John, who said yes from the beginning; and now, Fred, our closeness has eased the way of completing the circle and the book.

Chapter 1

Overview of Ozark Vernacular Houses

Time is running out for the ordinary and unpretentious houses that people in the rural Arkansas Ozarks built for themselves in the period from 1830 to 1930 and for our opportunities to observe them. Since the structures are overwhelmingly constructed of wood, they are deteriorating rapidly. Many are vacant; the simplicity and practicality that are their essence are also their undoing, for they are largely unappreciated both by the families whose forebears built them and by most preservationists who are accustomed to prizing buildings that are imposing and unusual, rather than ordinary.

While studies of traditional Ozark culture that focus on music, folk speech, and folk tales have flourished in recent decades, traditional houses in the countryside have been overlooked.[1] There are fundamental questions to be asked: What are the characteristics of traditional Arkansas Ozark houses? How do these houses relate to other vernacular houses in the Upland South? And what is the relationship of traditional houses to the predominant geographic subregions within the Arkansas Ozarks? Beyond this basic classifying activity, however, this work seeks to create a broader architectural history that links the dwelling with the farmstead, with construction materials and methods, with the traditional landscape, and with the way of life that the dwelling shelters.

The traditional rural Ozark dwelling never stands alone, but has its particular setting in the land and its own varying arrangements of fences and outbuildings. An underlying conviction of this entire study is that architecture is but a fragment of a larger whole—the house is inseparable from its inhabitants, and its inhabitants inseparable from their culture and their land. The goal is not simply to classify or describe but to illuminate the tapestry and the web of the whole.

Geographical Subregions and Their Relation to Architecture

The Arkansas Ozark region is one of the state's five clearly defined physiographic regions (fig. 1-1). Within the Arkansas Ozarks are three subregions: the Springfield Plain, the Boston Mountains, and the Salem Plateau (fig. 1-2). In conventional thought and speech and even in scholarly studies, however, the region is often treated as though it were homogenous. The areas chosen for the primary fieldwork—Stone County, Washington County, and portions of Madison County—were carefully chosen to represent the two major and most clearly differentiated subregions, the Springfield Plain and the Boston Mountains. A surprising correlation was found to exist between these two subregions and the distribution of certain house types. This will be discussed in chapter 4.

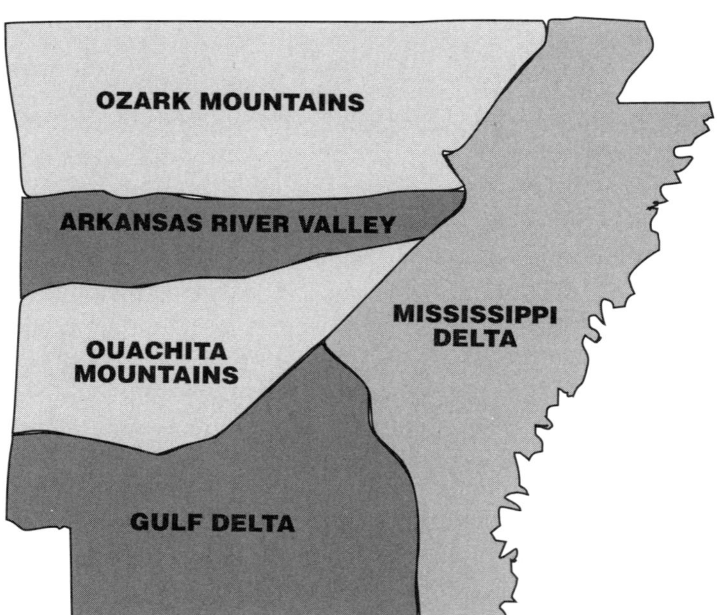

Fig. 1-1. Physiographic Regions of Arkansas. *Courtesy of Arkansas Historic Preservation Program*

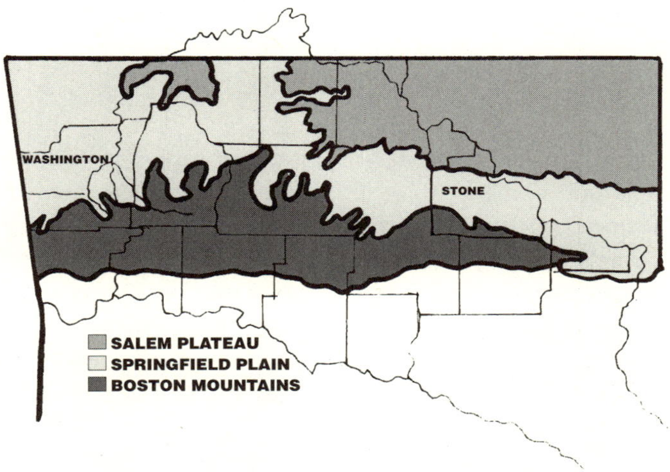

Fig. 1-2. Subregions of the Arkansas Ozarks. *Courtesy of Dr. Gerald Hanson*

The Choice of Locale and Chronological Framework: 1830 to 1930

Since a major purpose was to determine the indigenous characteristics of Arkansas Ozark houses, rural farmsteads were chosen for documentation because they reveal less self-conscious and more tenacious traditional architectural qualities. An underlying premise is that the Arkansas Ozarks region, as the flourishing study of Ozark folkways attests, is a veritable textbook of traditional culture. Nevertheless, through time traditional rural architectural forms give way to forms influenced from beyond the local setting through the medium of magazines, newspapers, and architectural pattern and plan books. The dates for this study, 1830 to 1930, were chosen to best illuminate the dynamics of this tradition of building vernacular houses. The year 1830 was the earliest time of settlement and 1930 marked a kind of cultural turning point around which time the bungalow house type, one of the first truly internationally popular houses, began to be introduced into the Ozarks (although it was introduced a couple of decades later than the time of its peak of popularity in urban areas of the United States).

Defining Vernacular Architecture

A central issue in this study is the definition and use of the term *vernacular architecture*. The word *vernacular* always connotes an association with the people of a particular place. A common usage of the word refers to the qualities in the ordinary speech of a given locality.

In the preface to their important anthology of studies on vernacular architecture, *Common Places,* Dell Upton and John Vlach note the difficulty of precise definition, remarking that vernacular architecture has more often been defined by what it is not rather than by what it is. Vernacular architecture is not sophisticated, not high style, not monumental, not designed by professional architects.[2] Positive definitions they offer are "that which is common in a given place at a given time" and "the architecture that groups of people make or have made for their daily use."[3]

All writers in the field agree upon the essential community aspect of vernacular architecture. As Upton and Vlach remark, in vernacular architecture the wishes and desires and the conventional tastes of common people are considered to be as significant as the act of building itself. The consumers of vernacular architecture are also important form givers, a circumstance that provides vernacular architecture with a strong popular or social identity. As the creation of local people, vernacular architecture presents not so much the wants of any single person but instead the wants that are communally sanctioned.[4] A complex issue, then, in the study of vernacular architecture is the varying degree of social representation of different vernacular forms. As Upton and Vlach observe, "the degree to which an artifactual set represents its residents can vary tremendously."[5]

In subsequent chapters, Ozark houses are divided into two types that are termed *traditional* and *popular* (or *nontraditional*). Despite this division, a basic assumption is that all the vernacular dwellings, both traditional and popular, of this region possess a high degree of the "intensity of social representation" because "the more self-sufficient and socially secure a community is, the more definite is its sense of identity and the more fixed are its architectural conventions."[6] As will be discussed in more detail later, the Ozarks are characterized by a high degree of self-consciousness as a region and by a tenacious self-sufficiency that resulted in a lingering of traditional culture longer than in many other areas of the country. Moreover, in the traditional Ozark culture most men possessed a high degree of woodworking skills, and in the early days of settlement they assumed responsibility for building their own log houses. Later, many assisted local carpenters in building their families' houses. Thus, Ozarkers were intimately involved in the building process as form givers; this was only one aspect of their highly developed self-sufficiency visible in many areas of Ozark traditional culture.

An important clarification with regard to the broad use of the term vernacular in this study is noted folklorist Henry Glassie's tripartite classification of objects as either "folk," "popular," or "elite/academic" (fig. 1-3). In Glassie's view, during the time of the construction of an authentic folk object, the tradition out of which it was produced cannot have been part of the popular (mass, normative) or academic (elite, progressive) cultures of the greater society with which the object's maker had contact and as a member of which he may have functioned.[7]

The folk builder, then, is one who is guided by the conventions of his locality. Along with function, tradition determines the size, shape, methods, and materials of construction.[8] For Glassie, the terms folk and traditional are nearly synonymous. As he remarks, "To be traditional, it must be old and acceptable to the group which produced it."[9] At the opposite end of this architectural spectrum is academic or high style architecture, which is designed by professionals attempting to set or to follow national or international standards of design.[10] In the middle

HENRY GLASSIE'S OUTLINE

Folk Culture	Popular Culture	Elite/Academic Culture
Vernacular		
Folk material exhibits major variation over space and minor variation through time		Popular and academic material exhibit minor variations over space and major variations through time
(study yields regions)		(study yields periods)
transmitted through collective memory; based on tradition of a group	pattern books plan books magazines	professional architects' designs; gentlemen architects' designs

Note that the above is a *continuum* and there may be great admixture of these three in any artifact, especially a building.

* This overview of three aspects of material culture is presented in Henry Glassie's book *Pattern in the Material Folk Culture of the Eastern United States.*

Fig. 1-3. Summary of Henry Glassie's analysis of objects' relations to culture.

of the spectrum is a wide-ranging category of architecture less easily pigeonholed, termed popular. In popular architecture, the designs are influenced by ideas imported from beyond the local setting through popular culture in magazines and newspapers dealing with domestic architecture and through nineteenth-century architectural pattern and plan books.

According to Glassie, folk material exhibits major variation over space and minor variation through time, while the products of popular or academic culture exhibit minor variation over space and major variation through time. The natural divisions of popular culture are temporal; that is, a search for patterns in folk material yields regions, where a search for patterns in popular culture yields periods.[11]

Folk architectural forms, then, will inevitably disappear with the previously mentioned influx of architectural ideas from outside the local tradition through popular books and magazines. This development accounts for the familiar observation that American traditional architectural forms began to fade in the post–Civil War period, disappearing to the extent that popular culture made inroads into previously self-contained areas. As noted earlier, however, the geographic isolation and the slow economic development of the Arkansas Ozarks region render it a veritable textbook of traditional architectural forms, for traditional designs were tenacious and viable in the region well into the twentieth century.

Finally, then, the term vernacular as it is used here is deliberately broad enough to include those designs at the folk end of the architectural spectrum with the greatest intensity of social representation of local tradition, which are here labeled traditional, and those designs that begin to be influenced by ideas from beyond the group tradition through popular-culture communications and which are here labeled nontraditional or popular. It is important to note that in the Arkansas Ozarks, however, these house types are not purely popular, but rather represent, in varying degrees, an overlay of popular-culture influence upon the traditional forms. The dynamics and the outcome of this process will be discussed in chapter 4.

Chapter 2

The Ozarks as a Geographical and Cultural Region

The Geography of the Ozarks

Located a few hundred miles southeast of the center of the United States, the Ozark region is the country's most centrally located highland. It is part of the Southern Highlands which consist of the Blue Ridge Mountains, the Allegheny-Cumberland Plateau, the Highland Rim, and the Ouachita Ridge. It shares with these regions a somewhat underdeveloped economic base, a degree of isolation from surrounding areas, and a decided Anglo-American heritage. The Ozark region is referred to by various names: the Ozark Mountains, the Ozark Hills, the Ozark Dome, the Ozark Highlands, and, because it is technically a plateau, the Ozark Plateau. The terms "Ozark Mountains" and "Ozark Plateau" are confusing because the region is composed of both mountains and plateaus. Following local custom, in this study the entire region will be designated simply as the Ozarks.

Geographers delimit the Ozarks as lying within four states: Missouri, Arkansas, Oklahoma, and Kansas, making up an area of about forty thousand square miles.[1] Most of the region lies within southern and central Missouri and northern

Arkansas (fig. 2-1). In a study of Ozark geography, Milton Rafferty states that the region is geographically identified by the following unifying criteria: greater relief and steeper slopes than surrounding areas; older surface rocks and the presence of chert; an abundance of karst features (springs, caves, and sinkholes) produced by groundwater action on bedrock; the prevalence of average to poor soils, except in stream valleys; extensive forests of oak, pine, and hickory; and an abundance of high-quality water resources, chiefly springs and meandering streams that are often accompanied by steep limestone bluffs.[2]

In terms of impact on the overall culture and economic development of the region, the negative factor of prevalence of average to poor soils is of overwhelming importance. Most of the Ozark soils are thin and poor in nutrients; these are characteristic of the Blue Ridge and the Ouachita Ridge as well.[3] A 1914 soil reconnaissance survey of the Ozark region cited not only the poor quality of the soil, but the presence of steep slopes, the susceptibility to erosion, and the frequent outcropping of surface rocks as detriments to large-scale agriculture.[4]

Exceptions to the generally average-to-poor soil fertility are the patches of prairie land interspersed throughout some areas of the Ozarks, ranging in size

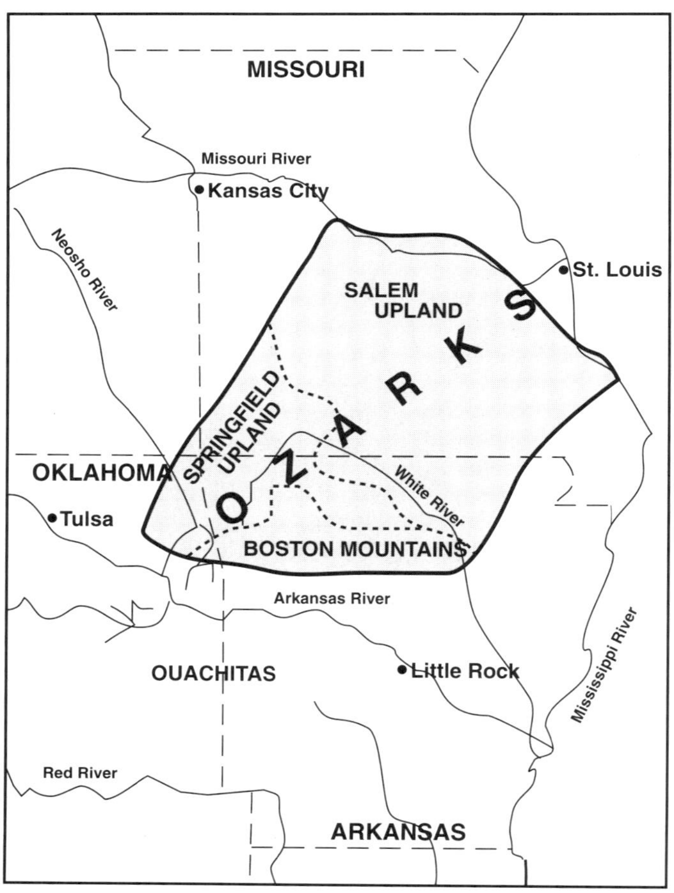

Fig. 2-1. Map of the Ozark Region. *Adapted from O. O. Maxfield, "The Geography of the Boston Mountains," figure II by Stacy Rennhoff*

from five to fifty square miles. These prairies were fertile and proved highly attractive to early settlers, both because of their fertility and because they did not require clearing.[5]

Reflecting its complex topography, the Ozarks are composed of four major subregions: the Boston Mountains, which are located in the southernmost part of the Ozarks in northern Arkansas; the St. Francis Mountains, located in northeastern Missouri; the Springfield Plain, which encompasses the western table land of the Ozarks, located both in northern Arkansas and south-central Missouri; and the Salem Plateau, which is located east of the Boston Mountains in Arkansas and north of the Springfield Plain in Missouri and which incorporates the remainder of the upland surface[6] (fig. 1-2).

The Boston Mountains

The southern edge of the Ozarks is the Boston Mountains, which lie in northern Arkansas and extend a short distance into northeastern Oklahoma. They form a relatively narrow belt some forty-five miles in width, extending east-west.[7] The northern boundary marks a sharp change in relief and is easily delineated, while the southern boundary feathers out more gradually (fig. 1-2). The rocks of the Boston Mountains are among the youngest in the Ozarks, with shales most abundant, sandstone second, and limestone third. In the Boston Mountains, the greater relief and the extensive forests create a picturesque area in which the celebrated wilderness character of the Ozark region is most pronounced. The maximum elevations of the entire Ozark region occur in the central section of the Boston Mountains, particularly in Madison and Newton counties in Arkansas, where elevations reach 2,578 feet at summit level.[8] The average elevation within these mountains is estimated at 1,800 feet, compared to other parts of the Ozarks where the average elevation ranges from 1,300 to 1,800 feet.[9] The Boston Mountain area is one of the most sparsely populated sections of the Ozarks. In a 1963 study, for example, no town within the Boston Mountains had a population appreciably greater than five hundred.[10]

The poorest conditions for agriculture exist in the areas where bedrock outcroppings are frequent and where mountain slopes are generally too steep for cultivation (fig. 2-2). A few exceptions to these poor soil conditions occur in bottomlands along streams and in what are termed lowland basins, the fertile valleys formed by the solution of limestone.[11]

The Springfield Plain

The Springfield Plain is a gently sloping surface that forms the western border of the Ozarks, bounded on the east by the Eureka Springs escarpment and the hills along the Pomme de Terre and Osage valleys. It lies to the north and west of the

Fig. 2-2. Rocky Outcroppings in the Boston Mountains Area. Farm studies have shown dramatic differences in the agricultural yield between the Boston Mountains and the Springfield Plain. When specialized farming became widespread in the early twentieth century, it clustered in the more fertile Springfield Plain areas.

Boston Mountains and is characterized by lower relief, better soils, and extensive but scattered prairies. Springfield, Missouri, and Washington and Benton counties in Arkansas are the most populous areas of the Ozarks and are located in the Springfield Plain. Several prairies are located in the Arkansas portion of the Springfield Plain, primarily in Washington and Benton counties. Although the native grasses were long ago plowed under, the place names of these prairies remain in local use.[12]

In his study of the geography of the Boston Mountains, O. O. Maxfield presents an illuminating comparison between the agriculture of the Boston Mountains and that of the Springfield Plain within Arkansas. Although the agriculture of the two areas is similar, that of the Springfield Plain is much more productive. For instance, while 80.6 percent of the Springfield Plain has been converted into farmland, only 35.8 percent of the land in the Boston Mountains has been converted to farmland. The average size of farms in the Boston Mountains is 131 acres, compared to 88 acres in the Springfield Plain. Most tellingly, in cash income per family in farm products in 1949, the amount for the Boston Mountains inhabitants was $587 compared to $2,910 for the Springfield Plain area. Because of better conditions for agriculture, a greater farm income on fewer acres was possible within the Springfield Plain (fig. 2-3).[13] To conclude, the relatively higher standard of living and the greater ease of communication in the Springfield Plain area made a significant impact on the types of rural dwellings constructed there, in ways that will be indicated throughout the rest of this study.

The Ozarks as a Cultural Region

Defining the cultural traits of a region is, of course, a more difficult process than delineating geographical features. Cultural geographers define traditional culture regions as being "self-contained, endogamous and stable cultural systems which manifest themselves physically and behaviorally in a number of ways." Regional self-awareness is another criterion that defines the culture of a region. Folklorist E. Joan Wilson Miller has identified a culture region in the Ozarks through intensive documentation of folk tales, speech, superstitions, Anglo-Saxon surnames, origins of settlers, and agricultural practices.[14] Scholars in several disciplines have studied the traditional culture of the Ozarks for several decades, as previously noted, and this book is not the place for an in-depth examination of folk culture.[15] Nevertheless, three of the aspects marking a distinctive cultural region seem especially pertinent and will be examined in some detail: regional self-consciousness, the origin of settlers, and agricultural practices.

Fig. 2-3. Springfield Plain Farming Area.

Regional self-awareness seems part of the strong sense of community that still exists in the Ozarks, a trait that has helped people survive in a land of meager resources, but, on the other hand, a trait that can create a sense of exclusion to newcomers. An interview with a farmer who had moved to the Boston Mountains area from elsewhere in Arkansas confirmed the sense of regional awareness. The transplanted farmer remarked, "I've been here twenty years now, but I'm still considered a 'comer-inner.'"[16]

It is well known that the Arkansas Ozarks were settled by predominantly native-born Americans of Anglo-Saxon origin from the Southern Highlands of Tennessee, Kentucky, Missouri, and North Carolina. As E. Joan Wilson Miller observed, they were searching "for the kind of topography, climate, water supplies, soils, grasses, herbs and timber that would be hospitable to customs, crops, tools and nostalgia for home."[17] Few people outside this group settled in the Ozarks, and this accounts for the overwhelmingly native-born, Protestant (often fundamentalist), Anglo-Saxon (often Scotch-Irish), homogenous character of traditional Arkansas Ozark society.

The census analysis of 1860 showed that immigrants in the United States tended to move west along the same parallel of latitude on which they had lived before. Other analyses indicated that, contrary to the popular romantic image of pioneers crossing the continent in covered wagons, most immigrants moved to adjoining states. Census records pertaining to settlement in the Arkansas Ozarks confirm this. Of the newcomers to the Ozarks from 1830 to 1880, the places of origin of the majority were Tennessee, which accounted for the most immigrants, and Missouri, which contributed the second-largest number of immigrants. After 1880, Missouri furnished the greatest number of new settlers, with Tennessee second.[18] In the Springfield Plain area, some large farms existed that early on practiced specialized agriculture, such as wheat growing or stock raising (like the William Wilson Farm near Prairie Grove [fig. 4-51]). These were, however, decidedly the exception in the Arkansas Ozarks. Instead, the small, self-sufficient family farm was the basic unit of settlement and, especially in the mountainous areas, this remained true during the entire study period, up to 1930. Because of the thin soil, the inaccessibility of markets, and the independent mind-set of the Ozark farmer, agriculture generally was for subsistence, and few surpluses were raised for shipments to markets. Moreover, as O. O. Maxfield observed, "The population pressure did not require intensive production; thus, only the most easily cultivated lands (prairies, valley bottoms, bench lands, and ridgetops) were cropped."[19]

In their richly informative study of traditional agricultural practices in the Arkansas Highlands, John Otto and Augustus Burns demonstrate that these farmers practiced methods well adapted to the terrain, to the scarcity of labor, and to their desired self-sufficient and somewhat leisurely lifestyle. Ozark farmers generally practiced what Burns and Otto term "safety-first" farming in which most of the acreage and the labor went to crops for the family's own use, primarily corn. Crops that were dependent upon the vagaries of the marketplace, like tobacco and cotton (both of which were grown with some success in the region), were generally avoided.[20] Ozark agriculture was based upon two traditional practices: open-range herding and patch farming. In open-range herding, free-ranging livestock subsisted on natural forage in meadows and woodlands. In patch farming, the entire farm was never cultivated. The farm was cultivated in patches instead: crops were planted for a few years, and when the soil began to be depleted, the field was allowed to revert to forest. These two practices were universal among small farmers in the Old South and continued through the 1920s in the Arkansas Highlands, in both the Arkansas Ozarks and the Ouachita Ridge.[21] A third and closely related traditional practice was a native-American technique called slash-and-burn cultivation. Instead of laboriously chopping down trees and clearing the land of stumps, settlers burned the undergrowth and merely girdled the bark on most trees. Within the first year, as the leaves fell, sunlight could penetrate to the forest floor and crops could be planted among the dead trees. Roots and stumps were often left in these fields, which were referred to as "deadenings."[22] This technique was appropriate for the thin soil of the highlands. When the undergrowth was burned, insects were killed and the soil was fertilized by ash; the deadenings retarded surface winds and evaporation and helped hold thin topsoil. Moreover, wood from dead trees in the fields could be utilized as firewood whenever needed.[23]

Both slash-and-burn cultivation and patch farming were well-suited to the thin soil and the sparse population of the Ozarks where labor was scarce. Patch farming did not overtax the poor soil; however, this method could support only a thinly dispersed population since most of the land was fallow or was wooded. In fact, Burns and Otto maintain that this practice in Appalachia was responsible for much of the westward migration. As early as the 1830s, the Appalachian hollows could not support the growing population, and, facing land shortages, many families began moving west to the trans-Mississippi Highlands to "a familiar rugged and wooded environment."[24]

The traditional Ozark farm, then, utilized cultivated land and woodlands that allowed the soil to replenish itself and provided natural forage for free-ranging livestock, primarily cattle and hogs. Because of the plentiful supply of game and fish, the availability of natural forage, and a thinly dispersed population, only a few acres needed to be cultivated. Cotton was a risky, labor-intensive crop that had to be hauled to market and was subject to market fluctuations. For maintaining a self-sufficient farm, corn was the ubiquitous, multipurpose crop. It could be eaten or fed to stock or made into whiskey; corn leaves could serve as fodder; the shucks could be used for making brooms, mattresses, chair bottoms, and dolls; the cobs could be used for fuel and for pipes. Before the ready availability of markets, families might raise wheat and oats along with garden vegetables and sorghum and honey for their own use. Sheep, cotton, and flax were sometimes raised for the production of cloth.[25] Cash was needed only for taxes and for a few goods like coffee and tobacco. To obtain cash, farmers could sell horses, cows, and hides or grow surplus corn, cotton, or tobacco, though tobacco was grown less frequently.[26] In sum, not only the kinds of crops but also the agricultural methods of the traditional Ozark farmer were well-adapted to the land and to a society that valued self-sufficiency, economic security, and leisure time above cash income.[27] With most of the livestock ranging free and only portions of the land under cultivation, farm work could be relatively undemanding, providing ample time for traditional Ozark activities enjoyed by the menfolk: hunting, fishing, swapping yarns, or playing the fiddle or banjo. Unquestionably, women were not so fortunate. The work required to rear large families, to cook and preserve food, to spin, weave, sew, keep house, and do the laundry must have been relentlessly demanding.

Ozark folklore is full of stories of the often condescending traveling "city-slicker" who is outsmarted by the "natives." Such travelers through the Ozarks—who often saw only the corn patches, the log houses, the wild hogs, and the homespun clothes—might term such a lifestyle "primitive." And so it was in some respects. But while the typical Ozark farm rarely allowed its inhabitants to rise above subsistence level, there were still many benefits beyond cash income, chiefly a rich traditional culture, a secure lifestyle, and freedom from indebtedness.[28]

In his observations about Ozark culture, Milton Rafferty has remarked that several obvious Ozark cultural traits are universally characteristic of rural societies, such as the prevalence of extended families and families living on the same land for generations; various means of work sharing (house raisings, cooperative harvesting, quilting bees, and the like); social lives that center around church and school; and a general stability of social systems and slowness to accept change.[29] Additionally, a tremendously important factor in the development of Ozark culture is the isolation of the region. In his 1920 classic study of the geography of the Missouri Ozarks, Carl Sauer discusses this isolation in terms of the entire region. Noting that the boundaries of the Ozark region are outlined roughly by navigable rivers (the Mississippi on the east, the Missouri on the north, the Arkansas on the south, and on the west the Arkansas, Neosho, and Osage rivers), he remarks,

> With regard to lines of communication the location of the area is singular. . . . Only two important direct lines of communication extend across the Ozarks, one between St. Louis and the Southwest, the other between Kansas City and the Southeast. One railroad trunk line from St. Louis to the Southwest, the 'Frisco', crosses the Ozarks. . . . The Ozarks occupy, therefore, an almost insular position with reference to great thoroughfares, being closely surrounded, but hardly invaded by them. This condition is due in part to the obstacles which the region presents to travel, but more largely to its accidental location outside of direct lines of communication between important points.[30]

The two lines of communication Sauer mentions are located in Missouri, not Arkansas, and, apart from the brief duration of the Butterfield Overland Mail (a stagecoach line that existed from 1858 to 1860) through Washington County, the Arkansas Ozarks were even more insular than the Missouri Ozarks.

In understanding the cultural traits of the Arkansas Ozarks, two more factors should be considered. The first (which will be discussed in the following chapter as well) is the "semi-arrested frontier" quality of the Ozarks. For a number of reasons, the frontier experience was not far removed in time or circumstance from the present. The other factor is the strong bond uniting Ozarkers in their shared experience of "the rigors of making a living in a region blessed with only modest resources," as Carl Sauer put it.[31] These factors, combined with the previously noted self-sufficiency, surely created a strain of anti-intellectualism. Ozark people esteemed their neighbors for their honesty, their character, and their ability to work hard and to live by their wits. Education and "book learning" were not especially valued and, indeed, were not readily available during much of the history of the Ozarks. A second and more admirable quality stemming from these factors is the egalitarian nature of Ozark society and the lack of class distinctions therein. Accordingly, few Ozarkers "put on airs." The most prosperous landowners had larger houses, but not elegant ones, and they seemed to have lived much like their neighbors. (See the discussion of the William Wilson House in chapter 8.) Finally, a practical outgrowth of the difficulty of wresting a living from the region is the well-known Ozark penchant for "making do." This is, of course, closely related to the disinclination for superfluity in one's home and possessions and for inflated self-importance. It is a trait that manifests itself in the present practice of "recycling" vacant houses and using them as hay-storage barns or adding them to existing houses; similarly, abandoned buildings are often moved to other farms for reuse; old schoolhouses become churches; old wagon wheels become fences when welded together; and old washing machines become flower planters (fig. 2-4).

In sum, then, the rural character, the ethnically and socially homogeneous population, the bonds of isolation, and the varying degrees of hardship within the Arkansas Ozark community created a conservative society with a persistence of traditional lifestyles; that these qualities also created a persistence of tradition-based architectural practices will be a continuing theme in this study.

Fig. 2-4. Washing Machines Used as Planters, Clark-Hill House (1880) Drake's Creek Vicinity, Madison County. In the well-known Ozark penchant for "making do," washing machines become planters, outbuildings are moved from one farm to another, and occasionally a small house may be moved to add on to an existing house.

Chapter 3

State and Local History

In fundamental ways, the history of the Arkansas Ozark region mirrors that of the state. A central fact about both has been slow development from the beginning. In his early history of the state, Malcolm Rohrbaugh described Arkansas as "an enduring frontier."[1] Similarly, economist Leland DuVall argued that Arkansas was an "economic colony" to the rest of the nation from the territory's beginning to the mid-twentieth century.[2] When describing the state at the close of the 1920s, historian David Tucker termed it "a rural, preindustrial society."[3] In any statistical rating of income or education in the United States, Arkansas has always ranked, and still ranks, at or near the bottom. And within the state, some of the poorest and least developed counties continue to be in the Ozark region.[4]

The Ozarks have been, in microcosm, what the state of Arkansas has been in relation to the rest of the country. Just as the frontier lingered longer in Arkansas than in other states, so the nineteenth century seems to have lingered longer in the Ozarks than in much of the rest of the state. One of the interesting consequences of this fact is the flourishing of studies of Ozark traditional culture. The reasons for this lingering presence of the nineteenth century are deep and multifarious; they can only be alluded to here.

It is significant that Malcolm Rohrbaugh used the term *frontier* to describe nineteenth-century Arkansas and that journalist Harry Ashmore used it again in reference to the Ozarks in the twentieth century. Ashmore, a native North Carolinian, was editor of the state's oldest and most prestigious newspaper, the *Arkansas Gazette,* in the 1950s and 1960s. Since he was well acquainted with Appalachia, he expected no surprises when he first visited the Ozarks around 1950; in reflecting upon that first visit, however, he said, "I could hear the same inflection and sounds in the Ozarks, and in the uncertain light from a cabin fireplace it would be hard to say these lean and shambling mountaineers were any different from the ones back home. But here there was a feeling of frontier, or still unrealized history."[5]

Arkansas's Lingering Frontier, 1819–1850

In 1819 when Arkansas became a territory and its present boundaries were established (with the exception of the western edge, which faded out into what was then oblivion and was to become Indian Territory), the number of its inhabitants was 14,000. Land was plentiful and cheap, ranging in price from $1.25 to $2.00 an acre, and cheap land continued to be an enticement through the 1880s, so squatters often ran ahead of surveyors.

Steamboat traffic greatly boosted the development of the territory. The arrival of the first steamboat up the Arkansas River to Little Rock in 1822 was the cause of much celebration. Nine years later, in 1831, the first steamer ascended the White River four hundred miles to Batesville, an early settlement that would thereafter become a thriving town near the eastern edge of the Ozarks. With access now available through both the White and the Arkansas rivers, settlement of the Arkansas Ozarks could begin in earnest. In May 1832, for example, the *Arkansas Gazette* reported that two steamboats passing through Little Rock on the way up the Arkansas River carried two hundred passengers who were journeying principally to settle Washington and Crawford counties, an area the *Gazette* termed "the Eden of Arkansas."[6]

Before the advent of the steamboats—and after their appearance on the smaller tributaries of the Arkansas and the White rivers—flatboats and keelboats hauled wagons and oxcarts that could then proceed overland.[7] Such water travel was of paramount importance because until well into the nineteenth century, roads in Arkansas were either bad, impassable, or nonexistent. As historian Walter Moffatt remarked, "Traveling in Arkansas between 1819 and 1840 was a strenuous and often hazardous activity."[8] Such conditions made the territory slow to develop and created isolated settlements with chronically irregular mail service.[9] The early settlements (with the notable exception of those settlements in what would become Washington County) were all situated along the navigable rivers, and travel by water was not superseded by wagon transport until after the Civil War.[10]

In 1836 Arkansas achieved statehood and was admitted to the Union (prematurely, according to some) as a slave state balancing the entrance of the free state of Michigan.[11] Yet, despite the steamboats, the cheap and plentiful land, and the heady experience of statehood, Arkansas's early years of settlement up to 1850 present a case study of retarded development. Its population in 1830 was only 30,388, while Missouri and Louisiana, its neighbors to the north and south, had 140,455 and 214,739 people, respectively. And Arkansas had only half the population of Michigan, its sister state at the time of statehood.[12] In his book, *The Trans-Appalachian Frontier,* Malcolm Rohrbaugh sums up the negative factors working against Arkansas's early development: it was remote, the roads were dreadful, the Indians were numerous, and the new settler was faced immediately with the extended swampland of eastern Arkansas, some of the most inhospitable terrain in the whole territory. "Arkansas was presumably no place for the energetic agriculturalist, especially one with capital. Lands in Alabama, Mississippi, and Louisiana had much more of everything to offer."[13]

In the 1840s, although an affluent cotton-based society had arisen around Little Rock, Arkansas was still in the process of development and much of the territory was still primitive. Even the Arkansas River Valley, which had been among the very earliest lands to attract settlers, retained the frontier population density, while to the north, in the adjoining state of Missouri, the Missouri River Valley had moved well beyond this point. As Rohrbaugh summed it up,

> Arkansas was a reincarnation of the American frontier traditionally associated with places like Kentucky after 1775 and Michigan after 1815. In Arkansas, the early frontier experience reappeared and lived on until well into the nineteenth century, immune from innovations of technology and forces of movement that overtook other frontiers after 1815 . . . it was typically Arkansan that these ameliorations in the frontier condition came later in Arkansas than elsewhere.[14]

It was in this formative period from 1830 to 1850 that two distinctive societies began to emerge in the state. In the south and east, a planter class based upon slavery and large-scale cotton production began to develop. In the northern and western sections, including the Ozarks, a society of small, independent farmers emerged. By raising corn and grains and grazing livestock, they were isolated by geography and economy from the cotton interests to the east. In 1836 this division was so well defined that the *Little Rock Times* described the two sections separately for prospective immigrants.[15]

Early Settlement in Stone and Washington Counties, 1819–1850

In 1828 a treaty with the Cherokee Indians resulted in their removal to the land west of Arkansas designated as Indian Territory. White settlement in Stone and

Washington counties began in earnest about this time. Most families arrived in the Ozarks through a combination of wagon and river travel. The only major waterway into the Ozark interior is the White River, which forms the eastern boundary of Stone County (fig. 3-1). Those settling in the eastern or central sections of the Ozarks traveled by wagon to the Mississippi River, then up or down it (with their wagons loaded on flatboats) to the mouth of the White. They then traveled up the White River to one of its navigable streams (most likely the North Fork or the Buffalo River) and finally by wagon overland to their destinations. Those settling in Washington County, or other western sections, bypassed the White River and traveled instead up the Arkansas River as far as Van Buren, then they traveled by wagon or oxcart in the laborious trek across the Boston Mountains into Washington County. Once there, however, the gentler terrain of prairies interspersed with rolling hills made travel northward to Benton County and even on to Missouri relatively easy.

Washington County was formed in 1828 with Fayetteville designated as the county seat. It originally included all of Benton County and half of Madison County. Its present boundaries were established soon after statehood in 1836.

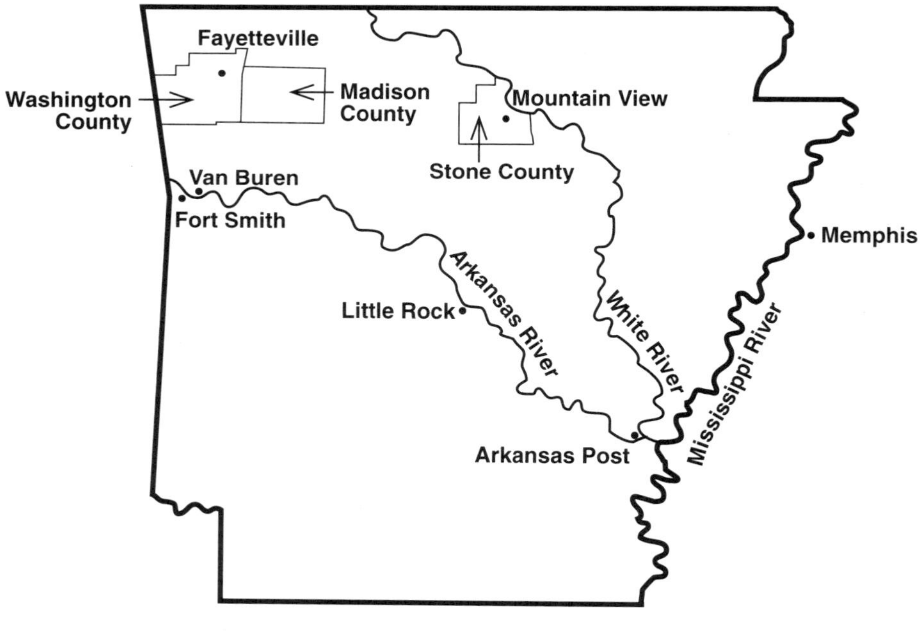

Fig. 3-1. Map Showing Location of the Three Counties Where Fieldwork Was Conducted and the Proximity of These Counties to Navigable Waterways into the Arkansas Ozarks. Washington County is an exception to the rule that the most populous early settlements were along navigable waterways since settlers there had to ascend the Arkansas River and then travel overland in a laborious trek across the Boston Mountains. Apparently, the moderately high elevations and the fertility of the countryside outweighed the lack of direct access to the county by river. *Courtesy of Dr. Gerald Hanson*

Washington County is an exception to the rule that the earliest settlements were along navigable waterways, for in 1838 Washington County was the most populous county in the state with 5,048 inhabitants. By contrast, Pulaski County, the seat of the state capital, had 2,473 residents.[16] An early newspaper account described Washington County's inviting landscape: "On the south and east the blue hills and mountains, with intervening prairies, present themselves as far as the eye can reach, and on the southwest there is prairie land of excellent quality."[17] Apparently, the relatively high elevation (which would safeguard against the ever-present danger of fevers that occurred in low-lying, marshy areas) and the relative fertility of the countryside outweighed the problem of the lack of direct access into the county by river.

Moreover, two military roads facilitated settlement. The first, established in the 1820s, ran along the county's western border adjacent to Indian Territory and linked Fort Scott, Kansas, to Fort Smith, Arkansas (located on the Arkansas River about fifty miles south of Washington County). A second military road, dating from 1835, ran from St. Louis to Fort Smith by way of Fayetteville. On this same route was an early trail that served cattlemen from Texas who were moving cattle to northern markets; it led from Van Buren over the Boston Mountains to Springfield and St. Louis, Missouri.[18]

For merchants, an additional impetus to early settlement in Washington County was the location of Indian Territory on the western border. The two oldest communities in the county, both established in 1828, are located in this western section.

Stone County was not formed until 1873; the townships it encompasses were originally the hinterlands of four adjoining counties: Independence, Izard, Searcy, and Van Buren counties. Initial settlement began at the same time as it had in Washington County, around 1828. Although the area that was to become Stone County was directly accessible from the White River, interior travel was hampered by the rugged, mountainous terrain, which slowed migration and hampered transportation and commercial and agricultural development throughout the entire century. The early settlers relied heavily on secondary waterways for transportation into the interior. Unlike Washington County, where settlement clustered in the west, settlement in the Stone County region seems to have been evenly distributed in the good bottom lands and the more fertile sections of plateaus and valleys. By the late 1840s, settlements existed at Buckhorn (in the east), at Richwoods and Blue Mountain (in the central section), and at Big Springs and Locust Grove (in the west).[19]

The population statistics for the area of Stone County are difficult to determine for the early nineteenth century since the region's townships were split among four counties, but some comparison with Washington County can be illustrated by the fact that in 1829 three post offices had been established in Washington County, while the first two in the Stone County region were not established until 1837, and by 1860 the region had only seven post offices, while Washington County had twenty-four.

Although more sophisticated communities—for example, Cane Hill and Fayetteville—existed in Washington County than in the Stone County area, the lifestyle in rural areas was surely similar in both locales. It was largely an economy of small, self-sufficient farms since the lack of transportation facilities limited the exportation of farm commodities. Farming was augmented by hunting and gathering. The varied crops included corn, potatoes, sweet potatoes, wheat, oats, and beans. The livestock raised included swine and cattle. In addition, the early farm census indicates that considerable amounts of honey, cheese, tobacco, cotton, and wool were produced for home consumption. (After 1910 these goods would rarely be listed in the agricultural census.)[20] In the countryside, most of the commercial activity clustered around the mills constructed on the many streams. These mills doubled as flour mills and as sawmills. In true Ozark self-sufficient fashion, much of the machinery for these mills was made by the operators themselves. The water wheels, shafts, pulleys, and flumes were built of seasoned wood. Native stone was cut for burrs, while cowhide was used for belts.

Despite the scattered sawmills available, most rural houses during this early period were probably of log construction. An early oral history of the prosperous West Fork community in Washington County concluded, "Not until after the Civil War was there a plank house. Mr. Jett said when he came to this community in 1857, there was not a frame house between West Fork and Fayetteville."[21] Another indication of Ozark self-sufficiency can be gleaned from early store ledgers that recorded a flourishing barter system, making cash unnecessary for purchasing items that could not be made or grown at home. An 1837 ledger in Washington County indicates that such items as sugar, salt, nails, Bibles, calico, shoes, boots, "specks" (eyeglasses), cups and saucers, and Walker's *Dictionary* were all purchased by means of various credits, including "use of wagon, $5.00 credit," "credit by lumber $13.20," "credit by labor done," "credit by cotton sold." Many listings indicate women's contributions, such as "credit by butter" and "credit by socks."[22]

Antebellum Arkansas, 1850–1861

Arkansas in this period was characterized by the rural nature of its population, an agricultural economy, and, in major agricultural areas, a slave labor system. In 1860 Little Rock was the largest town with 3,727 inhabitants; Fayetteville was the fifth largest with 967, but the state was, by present census standards, almost 100 percent rural.[23] As historian David Tucker describes it, "Much of Arkansas still appeared to be a new country in 1860. The main dirt road from Memphis remained impassable through the east Arkansas swamps for much of the year. Only 2 million of the state's 33 million acres were 'improved.' Arkansas remained predominantly a forest without cities, without canals, banks or railroads, although a rail connection with Memphis was under construction."[24]

And yet this first twenty-five years of statehood is generally considered the most prosperous period Arkansas has known up to modern times. Although there were no railroads, river traffic grew steadily and stagecoaches came into regular service. The principal towns were bustling; Little Rock, for example, could boast of having three newspapers and what was claimed to be the largest flour mill west of the Mississippi. Fayetteville was the commercial center of northwest Arkansas, and in addition to three schools, in 1854 it supported six dry goods stores, a cabinet shop, a cotton gin, and a carding factory for wool, besides a hotel and several taverns.

The bustling of the towns was directly dependent, however, upon the surrounding agrarian countryside, as the towns were primarily service areas for rural people and products. For whether in town or countryside, almost every Arkansan, directly or indirectly, owed his livelihood to the farm. Corn and wheat were produced all over the state, and in the Delta cotton was the most important cash crop. The two major types of agricultural units were the small, self-sufficient farms and the plantations, and while the plantation was clearly the most productive unit, on the whole, most farmers (as in the period of early settlement) continued to run self-sufficient farms, rather than relying upon slave labor and the market system.[25]

While slavery was a major component in the antebellum agricultural economy of Arkansas, providing the primary labor source for the large farms and plantations (and slaves made up 20 percent of the state's total population in 1860), there were never many slaves in the Ozarks. As Milton Rafferty remarked about the entire Ozark region, "Only a few areas were fertile enough to attract slave owners."[26]

Apparently one of these fertile areas was Washington and Benton counties, especially the river valleys of the White and Illinois rivers. Slaveholders in Washington County were among the earliest settlers, and in 1860 more than 300 owners had 1,486 slaves who made up 10 percent of the population. Slavery in Washington County seemed out of its natural habitat; the region, far from the slaveholding centers of Arkansas, was composed of small farming communities that practiced crop diversification. A recent study has shown, however, that slaveholdings were generally small, not exceeding 4.6 per owner in 1860, compared to 33 per owner in the major cotton-growing region of Chicot County in southeastern Arkansas. Many slaves were apparently engaged in nonagricultural types of work in Fayetteville, which had 294 slaves out of a population of 967 in 1860.[27] Washington County fulfilled its earlier promise of prosperity in this period, becoming the leading producer of wheat and corn in the state by the end of the 1850s. Another source of agricultural income was stock raising. Since livestock could "ship themselves" to markets, the lack of transportation facilities was not as critical as it was to perishable crops.[28]

In 1858 a dramatic improvement in the transportation and communication network occurred with the establishment of the Butterfield Overland Mail system, the southern route of which traversed the entire north-south distance of Washington County. Originating in St. Louis, the stagecoaches carried nine passengers who could travel from St. Louis to San Francisco for two hundred dollars, or shorter distances for ten cents per mile. The route through the Boston Mountains was considered the roughest ten miles of the entire trip. Two local stagecoaches also operated between Fayetteville, Cane Hill, and Bentonville, and the first telegraph in the county was established along the Overland Mail route in 1860.[29]

While transportation began to approach higher standards, the extent and quality of education in antebellum Arkansas was generally low. Arkansas was the only state before the Civil War without a school tax, and what Arkansans called public schools required tuition payments just as the private academies did. Education in Arkansas consisted of one-room, one-teacher schools that operated about four months a year, or of scattered academies with 1.5 teachers each.[30] Within this bleak picture, Washington County continued to lead the state in education with 57 of Arkansas's 632 schools located within its boundaries.[31]

The area that is now Stone County existed in relative isolation. There were no public schools and no communities in the county that even approached the sophistication of Fayetteville in Washington County. The primary commercial center was Riggsville, which supported a mill, a blacksmith shop, a store, and a church in the years before the Civil War.

The average farm in the Stone County region contained about 80 acres with approximately 35 acres improved for agriculture. Larger farms were located in the bottom lands and fertile valleys, especially adjacent to the White River, where the terrain is least mountainous. In the least mountainous areas, the largest farms averaged about 160 acres, about 50 of which were in cultivation. Other large farms were located in Richwoods, Timbo Valley, and along the White River north of Mountain View. Both tobacco and cotton were grown in the antebellum period, with tobacco production exceeding cotton production. In both counties, the agricultural census indicates the importance of several kinds of livestock: a horse, mule, or ox for farming and transportation; pigs and cattle for meat; cows for dairy products; and sheep for wool.[32]

What few items could not be made or grown locally were brought by steamboats on the White River and then transferred to wagons and hauled inland to merchants and farmers. Such freight was unloaded at Walls Ferry (near Marcella), Round Bottom, Hell Creek, Sylamore, and Rocky Bayou landings.[33]

In 1860, despite the presence of the steamboats, the ladies' academies, and the stagecoaches, most Ozark farm families could still be considered pioneers. Land was still being cleared; houses were generally made of logs; clothes were usually homespun; luxuries were few and life was rough. Still, within a certain framework, it was a secure life, and the standards for judging the new territory were much different from the standards of today, as Carl Sauer discusses in his classic book on the Missouri Ozarks. In remarks equally applicable to the Arkansas Ozarks, Sauer writes,

> The activities of the pioneer were not directed toward the production of specialized commodities. Because of his isolation he was forced to produce

> whatever things were necessary to the sustenance of his family. . . . The intermediate climate . . . the favorable association of forests and grassy tracts, the abundance of springs, the many mill sites, and the varied mineral resources enabled the pioneer in most localities . . . to live in almost complete independence. . . . This diversity of resources was more important then than now, and caused many sites to be more desirable for settlement to the pioneer than they are to the farmer of today.[34]

Civil War and Reconstruction Period, 1861–1874

Arkansas seceded from the Union on May 6, 1861. Union sentiment was strong in northern Arkansas, especially in the Ozarks. In the final secession convention, a lone Ozarker, Isaac Murphy from Madison County, stubbornly refused to change his vote to make the secession decision unanimous. An estimated 15 percent of the white males in northern Arkansas fought for the Union. Secret peace societies with several hundred members extended through nine northern Ozark counties.[35] Ironically, then, it was the people of northern Arkansas who bore the biggest brunt of the war, at least early on. One of the earliest battles took place in the Ozarks at Pea Ridge in Benton County. The decisive Union victory there opened up all of the northern part of the state to Federal troops. Three days before the battle, Confederate General McCullough ordered all public buildings and vacant dwellings in Fayetteville to be burned. The town served as both a staging area and as a line of retreat for troops of the Union and the Confederacy.[36] The Battle of Prairie Grove, near Fayetteville, which was won by the South in December 1862, resulted in 2,508 casualties in one day.

Throughout the war, a stream of both Union and Confederate armies crisscrossed the state. Besides the burning and foraging by both Union and Confederate soldiers, people in the countryside were terrorized by the murderous plundering by rival bands of irregulars. These irregulars were called Jayhawkers when they professed Union allegiance and Bushwhackers when they purportedly were Confederates.

When the war ended in April 1865, blackened chimneys and empty smokehouses dotted the bleak landscape. As one northern Arkansas woman expressed it, "This country was very poor at the close of the war; houses and horses gone. No food. Everything was leveled down. Rich and poor were all one class. All poor."[37]

Then, for almost another decade, Arkansans endured the double burdens of another "war": one burden was the struggle for political control of the state; the other was the general economic depression at the war's end. In an attempt to solve the critical problem of restoring Arkansas's agricultural productivity in a system with newly emancipated blacks and bankrupt whites, sharecropping was born. It was a system that would prove "a blight to whites and blacks alike in the years to come."[38]

At this time, being an Ozarker seemed to have unexpected advantages. Ozarkers, with their long tradition of self-sufficiency and general forgoing of slave labor, were able to resume normal lives more easily than planters and farmers elsewhere who had become dependent upon slaves in their agricultural enterprises.

1861 to 1874 in Stone and Washington Counties

The despised Republican or "Carpetbagger" state government, in power from 1868 to 1872, achieved two noteworthy goals: it completed a systematic construction of railroads and of free public schools. The shocking prewar neglect of public education had resulted in only twenty-six free public schools having been built in the state, and, at the beginning of Reconstruction, an estimated one-third of the white voters could not write their own names. In contrast, in four years of Republican leadership after the war, 1,146 schoolhouses were constructed.[39]

One of these newly established schools was the first state institution of higher learning, the University of Arkansas, which opened its doors in Fayetteville in January 1872. This sought-after plum was awarded to Washington County because of its previous support of educational institutions and because Fayetteville supplemented the county's offer of $100,000 in bonds with $30,000 plus 420 acres of land.[40] Soon thereafter, a census in 1874 showed that Washington County ranked second in population among all the counties in the state.

Between 1873 and 1875, one of the most imposing high style buildings in the state was being constructed on the Fayetteville campus, the university's high Victorian, Second Empire style landmark, Old Main. Old Main was only one of many brick edifices (both public buildings and houses) constructed in Washington County during the Reconstruction period. This boom in construction was triggered by the need for rebuilding after the war and by the arrival of new brickmaking machines (see chapter 7).[41]

As normalcy returned after the war, farmers had some prosperous times, aided by good weather and a rise in cotton prices to a high in the early 1870s of fifteen cents a pound. This prosperity led to Stone County's farmers increasing their cotton production fivefold, with a corresponding decrease in wool and tobacco production.

In 1873 Stone County was formed. Its area was carved largely from Izard County, with smaller parts taken from Independence, Searcy, and Van Buren counties. Mountain View was chosen as the county seat because of its central location. It became, almost literally, a town carved out of the woods. Predictably, the first courthouse was a log building.

Stone County generally prospered during this time, especially in the areas along the White River that served as ports for transporting cotton to markets elsewhere. The once-flourishing river port of Hesstown (now Marcella, and site of the two fine Hess family houses seen in figs. 4-49 and 4-57) was established during this period. A number of new sawmills were built in the county as well.

In sum, as this period ended, some obvious comparisons between the two counties can be made. While Washington County was sufficiently well established to have Fayetteville, its county seat, designated as the site of the new University of Arkansas, Stone County was not formed until 1873, a year after the university opened its doors. Washington County enjoyed a brick-building boom, especially in houses, in both town and countryside, while a 1984 architectural survey of Stone County showed that if there were brick houses constructed in Stone County in the nineteenth century, none remain. Washington County ranked second in the state in population in 1874, while, like the other mountain counties, Stone County lagged far behind in population.

In her study of the Ozarks, E. Joan Wilson Miller, using the traditional measure of designating frontier areas as those which had a population density of only two to six persons per square mile, asserts, "By 1870 the roughest parts of the Ozarks . . . were still to be classified as frontier. . . . The frontier density remained unchanged for more than twenty years in spite of the Pre-Emption Act of 1841 and the Graduation Act of 1854, which provided opportunities for the easier purchase of small farms. . . . By 1890, the density of population was still low, ranging from six to eight persons per square mile."[42]

Far from being an anomaly, then, Stone County's sparse population and retarded development were more typical of the Arkansas Ozarks than was the vaunted progress of Washington County.

Late Nineteenth Century, 1875–1900

Like other southern states after the turmoil of the Civil War and Reconstruction, Arkansas entered the last quarter of the nineteenth century at a disadvantage. It was able, nonetheless, to share somewhat in the general prosperity and industrial development of the country as a whole. In the decade 1880–90, the census indicated that, having passed one million in population, Arkansas had outstripped all other southern states (except for Florida) in percentage of population increase. Two factors contributed to this growth: federal and state lands were still for sale at cheap prices; and the state's railroad system more than tripled during this decade, making these lands more accessible.

The railroads tied Arkansas to the rest of the nation, making it possible for certain crops, such as strawberries, apples, and peaches, to be grown for northern markets. But the boosters and promoters who envisioned an Arkansas landscape dotted with cities and factories were disappointed. The state remained unquestionably a rural, agrarian one, and, aside from some manufacturing in the larger towns and some coal mining in western Arkansas, the only major new industry resulting from the railroad was lumbering. Lumbering companies were generally established by northern capitalists who, having depleted the forests of the north and east, now moved south to the Mississippi Valley and the extensive forests of

Arkansas. In a few decades, lumbering would become the state's major industry. Arkansas contributed cheap land and cheap labor to this enterprise.[43]

In the long run, the railroads proved to be a mixed blessing. By creating a national market, they forced Arkansas farmers to compete not only with the produce of other American farmers, but also with the produce of other nations as well. Moreover, the railroads took over as the dominant special-interest group in Arkansas politics, replacing the planter-politicians who had for so long held sway. As Harry Ashmore summarized it, Arkansas's leadership "was not equipped to deal with the likes of Jay Gould. . . . They yielded their own and the state's long-range interests in return for immediate gain, and often didn't realize even that."[44] It was Arkansas's confinement to a secondary role while much of the rest of the country was developing a high-profit corporate economy that led economist Leland DuVall to describe the state as an "economic colony" for most of its existence until around 1950. "Just as the New World had provided factory fodder to the plants in Europe, Arkansas (and much of the South) supplied agricultural and industrial raw materials to the manufacturing complex of the United States. . . . "[45]

The reasons for this long-entrenched economic position are complex and outside the scope of this book. Suffice it to say that throughout the nineteenth century agriculture remained the major component of the state's economy, while mechanization, the opening of local markets to outside goods through railroads, and the fierce competition for credit made the late nineteenth century a difficult time for Arkansas's farmers. To make matters worse, the price of cotton fell drastically. Such economic suffering spurred the formation of agrarian reform organizations, and the state became a center of similar organizing efforts. These efforts were to little avail, however, for agricultural depression characterized the condition of Arkansas's rural population into the twentieth century.[46]

In many parts of the state, Arkansas farmers were trapped in a debt-ridden, one-crop (cotton) economy. Against this dismal scene, one can see that the Ozark farmer, who tilled only a fraction of his land, who depended only minimally upon the cotton market, who avoided debt like the plague, and who had a proud tradition of independence, was in many ways prosperous, if not in terms of worldly goods, at least in terms of peace of mind. Harry Ashmore recognized this irony when he observed:

> Hardships and subsistence living were accepted as a valued way of life by those who settled in the mountains. . . . They raised or hunted their own food, grew tobacco and made whiskey . . . entertained each other with homemade music and oft-told tales, drew solace from the old-time religion and generally looked upon change as a threat to their ordained way of life. Their situation was significantly different from that of equally impoverished lowlanders, the black and white sharecroppers who accepted economic bondage as the only means they knew that would permit them to cling to the edge of subsistence.[47]

The Late Nineteenth Century in Stone and Washington Counties

On June 8, 1881, the Frisco (the St. Louis–San Francisco line) became the first railroad to run through Washington County. An early resident of West Fork recalled, "This was a holiday for everyone living within miles of the railroad since few people had ever seen a train."[48] The opening of the railroad had an especially positive impact upon this relatively fertile area, enabling fruit growing to develop into a prosperous enterprise. The double attractions of a flourishing fruit-growing enterprise and still-available land led Arkansas boosters to seize upon the charms of Washington County, as an article in a St. Louis newspaper in 1897 demonstrates:

> Washington County's 70,000 Rich Acres Open to Homestead Entry
>
> People are just now obtaining a more extensive knowledge of her alluvial lands, navigable streams, water power, vast and varied timber and mineral resources, wonderful springs, delightful climate, rapid transportation facilities . . . mountainous northwest Arkansas is especially adapted to fruits.

The article further reports that prize-winning apples at two World's Fairs, including the 1893 Columbian Exposition in Chicago, had been cultivated in Washington County, which could boast of growing 130 varieties[49] (fig. 3-2). The railroad was essential for transporting these apples and other produce to national markets. In the early 1880s, an estimated 125 railroad cars of wheat, 100 cars of apples, and significant amounts of eggs and other produce were shipped out of the county in one year. This was, of course, in addition to the carloads of timber, which had spurred construction of the railways in the first place.[50]

Although the railroad lines within Washington County were not extensive, they connected with other major lines just over the borders of Oklahoma and Missouri. This network, besides benefiting fruit growers, aided farmers who raised livestock, especially in the western and central sections of the county. An oral history of the Summers community (in western Washington County) describes how Mr. D. C. Price sold a hundred hogs in 1877: he rounded them up after they had pastured on the open range, fattened them in fenced pastures, and then drove them overland to Neosho, Missouri, where they were shipped by railroad to St. Louis.[51] Benjamin Franklin Johnson, whose handsome Italianate house of 1878 (fig. 4-54) is discussed in chapter 4, also depended upon a railroad connection in his hog and cattle operation. "I would drive my hogs and cattle to the spur north of Harris and we would load them on the train. Then I would ride with the cattle to St. Louis. When I got the money for the livestock, I would save half of it and invest the other half."[52]

Fayetteville, where the state university had opened in 1872, prospered culturally as well as economically. By the 1890s, newspapers recounted a surprising

Fig. 3-2. Barrelling Apples in a Washington County Orchard. *Shiloh Museum of Ozark History (L. W. Searcy Collection)*

range of cultural events, especially concerts and recitals. In 1888 the Fayetteville Electric Light and Power Company held a grand Electric Ball to commemorate the lighting of the city. It would be several decades, however, before electricity reached the rural sections of the county.[53]

Both Fayetteville and the hamlet of Winslow (to the south in the Boston Mountains) became popular summer resorts at this time for people from Oklahoma, southern Missouri, and the Arkansas lowlands. A short railway ran between Fayetteville and Winslow for the convenience of these summer visitors, many of whom maintained summer cottages in Winslow until World War II.

Little changed in Stone County, however, as the railroad remained only an often-promised eventuality, and the county continued to rely upon White River steamboat traffic for transportation to the outside world. Areas in this vicinity continued to prosper. The small community of Marcella (formerly Hesstown) on the banks of the White River, provides an example. Thomas M. Hess established a river port, a ferry, a cotton gin, and cotton warehouses on the Marcella site. His fine central hall house, its furnishings shipped upriver from New Orleans, was constructed in 1868 (fig. 4-59).

Despite Stone County's isolation from a rail network, it enjoyed a steady growth in the post–Civil War decades. Farming continued to be the primary enterprise, and, except for an increase in cotton acreage and the establishment of orchards, both the kinds and quantities of crops grown were similar to those grown in the prewar period.

Having been established relatively late as the county seat in 1873, Mountain View was still developing into a commercial center. The original log courthouse was replaced in 1888 by a two-story frame courthouse on the site of the present courthouse square. Businesses began to cluster around this square, as they still do.

The cultural lag between Stone and Washington counties is increasingly marked from this time on; certainly the establishment of the university and the arrival of the railroad in Washington County were turning points in this divergence in progress. An indication of this lag is the fact that Stone County's first school was not established until 1890 in Mountain View and the first public school was not established until 1895, while Washington County, as we have seen, had been a leader in terms of the number and the quality of schools since Arkansas's early settlement period.

An interesting glimpse into the social life of late nineteenth-century Mountain View is provided by an account of an important social event, the construction of the First Baptist Church in 1894. It is recorded that the sills and sleepers for this edifice were hewn from white oak timbers by the pastor of another Baptist church, the Rev. Jacob King (whose own log house is shown in fig. 4-19). The timbers had been rafted down the White River from their source at Optimus, then hauled to the site by ox-drawn wagons. The congregation held pie suppers and dinners and performed a play, *Uncle Tom's Cabin,* to help pay for their new church.[54]

The Progressive Era, 1900–1930

In 1915 Arkansas completed the construction of its elegant neoclassical state capitol, an effective symbol of the state's progress in public services, especially education. Under three progressive governors from 1900 to 1913, the belatedly established public school system was improved by strengthening financial support, by passing compulsory schooling laws, by lengthening school terms, by providing teacher training, and by raising scholastic standards. Moreover, important strides were made toward developing a modern highway system; from 1917 to 1921, bonds were authorized for the first paved roads in the state.

Arkansas as a whole enjoyed significant economic growth through the 1920s, with increased agricultural, mineral, and manufacturing production. Bauxite mining, which Arkansas virtually monopolized, surged before and after World War I. Lumber and cottonseed oil led factory production. Oil was discovered in southern Arkansas in 1921, and Arkansas placed fourth in the nation in oil production that year. In many rural areas, because of mechanized farming and railroads that provided access to markets, farmers shared in the general prosperity as farm prices climbed once again. There was a growing shift from subsistence farming to general farming in areas where it was feasible.

But, for a balanced outlook, the negative side of the ledger must also be examined. Despite the burst of energy for progress and reform, by 1929, the time of the great crash, 80 percent of Arkansas was still rural and cotton was still king, despite all its debt-ridden drawbacks. The timber companies (which by the late 1920s had logged out most of the extensive forests) were pulling out, dealing a terrible blow to the economy. They left behind abandoned rail tracks, factories, mills, and diminished opportunity for rural people to supplement their meager farm incomes. Moreover, serious damage had been inflicted on the environment: the destruction of forests diminished the wild game populations and accelerated the already serious problem of soil erosion. By reducing the organic material covering of the earth, the timber companies had caused many springs to go dry.[55] By 1930, the state was seriously in debt because of the highway bonds and only half of the new highway system had been implemented. Most roads remained in terrible condition. In short, the conditions were being set for the great out-migration of the 1930s and 1940s in which 40 percent of Arkansas's rural population left the state, a figure exceeding the southern average.[56] The poor living conditions that David Tucker describes, although tolerated for decades, finally became impetus to move on:

> The hard time of the thirties . . . drove thousands of Arkansans to reconsider their local attachments. They lacked not only the income for obtaining basic necessities but also all the modern conveniences. The upland farmers lacked electricity. Not even two-percent of Arkansas farms had electric power and the private power companies had no interest in extending their lines into rural areas . . . neither did farm homes have indoor plumbing or telephones. Women especially wanted to have the modern household conveniences and urged their husbands to move when jobs became available.[57]

Stone and Washington Counties, 1900–1930

Since the Ozarks are so heavily forested, the timber industry had a significant impact. In the 1890s, two-thirds of Arkansas was covered with forests. The peak year for the timber industry in Arkansas was 1907, when the state was the fourth largest producer of lumber and wood products in the nation.

As Milton Rafferty explains, "Railroads were essential for profitable lumbering; where rails led, lumbermen followed."[58]

> Large acreages of short-leaf pine and oak were purchased by eastern investors. It was clear that the Ozark forests could supply lumber and railroad supplies for both the Great Plains and the East. The cost of stumpage was low . . . and the open winters permitted year-round logging. Following well established practices, lumber companies often set up complete manufacturing facilities, constructed logging railroads, and began cutting timber. Short-leaf pine forests were exploited for construction lumber, while oak was used for flooring, barrel staves and railroad supplies.[59]

Such activity began in Washington County in the late 1880s with the arrival of the railroad (fig. 3-3). Soon after the Frisco was established, a short line was extended from Fayetteville to Pettigrew (in Madison County), forty-five miles eastward. Within a few years, more than twelve lumber or stave mills had been constructed in the area. But rural people could profit even when a mill or railroad was not in close proximity. When, for example, the Eagle Pencil Company in remote, mountainous Newton County created a demand for cedar, cedar logs were harvested along the Buffalo River and floated down to the North Arkansas Railroad. In Stone County, which lacked the railroad network Washington County enjoyed, logs could be placed on the White River ferry and transported to the railroad just on the other side of the river in adjoining Cleburne County. Or, logs could be transported by wagon to Shirley in Van Buren County, meeting the railroad there. Several lumberyards were established in Stone County, usually near the White River.

For rural Ozark folks, the timber industry was great while it lasted. By farming in the spring and summer and cutting timber on their own land in the winter, they could obtain cash income without seriously challenging their preferred and by now well-established way of life. David Tucker states that a man could hew twelve to twenty railroad ties of rot-resistant white oak daily, and "an estimated million ties a year came out of the Ozark hills, making tie-hacking the most common occupation next to farming."[60]

In his fascinating reminiscences about growing up in Cajun Creek, a remote area of Stone County, Clarence Jetton recalls that his father's only cash income

Fig. 3-3. Steam Saw Mill at Skinner Gap, Washington County. *Shiloh Museum of Ozark History (Wayne Martin Collection)*

was from the sale of barrel stave bolts and white oak hubs that were made into wagon wheel hubs. These were cut on Jetton's land and hauled by wagon to the nearest lumberyard, where they awaited the buyers who hauled them out by barge on the White River.[61]

When the cheap timber ran out, the mills were closed, the machinery was sold, and investment capital was withdrawn from the Ozarks for more lucrative ventures elsewhere. The unfortunate results, both to the local economies and to natural resources have already been noted.

The methods by which the companies disposed of the logged-out land varied. In a few areas, large amounts of land were sold, sight unseen, in a nationwide advertising campaign. One especially eloquent brochure described the Ozarks as "a land of peace, happiness, independence and contentment. It is the country of the little red hen and the much read Bible."[62] Eventually, much of the cutover land became tax delinquent and was purchased in the 1930s by the U.S. Forest Service. Ozark National Forest in the Boston Mountains, for example, comprises mostly cutover lands.[63]

Another development with widespread impact on the entire Ozark region had a happier ending—the shift from subsistence to general or specialized (one crop) farming. The type practiced in the pioneer stage of development, subsistence farming, in which the farmer raised both crops and livestock only for his family's consumption and was not dependent on markets, had lingered in many parts of the Ozarks. Because not all of the land was cultivated at one time, but was rotated instead, subsistence farming required large acreages as well as acres of woodlands where stock and hogs could forage on the open range. Crops were grown primarily for the family's own use with few surpluses, so distance from markets was of no concern. Corn was a favorite crop because of its multiplicity of uses.

General farming, in which a farmer grew both crops and livestock on a larger scale than for the family's use, was dependent on market access. As geographer Milton Rafferty has noted, the shift to general and to specialized farming, however, occurred only in certain geographic areas—those that had smoother topography, better soils, and transportation facilities: "In the interior of the Ozarks residents practiced general farming in the valleys, where conditions were favorable, but in the hill country the farms continued to be of the subsistence types."[64]

The shift to general farming had begun in the late nineteenth century in the good farming areas, such as the river bottoms, the valleys, and the Springfield Plain. Access to railroads was essential. Before the arrival of the railroad, a farmer who did not have access to boat transportation would have found livestock the only feasible product because livestock could be driven north to markets. With the railroad, however, wheat, corn, and other grains, fruits, and vegetables could profitably be grown for markets. General farming led to smaller farms and more intensive use of the land, with a corresponding concern for mechanization and soil fertility.[65]

In the Arkansas Ozarks, specialized farming, or one-crop farming, which was heavily dependent on access to markets, occurred primarily on the Springfield

Plain. This usually involved fruit growing, and Washington and Benton counties led the state in this enterprise. The specialty crop might be apples, strawberries, peaches, or grapes. In 1920 orchard production in Washington County was at its peak with 46.2 percent of the state's total output. That year was the banner year for apples, with 1,952,979 bushels harvested.[66] Many acres were planted with grapes, strawberries, and peaches as well.

The 1930 agricultural statistics for Washington County indicate that general farms were the most numerous; they made up 34.8 percent of the total. Farms specializing in fruit growing ranked third with 17.5 percent of the total. Significantly, even in Washington County, with its open landscape and a railroad network, the old-fashioned subsistence farms ranked second and accounted for 21.8 percent of the total farms. (Other types of farms that represented smaller percentages were stock-ranch, poultry, and dairy farms.)[67] Similarly, in Stone County self-sufficient farms were also ranked second with 25 percent of the total. Cotton farms ranked first with 36 percent of the total, and general farming ranked third with 23 percent of the total. Fruit growing was minimal.[68]

With such statistics in mind, then, it's not surprising that geographer W. A. Browne has found that "frontier conditions" still prevailed on farms in the mountainous sections of the Ozarks (in both Missouri and Arkansas) as late as 1929. In a fascinating article, Browne reported that his survey found most farms were still the self-sufficient type, with crops grown mostly for the family's use. Hogs were still foraging on the open range as the principal meat source, supplemented by wild game. Farm buildings were still being constructed of logs, although occasionally a small, portable mill might move in to saw logs for construction throughout the neighborhood. Farm wives still raised sheep and spun their own yarn for knitting items of clothing, but weaving cloth on floor looms was less common than formerly. A few beef cattle were grown as cheaply as possible by grazing them on the open range, then fattening them on summer forage before selling them in the fall. Railroads had avoided these areas because of the rough terrain and the limited amount of products available for shipment. Thus, the few market products that were raised had to be hauled in wagons for long distances over roads that as late as 1929 were "scarcely more than trails," according to Browne. He concluded, "These conditions naturally result in little contact with the outside world."[69]

Wheat was still an important crop in both subsistence and general farming. Mechanized threshers became common at this time, adding excitement as well as efficiency to farm life. In Washington County, Ruth Holt Payne recalls:

> Many of us remember hearing that puffing and chugging steam-engine as it pulled the huge, dinosaur-like thresher with its long neck along the road, as we followed it to the field to watch its performance. It was moved from farm to farm, leaving great stacks of straw behind for the stock to munch on all winter. The straw was used to refill flattened straw ticks, to make hen nests, and to pad hog houses. During threshing, neighbors swapped work, and the women gathered at each stand to cook the mountains of good food. Not to mention the "camp followers" who were present at every stand to get in on the good eats.[70]

The threshing activity involved work-sharing arrangements and the "waste not, want not" philosophy, both of which helped Ozark people survive. In Stone County, the Kocher family began threshing wheat around 1916. Their thresher was pulled by a gasoline engine that moved from farm to farm. They were paid by toll, receiving one bushel out of every eight bushels harvested. The thresher workers slept in barns and were fed by the people who owned the farms. When a family hadn't produced enough wheat for them to get their bushel, they threshed anyway without pay. According to Stacey Kocher,

> The first engine that the Kochers purchased was bought for $120.00 from Montgomery Ward. They put it in the top of Dominic Kocher's cellar and didn't anchor it down. When they started it up, it started vibrating and scared all the men. They jumped out of the cellar window and doors. Will Williams finally jumped on it and straddled it to hold it down. Then they decided it had to be bolted down.[71]

In both counties this was the heyday of the one-room schoolhouses, which dotted the countryside. Their modest appearance belied their importance, for they were significant landmarks that lent identity to communities (fig. 3-4). Local people built the schoolhouses of weatherboard. They resembled the form of a large single pen or double pen house with a gable roof. For schoolhouses the gable end was turned toward the front, creating an entrance in the short gable end. This was a configuration that vernacular houses almost never assumed. One-room schoolhouses, like vernacular houses, made multipurpose use of interior space. Community meetings, social events, singing schools (held on weekends and evenings), and sometimes religious services were all held in schoolhouses.[72]

In the early 1900s, the curricula of these rural one-room schools did not go beyond the eighth grade. High schools were located only in the county seat, although an occasional private academy might be established elsewhere. At Lincoln, a prosperous apple-growing community in Washington County, a relatively early high school was established in 1910, but the twelfth grade was not offered until 1922. Mountain View's public school was not expanded to include a full twelve-year program until 1928.

Rural churches were usually one-room structures painted white, and they were architecturally almost identical to schools. Even the presence of a belfry did not help to distinguish them from schools, since schools sometimes had belfries, too. Churches were an important focus for social as well as religious life. They were as plain as the houses and schools, since there was little money or time for unnecessary frills. Many of these churches are still in use and they seem remarkably austere to a modern visitor. Their austerity stems in part from the fact that the Baptists, Methodists, and Pentecostals who built the churches saw them as meeting houses primarily and not as sanctuaries where God was present in any special way.

The weatherboard cladding of these churches lends them a special old-fashioned quality, with all the horizontal shadow lines and the texture and "feel" of the wood. Unfortunately, many of these churches have undergone the indignity of

Fig. 3-4. One-Room School, Washington County. Rural one-room schools and churches were architecturally interchangeable and, appropriately, as schools have consolidated and closed recently, some schools have become churches. *Shiloh Museum of Ozark History (Willard Graham Collection)*

being clad in brick veneer or aluminum siding, destroying the pleasing old-fashioned wood aesthetic qualities. Still visible outside some churches are the old wooden frames that were set upon on the land around the churches. Boards were laid across these frames to form long wooden tables on the days when there was "dinner on the grounds."

Revival meetings were popular during this period; in the summer, these were sometimes held outside in brush arbors. Camp meetings, too, continued to provide outlets for socializing as well as for fostering religious experiences.

Washington County, 1900–1930

Washington County was an anomaly in this period: It was the only Arkansas county to gain people instead of losing them during every decade from 1900 to 1940. In addition to agricultural prosperity, the rail network, thousands of acres suitable for fruit growing, fruit processing and canning plants, and the presence of the University of Arkansas all contributed to Washington County's population gains, even in the period of the greatest out-migration from the rest of the state.

Washington County's prosperity is illustrated by the arrival of the automobile age in Fayetteville in the 1920s, which brought several miles of paved roads within Washington County and an automobile population of a thousand by 1927.

A leading Little Rock architect, Charles L. Thompson, designed Fayetteville's stylish new Renaissance Revival stone courthouse, which was erected in 1904. That the good people of Fayetteville had not lost touch with their rural roots, however, is evident in the fact that in the shadow of the new courthouse, people were raising their own cows, chickens, hogs, and, of course, vegetable gardens, all of which were permitted by municipal ordinance. During the Depression, the entire community benefited from these customs, for, as one resident recalled, "People took care of each other; there were no soup lines in Fayetteville."[73]

In 1910 the last major railroad in the county was completed, enabling the Chamber of Commerce to boast that Fayetteville was served by five railroads with easy access to the leading markets of the West, Northwest, South, and Southwest.[74] It would be difficult to overestimate the economic benefits Washington County families derived from the transition from subsistence farming to fruit growing, especially apple growing. As local historian Conrad Russell observed, "Apples once held the same position in the economy of this area that poultry holds today."[75] The year 1907 had been a record year for apples, but, as noted earlier, 1920 became the all-time banner year with 1,952,979 bushels harvested. Small outbuildings, called apple dryers, sprang up on farms, and large commercial evaporators assumed an importance that mills had formerly had. Many old photographs show men working in the orchards and men waiting to unload lines of wagons filled with fruit onto boxcars. Profitable fruit growing was made possible not only by soil and climatic conditions, but also by the presence of a railroad network. Conrad Russell explained how the process worked in Washington County:

> Many apples were culled and barreled in the orchard. A vacant store in Cane Hill was used by some of the buyers for culling and barreling. Lines of wagons waiting to unload were a daily occurrence. . . . The culls from the packers were taken to the many evaporators in the area. Dried fruit was hauled into the towns where buyers would bid and buy. . . . By the 1940s the orchards were becoming less profitable and as the trees were removed they were replaced (in some cases) by polled Hereford cattle.[76]

Stone County, 1900–1930

Despite several near-miss schemes, the railroad largely passed Stone County by. In 1907 the Missouri and North Arkansas Railroad cut across the southwest corner of the county, establishing the county's only railroad town at Arlberg. The rugged Blue Mountain range, however, isolated this corner, preventing the railroad from having an enlivening impact on the entire county and its economy. Many of the area's residents were hopeful that the Missouri and Kansas City

Railroad would run through Stone County, but instead it ran on the opposite side of the White River through Independence County, accessible to Stone County only by ferry.

Nevertheless, Stone county enjoyed a relatively prosperous time by sharing in the general farm prosperity of the entire state until World War I. Certainly it was possible, if not particularly convenient, to haul goods to neighboring railheads in adjoining counties by wagon or by ferry. Stone County farmers had grown cotton in significant quantities as a readily marketable cash crop since the post–Civil War decades. Longtime residents can recall seven cotton gins in the county at one time.

However, general misfortune occurred in the last decades of this period when much of the land became "cottoned out," that is, drained of nutrients from lack of adequate fertilization methods. Losses occured from soil erosion as well. (It was not until the Agricultural Adjustment Act of 1932 that the radical measures required to improve this situation could be implemented.)

Ironically, the arrival of the railroad in the county, even to such a limited degree, effectively brought about the demise of the steamboat commerce networks along the White River, enterprises which had brought some degree of prosperity to parts of the county for many decades.

Many Stone County citizens had benefited from the timber industry, however, in 1907 the Ozark National Forest was created in Arkansas. It encompassed the northern portion of Stone County and thereby prevented this sizable section from being developed further.

Mountain View, the county seat established in 1874, finally came into its own as the county's leading commercial center, aided by the demise of the river ports. The old frame courthouse was replaced by the present three-story sandstone structure in 1922. With its simple details, its broadly overhanging eaves, and its rustic quality, it still forms an appropriate center for the courthouse square. Ringed by other sandstone commercial buildings, the courthouse forms an attractive setting for the traditional music played regularly on the courthouse grounds during the summer.

Throughout the county, especially in the mountainous sections, roads were still bad and travel was difficult. Community histories collected by the Stone County Historical Society often reflected the isolation many residents felt. In the still-isolated community of Herpel, one resident recalled when the mail route was established there in 1907 with delivery three times a week: "If people needed something, they would put a list and money in the mailbox and the carrier would pick up the items and bring them back next mail day."[77] The rugged, isolated quality of Ozark landscape is also manifested in a history of School District Number 54 that recounted the construction of its one-room schoolhouse by local people in 1909. The school had eight grades and a three-month term with twenty to thirty students ranging from age six to age twenty. The schoolhouse was located at Iron's Point on one of the highest mountains in the area. One teacher who was unfamiliar with the mountain (and who was boarding with a local family, as was the custom) became lost the first day on the way home from school. The search party, after looking everywhere for her, found she had returned to the schoolhouse to spend the night.[78]

Conclusion

For the researcher this is a fascinating period because older residents can flesh it out with their memories. Despite the fact that many of these families lived below the poverty level by modern standards, these times are remembered with nostalgia. Two themes constantly emerge: the importance of self-sufficiency, or pride in "making-do," and the importance of neighborliness. Regarding the latter, Renzo Hurst of Cove Creek in the isolated, mountainous southern section of Washington County recalls that community house raisings were held until 1940, and that "in the old days this country was like a big family. Everybody was in need back then. My daddy died when I was fourteen and all the neighbors came in one day and cut enough wood to do us half the winter."[79]

With regard to self-sufficiency, W. A. Lower of Washington County recalls, "If we just had $150.00 for the winter, we'd do just fine. Taxes would be $8.00 to $10.00, and then we'd have only flour, cloth and shoes to buy." He describes a good barter system at the crossroads store where farm people could also sell cream, butter, and milk for cash to the store.[80]

Mrs. Agnes Pierce of Cove Creek recalls hauling garden produce, chickens, and eggs in a wagon fifty miles down the mountains to Fort Smith. Accommodations for such travelers were provided at no cost. "Every town had a wagon yard with a little camp house. You just brought your own bedding and spent the night."[81]

In sum, as this period closed in 1930, the Arkansas Ozarks enjoyed improvements in public services, most notably in public schools and somewhat erratically in road improvements. Farms generally became more prosperous, especially in areas doubly blessed with fertile soil and a railway network.

Yet, as we have seen, many people in the remote sections of the Ozarks were living in ways more characteristic of the nineteenth century than of the twentieth. Isolation was still a limiting factor for many. Nearly all lived without electricity or running water or roads that were dependable in all weather.

Despite the addition of high-school curricula including twelve grades, generally only one high school existed in each county, so it was difficult for young people in outlying areas to avail themselves of a high-school education. Accordingly, the cultivation of practical skills and the tradition of living by one's own wits continued to be more important than developing one's intellect or acquiring a formal education. The traditional work-sharing and barter systems continued because they were still important in helping people survive.

Most significantly, this is the period in which the great out-migration began and thousands of Ozarkers moved elsewhere, no doubt seeing themselves as moving out of the nineteenth century and into the twentieth. What made some people stay? They were not necessarily the least ambitious, surely, but rather those most skilled in the Ozark ways of "making do" and those whose roots ran too deep to be transplanted. As Harry Ashmore observed, these are the people "for whom the land provided a benison, sustaining an optimism and vitality that could be transmitted from generation to generation." Even as their neighbors left in droves, they must have known "that the bluebird of happiness nested in the backwoods of Arkansas at least as frequently as in the crowded neighborhoods of the . . . industrial cities."[82]

Chapter 4

House Types in the Arkansas Ozarks

Background to the Study of American Vernacular House Types

The delineation of house types is a basic foundation for vernacular-architecture studies. For example, cultural geographers have studied house types to determine cultural-geographic regions since 1936 when geographer Fred Kniffen published his pioneering article, "Louisiana House Types." As Kniffen commented, "The humbler buildings by reason of their adherence to type and numerical superiority are far more important as markers of basic cultural processes than are uniquely designed individual structures."[1]

It is indicative of the paucity of scholarly attention to the vernacular architecture of the Arkansas Ozarks (and, indeed, of all regions of the state) that at the end of the twentieth century this basic classifying activity has scarcely begun. More than twenty years have elapsed since Diane Tebbetts published the single scholarly article on traditional houses of Independence County, Arkansas, that identified vernacular house types in Arkansas.[2]

In a second influential publication from 1965 entitled "Folk Housing: Key to Diffusion," Kniffen expanded his study to include the eastern United States, concluding that initial occupance patterns established by migrants from three eastern seaboard source areas could be discerned through folk-housing patterns (fig. 4-1).[3] In 1968 folklorist Henry Glassie elaborated upon Kniffen's thesis in his *Pattern in the Material Folk Culture of the Eastern United States.*[4] Subsequent work by geographer Pierce Lewis and several others has substantiated Kniffen's and Glassie's theories so that, with the caveat that the model requires testing, especially in the Midwest and the South, the scholarly consensus "is sufficient to yield a common model of architectural diffusion for the eastern United States."[5] Kniffen's model of diffusion indicates that by 1790 three well-defined source areas were operative on the Atlantic seaboard: New England, the Middle Atlantic (centering on southeastern Pennsylvania), and the lower Chesapeake (centering on Tidewater Virginia) (fig. 4-1).[6] The diffusion from these source areas formed the characteristics of the present major folk-culture regions of the eastern United States—the North, the Mid-Atlantic, the Midwest, the Upland South, and the Lowland South—as defined by Glassie (fig. 4-2).[7]

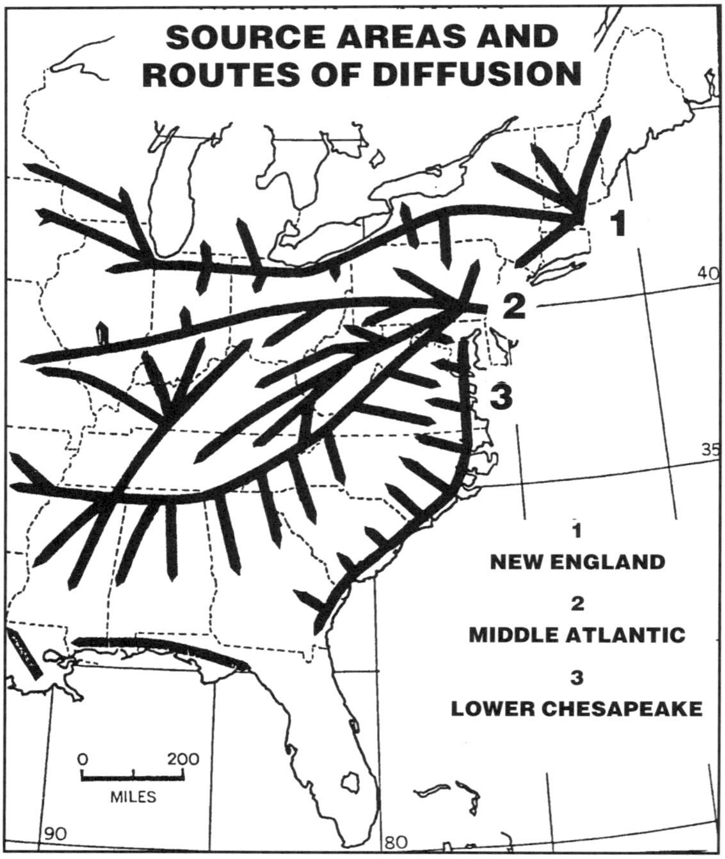

Fig. 4-1. Atlantic Seaboard Source Areas and Route of Diffusion of Vernacular House Forms. *Adapted from Fred Kniffen, "Folk Housing: Key to Diffusion," figure II*

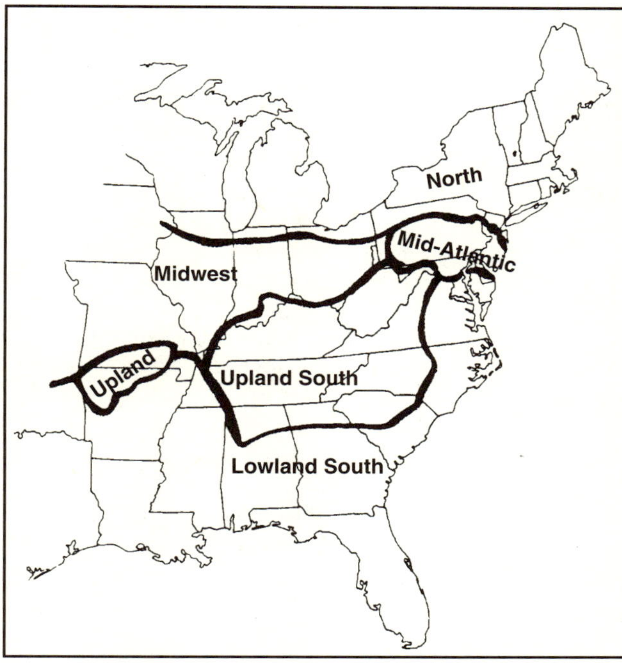

Fig. 4-2. Material Folk-Culture Regions in the Eastern United States. *Adapted from Henry Glassie,* Pattern in the Material Folk Culture of the Eastern United States, *figure 9*

Of the original source areas on the Atlantic seaboard, the Middle Atlantic culture hearth had the most widespread influence, affecting, as it did, both North and South (fig. 4-1). As Kniffen summarized it, from the Middle Atlantic region,

> The major directions of propagation were southward along the Appalachian axis, with offshoots in every direction, and westward across from Pennsylvania, eventually to dominate everything south of the New England stream, except for a generally thin Tidewater strip along the outer coastal plain.[8]

Emanating from the Middle Atlantic culture hearth, then, was the southern Appalachian-Kentucky Bluegrass stream, which is the major source of influence for the vernacular architecture of the Ozarks. Indeed, the traditional Ozark house types are so typical of the model of Upland South vernacular architecture patterns that the Ozark region holds few surprises for those familiar with the work of Kniffen and Glassie.

There were three major architectural contributions from this Middle Atlantic source area: German log-construction techniques, the English I-house form, and basic German barn types.[9] Each of these will be discussed subsequently.

The elemental dwelling form spreading from the Middle Atlantic culture hearth was a single pen log house, the chimney of which gradually moved away from a German central chimney to the Tidewater English end-chimney. Thus, the traditional house types that the early settlers developed and that the westward moving migrants carried with them as part of their heritage were house forms that emerged as pragmatic solutions to the problem of making additions to a single-room log structure.

Construction exigencies played a crucial role in the way builders thought about traditional house types. As Martin Wright explains it,

> Consider the restrictions upon pioneer construction. . . . The size of the home was determined by the length of the logs which the men could handle. Lengths of logs which could be raised by two men varied from twelve to eighteen feet, depending chiefly upon the thickness of the log. Consequently, the erection of a single log pen resulted in a crib of logs between twelve and eighteen feet square. If enlargement of the house was required and logs were the only building material, the pioneer was faced with a knotty problem. Two obvious solutions presented themselves. First of all, the walls might be extended by adding logs. This, however, would require the interlocking of new logs in the old walls, an extremely difficult procedure. . . . The second obvious possibility was to extend his old walls upward and form a second story, but this required the removal of the roof. . . . From the pioneer's viewpoint, then, the single log pen was an indivisible unit. In order to expand, another had to be built.[10]

All the traditional Ozark house types then, as we shall see, can be viewed as mental constructs based on seeing a house as a combination of indivisible single pens. This way of conceiving of house construction developed in the diffusion westward as solutions to the problem of constructing additions to single log pens (figs. 4-3, 4-4). The additive nature of the design process is apparent in all the traditional house types and clearly influences the adaptation of popular house types in the region as well.

Underlying the entire endeavor of studying house types to determine cultural-geographic regions is, of course, the remarkable persistence of forms in tradi-

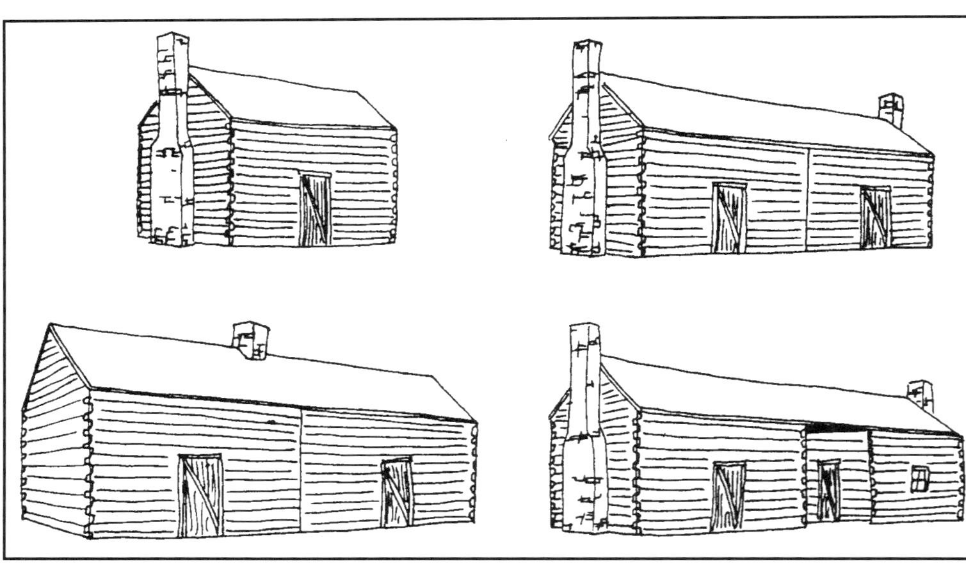

Fig. 4-3. Standard Methods of Adding On to a Single Pen Log House. Together with the houses in fig. 4-4, these houses constitute the six traditional Arkansas Ozark house types. *Adapted from Doug Swaim, "North Carolina Folk Housing,"* Carolina Dwelling, *Figure 6*

Fig. 4-4. Arkansas Central Hall House and I-House. Together with the four traditional houses in fig. 4-3, these constitute six traditional Arkansas Ozark house types. *Drawing by Stacy Rennhoff and Janet Boyeskie.*

On the basis of field work, the houses in figs. 4-3 and 4-4 have been identified as the six traditional Ozark vernacular house types. Although they stem from different origins (the first four from log construction and the second pair from high-style influences) strong commonalities bind them. They appear in both log and frame construction, early and late; all follow the English folk tradition of being one room deep (not counting the variable rear shed or ells); all have gable-end roofs and entrances transverse to the ridgepole; all have balanced or bilaterally symmetrical facades. Most importantly, all are conceived of simply in terms of additive "units" with only a few variables possible. This concept of constructing in additive units was doubtlessly dictated originally by the inherent inflexibility of log construction, but since the same additive approach persisted long after the infinitely more variable balloon frame was introduced, we can conjecture that this quality satisfied a conceptual and aesthetic urge. These constitute the shared house models found in all tradition-bound societies. Since the knowledge of the models is shared by all, there is no need for drawings or plans.

tional architecture. An elderly Ozark man who lived in a traditional double pen house with double front doors was persistently asked by the interviewer where he and others of his generation got their ideas for designing houses. He finally remarked impatiently, "We just built them out of our heads the way we wanted them." The way they wanted them changed little over the generations.

Many scholars have commented upon this continuity. Pierce Lewis related the continuity to the desire for community,

> Most people avoid building eccentric houses for the same reason they avoid eccentricity in hair cuts, clothing styles, speech patterns and religion. Each is such a basic expression of unspoken cultural values that deviations from accepted standards are taken as evidence of an unstable and untrustworthy personality and invite unfavorable comments from one's neighbors.[11]

Henry Glassie related the form concepts of traditional architecture to traditional music, remarking that "the number of folk house types in any area of the U.S. is surprisingly small. . . . The Anglo-American folk performer's practice was to ignore many of the chances for variation theoretically open to him, to perfect a form and then to repeat it over and over again. . . . The measure of . . . the folk performer's success is repetition, not innovation."[12]

These two views seem complementary, rather than mutually exclusive; both address the fact that people take comfort in the familiar, particularly in somewhat isolated locales like the Ozarks.

In his profound study, *House Form and Culture*, Amos Rapoport only commented upon the difficulty of defining vernacular architecture, instead, he preferred to speak of the process by which vernacular houses are built. For Rapoport a "shared model" is the essential ingredient in the vernacular building process,

> The vernacular design process is one of the model and adjustments or variations. . . . One starts with the simplest outline, the main features, and adds and elaborates the details and makes adjustments as one proceeds. *The outline is in the mind's eye at the start,* and even the execution involves the use of principles applicable to every building; the form also adjusts to given problems and available means without *conscious* aesthetic striving or stylistic interests. Such buildings are based on the idea that a common task should be performed in the simplest, most unobtrusive and direct way possible. This can only occur in a society which is tradition bound, where the few changes that occur happen within a frame of a given common heritage and hierarchy of values reflected in the building types.[13]

It should be noted, as Upton and Vlach were careful to point out, that vernacular houses are not simply repetitious of one another or built by rote; indeed, there are no two exactly alike.[14] But the changes are in variations of and adjustments to the shared model; as Rapoport said, "It is the individual specimens that are modified, not the type."[15]

The process described by Rapoport rings true with regard to the Ozarks. There were limited models for smokehouses, barns, corn cribs, and houses as well. The limited choices involved, it seems, only decisions about the size of the house (one story or two), about the choice of the double pen plan or central hallway plan, and about whether a central passageway was to be open or closed.

Traditional House Types in the Arkansas Ozarks

Six traditional and three nontraditional house types were identified in the fieldwork. The six traditional types are the single pen, the double pen, the saddlebag, the central hall cottage, the dogtrot, and the I-house. Each of these styles originated from the architectural conventions developed and passed down within cultural groups. They represent the folk-tradition end of the architectural spectrum; they have the most intense degree of social representation in that they represent

Ozark architectural traditions with little outside influence from the larger popular culture.

The standard methodology for classifying traditional house types is based upon the basic floor plan and height. Although appearing on almost all houses, porches, rear sheds, or rear ell additions are not taken into consideration, since these are variables and contrast with the otherwise constant basic floor plans (figs. 4-5 and 4-6 illustrate rear sheds and rear ells).

Several generalizations apply to all the Ozark house types designated as traditional. All appear in both log and frame construction. All follow the English folk tradition of being one room deep (again, with the exception of rear shed and rear ell additions). Finally, all have gable-end roofs and entrances transverse to the ridgepole. Typical of Upland South houses, most had exterior gable-end chimneys, which were generally constructed of stone rather than brick.

By moving beyond construction details to a more profound level of observation, however, one sees underlying aesthetic concepts that relate Ozark houses to more general qualities observed in vernacular architecture of both the Anglo-American tradition and worldwide folk practices. First is the ubiquitous frontality, which Henry Glassie remarked, is "one of the great principles of the Western folk aesthetic."[16] Second is the consistently displayed urge toward bilateral symmetry in the facade openings and in the overall massing when viewed frontally. Glassie noted that in order to satisfy this urge, Anglo-American folk builders departed from the English tradition of placing appendages on the sides of the original house. Thus, "unconfused by lateral appendages . . . the house's symmetry

Fig. 4-5. Typical Rear Shed, Burl Brown House (1910), East Richwoods, Stone County. Rear shed additions are typically found on modest houses of one story.

Fig. 4-6. Typical Rear Ell, Parks Station (1857), Hogeye, Washington County. Rear ell additions are typically found on houses at the upper end of the economic scale, as in central hall or I-house types.

stood out clearly and simply, presenting like recent minimalist art, an image of artificiality and control."[17] The third quality is that of additive composition, which, Amos Rapoport observed, characterizes vernacular architecture throughout the world. In the case of Ozark vernacular houses, this additive composition is exemplified by the multiplication of the indivisible pen. This unspecialized, open-ended nature of vernacular architecture "enables vernacular buildings to accept changes and additions which would visually and conceptually destroy a high-style design."[18] As noted earlier, this concept of constructing a house in additive units was doubtlessly originally dictated by the inherent inflexibility of log construction. Nevertheless, since the same additive approach persisted long after the infinitely more variable balloon frame construction was introduced, we can reasonably conjecture that this quality satisfied a conceptual and aesthetic urge.

Single Pen Houses

The one-room structure, the most elemental form of shelter, was built as a temporary dwelling by settlers all over the United States. According to Glassie, this type, composed of a single construction unit fewer than two stories high, is properly termed a cabin. As he observed, not all cabins are log; they were constructed of stone in Pennsylvania, of brick in Virginia, and of adobe in Utah, for example.[19]

Current scholarly consensus decrees that a square cabin reflects the English folk tradition, while rectangular cabins stem from a Scotch-Irish or German tradition. In the Middle Atlantic colonies the Scotch-Irish and Germans built rectangular log houses, while the English in Virginia introduced the one-bay house of old England, which was traditionally sixteen feet square.[20] The English built this small house in frame construction, but it was copied in log in areas where the Tidewater and the Middle Atlantic architectural traditions mixed. Most of the single pen houses documented are square and, if further study confirms this, it represents one of two elements of Tidewater rather than the common and predictable Mid-Atlantic traditions in the Ozarks.

All the documented cabins were of wood construction, with logs being the most common material. Several early twentieth-century cabins of box construction (an economical studless construction method popular in the early twentieth century, discussed at length in chapter 7) were also recorded. The span of dates for the single pen house was from 1837 to 1920. Typical floor plans for the single pen houses recorded are illustrated in figs. 4-8, 4-9, and 4-10. Fig. 4-7 is a key that should aid in interpreting the floor plans. Lofts were often used as sleeping areas in these small dwellings, but because of remodelings or advanced stages of deterioration, none of the original stairways remained.

The twentieth-century box construction houses had stove flues instead of chimneys, but all the earlier cabins had an exterior stone chimney on the gable end. Most had small shed room additions in the rear.

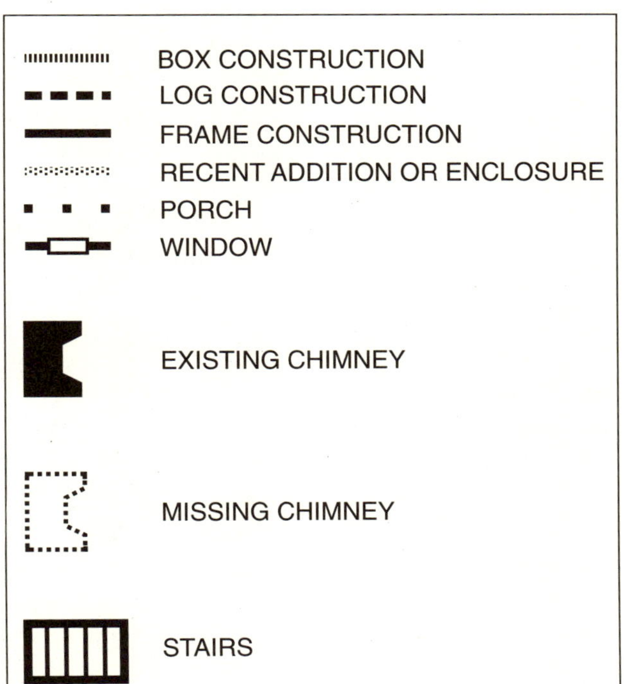

Fig. 4-7. Key to Construction Symbols Used in Plans. *Drawing by Stacy Rennhoff*

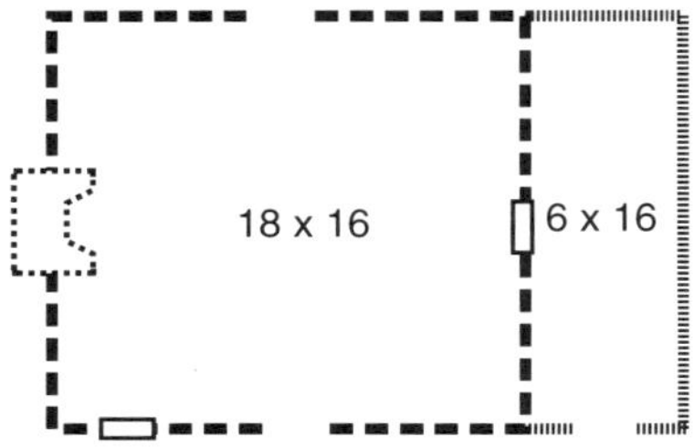

◀ Fig. 4-8. Single Pen Log House Plan: Isaac P. Looney House (c. 1850), Timbo, Stone County. *Drawing by Stacy Rennhoff*

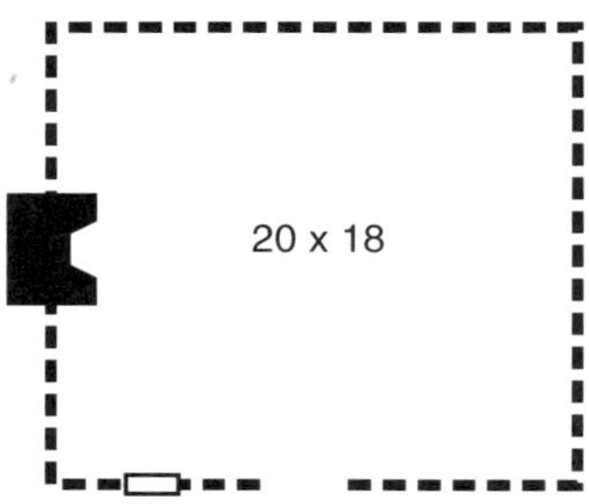

▲ Fig. 4-9. Single Pen Log House Plan: William Dillard House (c. 1860), Round Bottom, Stone County. *Drawing by Stacy Rennhoff*

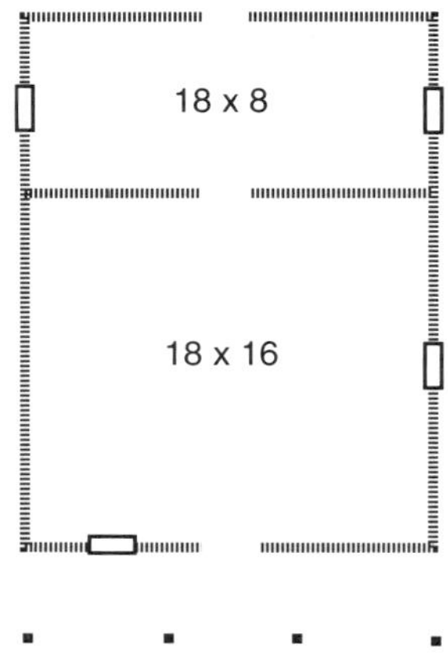

▲ Fig. 4-10. Single Pen House Plan: C. F. Williams House (1910), Herpel, Stone County (box construction). *Drawing by Stacy Rennhoff*

The square or approximately square floor plan definitely prevailed in these single pen houses.[21] About half were square and the other half were approximately so; common measurements were sixteen feet by eighteen feet, sixteen feet by seventeen feet, and eighteen feet by nineteen feet. In the Arkansas Ozark region as a whole, two-story houses are uncommon, and two-story single pen houses are rare; however, two single pen two-story houses of log construction were documented in Washington County.[22]

Because of the single pen's cramped living quarters, as soon as a family could afford to do so, they either moved into a larger house or enlarged the original pen. Literally hundreds of traditional Ozark houses still have, beneath their weatherboard exteriors, the single pen log unit that forms the core of the newer and larger house. Most extant log cabins are now being used as barns.

Usually the single pen house became a double pen or a dogtrot house; figs. 4-11 to 4-14 illustrate four different configurations resulting from additions to single pen houses: dogtrot, double pen, saddlebag, and an atypical arrangement in which the newer log pen was placed to the rear and perpindicular to the original pen. The three typical configurations precisely match those documented in a study of North Carolina vernacular houses.[23]

As the postcard entitled "A Native's Cottage" suggests, the single pen house type (especially in log) has symbolized the dwelling of the poor, ignorant, stereotypical "hillbilly" in the popular imagination (fig. 4-17). In reality the situation was much different: the 1880 photograph of Rebecca and Charles Henry Holcomb's single pen house (no doubt a log cabin covered with weatherboard), complete with a counterpane on the bed, curtains at the window, ornamental vines and tiger lilies in the yard, in addition to a brick chimney, proves that this smallest of all house types was a perfectly respectable dwelling for Ozark people of whatever class (fig. 4-18). Six examples of single pen houses are shown in figs. 4-15 to 4-20.

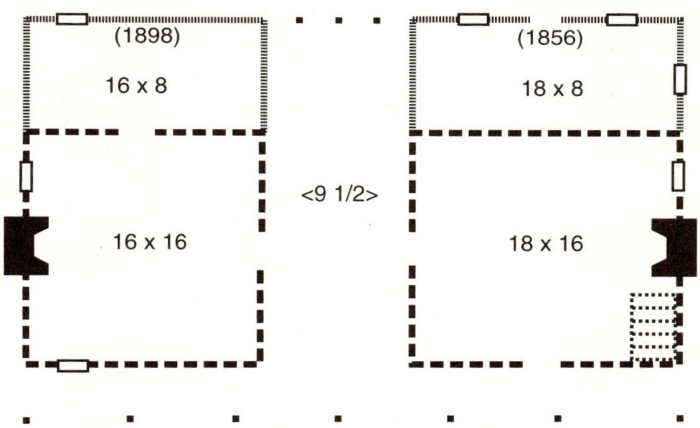

◀ Fig. 4-11. Addition to Single Pen Log House to Form Dogtrot Plan: Zachariah Ford House (1856, 1885), St. James Vicinity, Stone County. *Drawing by Stacy Rennhoff*

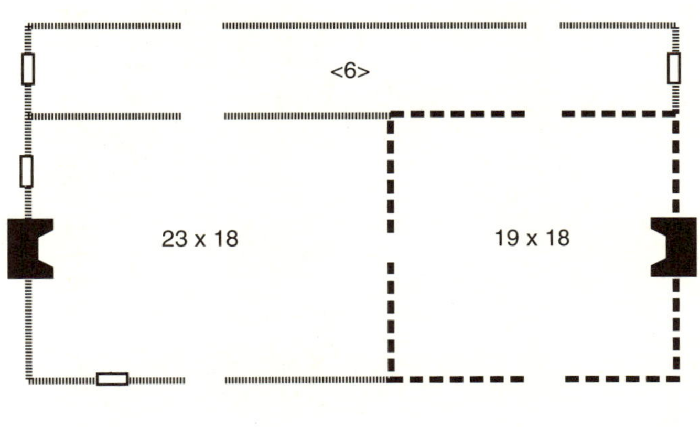

▶ Fig. 4-12. Addition to Single Pen Log House to Form Double Pen Plan: Henry Nolan House (no date), St. James Vicinity, Stone County. *Drawing by Stacy Rennhoff*

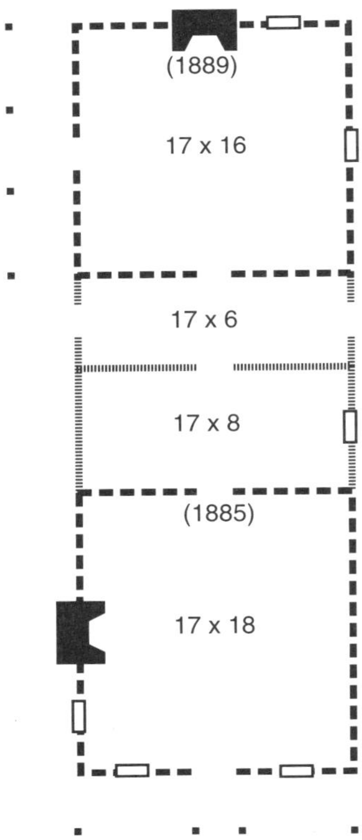

◀ Fig. 4-13. Addition to Single Pen Log House to Form Atypical Double Pen Plan: Clark-King House (1885, 1889), Mountain View Vicinity, Stone County. *Drawing by Stacy Rennhoff*

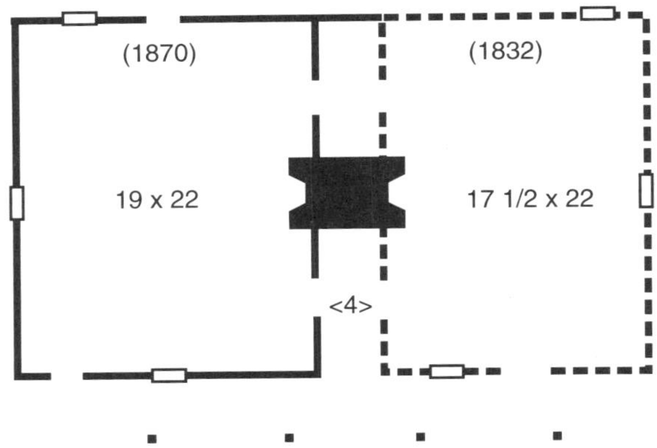

▲ Fig. 4-14. Addition to Single Pen Log House to Form Saddlebag Plan: McGarrah-Reed House (1832), Elkins Vicinity, Washington County. One of the finest antebellum log dwellings constructed in Washington County, this house is now partially reconstructed and furnished inside the Shiloh Museum of Ozark History, Springdale, Arkansas. *Drawing by Stacy Rennhoff*

Fig. 4-16. Isaac Preston Looney Log House (1850), Timbo Vicinity, Stone County.

◀ Fig. 4-15. Daisy and Albert Blair Single Pen Log House (c. 1800, nonextant), Pleasant Grove, Stone County. This small log house with its eighteen-feet square front room, gable-end stone chimney, and rear kitchen shed addition has all the qualities of the typical Ozark log cabin. In 1910 Albert and Daisy Blair purchased it from unknown previous owners and lived in it until they built their frame double pen house adjacent to it in 1926. A daughter, Mrs. Novelle Blair Baumert, who grew up here, has described its interior and the family's activities in this house in great detail, including drawing a furnishings plan. (This is discussed in chapter 8, and her interview is reproduced in the appendix.) *Courtesy of Novelle Baumert*

Fig. 4-17. Postcard of Ozark Single Pen Log House Entitled "A Native's Cottage." As the caption on this postcard indicates, the rough, poorly constructed single pen log house embodied all the stereotypical qualities of its allegedly lazy, ignorant, shiftless inhabitants—"hillbillies" all. But as the following photograph indicates, a small single pen log structure could house perfectly respectable inhabitants as well. *Shiloh Museum of Ozark History*

Fig. 4-19. Clark-King Single Pen Log House (1885 and 1889), Mountain View Vicinity, Stone County. Located at the end of a dirt road that is little more than a trail and still without electricity or running water, this single pen log house with half-dovetail construction notching, full front porch, and large stone chimney, seems the quintessential Ozark log cabin. Its unusual building history, however, has formed an atypical double pen house. In 1885 P. C. Clark built the front single pen facing south. Four years later the second owner, Rev. Jacob King, built a second single pen log house facing east about fifteen feet away from the first. The space between the two houses was enclosed with board-and-batten box construction and partitioned into two sections. The section nearest the kitchen was called the breezeway and was used to cure meat, while the area nearest the front pen was called "the lean" and served as a bedroom. Reverend King, a circuit preacher, was a well-known figure in Stone County. He served in the state assembly in 1891–1893, 1897–1901, and was elected as a state senator in 1901. (The plan is seen in Figure 4-13.)

◀ Fig. 4-18. Rebecca and William Henry Holcomb Single Pen House (c. 1880), Elm Springs Vicinity, Washington County. The small dimensions of the house and its rather diminutive door and window indicate that this dwelling was probably a log house covered with weatherboard. The brick chimney, the curtains at the window, and the counterpane on the bed, along with ornamental plants, such as tiger lilies and ivy, reflect a concern for propriety. (Note the typical wood shingled roof and the proximity of the log smokehouse to the rear of the house.) *Shiloh Museum of Ozark History (Kennedy Deaver Collection)*

Fig. 4-20. Austin Crymes House (1920), Newnata, Stone County. This small single pen house is of box construction, the flimsiest and least expensive type. Several features make it a typical early twentieth-century Ozark dwelling: its board-and-batten exterior masking box construction; its proportions in which the rear shed kitchen addition is half the width of the principal room (seven by fourteen feet and fourteen by fifteen feet) and its stove flues, which substitute for the traditional stone chimneys. It represents the early twentieth-century alternative to the single pen log cabin as a basic and inexpensive dwelling.

Double Pen Houses

This rather homely little house type, which always has two front doors, is so common it could be designated the quintessential Ozark house. (Called a "duple" first by author Donald Harington in his novel *The Architecture of the Arkansas Ozarks,* the term was then popularized by architectural historian Cyrus Sutherland of the University of Arkansas.) The double pen house is a one-story gable-end roof structure with two adjoining rooms of approximately equal size across the facade. A connecting door is located in the dividing wall between the two rooms, and each pen has a front door. The double pen type could be formed by adding a second pen onto the gable end opposite the chimney of a single pen house (fig. 4-3). In most cases, however, the two pens were built simultaneously.

Widely found throughout the United States, the double pen house is an especially common rural type in Mississippi and in Middle Tennessee.[24] The Independence County, Arkansas, survey ascertained that this type (often in box construction) is the most common folk house.[25] It is quite common in the Ozark study area as well.

Scholars agree that the type originated in the British Isles, but differ on the question of whether the form was disseminated by the English in the Chesapeake Tidewater districts of Virginia and Maryland or by the Scotch-Irish in Pennsylvania. Because of its early prominence in Middle Tennessee, this double pen type with two front doors has been labeled the Cumberland House. Occupants of double pen houses cited three reasons for the one design element that might seem peculiar, the two front doors. Having two front doors was useful for extra cross-ventilation, for easy escape in case of fire, and for additional privacy in making essential trips outside during the night, since both front rooms were often used as bedrooms. As Terry Jordan noted, since the type is so widespread, multiple origins are possible.[26]

The arrangement of doors and windows varies, but never completely departs from a bilateral symmetry or at least a balanced facade. All have four- or six-bay facades.

The double pen house in the study area spans the dates 1830 to 1929, with the earliest example being a log version, the George Morrow house in the Morrow community of Washington County. This type was built by families of moderate to poor economic status, and, predictably, they rarely display any form of exterior ornamentation, and generally have exterior stone chimneys and rear shed additions. In houses constructed after 1880, however, stoves might be substituted for fireplaces, with stove flues visible on the exterior rather than the more picturesque stone chimneys. Almost all have a full front porch. (Examples of double pen houses are shown in figs. 4-21 to 4-25.) Because of the difficulty of joining two log pens, most double pen houses are of balloon frame construction.

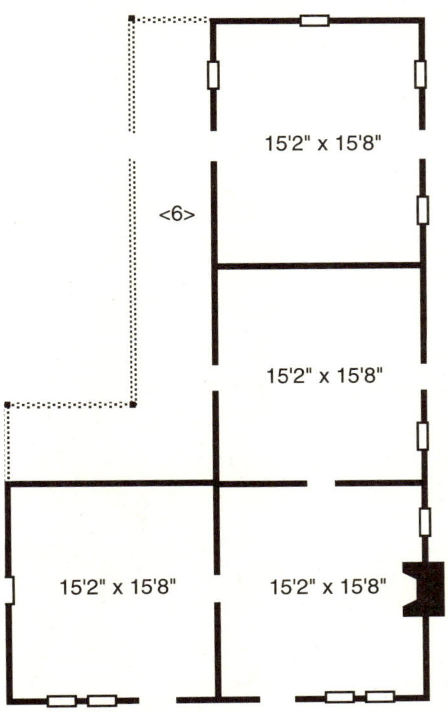

◀ Fig. 4-21. Double Pen House Plan: Henry Copeland House (c. 1900), Pleasant Grove, Stone County. *Drawing by Stacy Rennhoff*

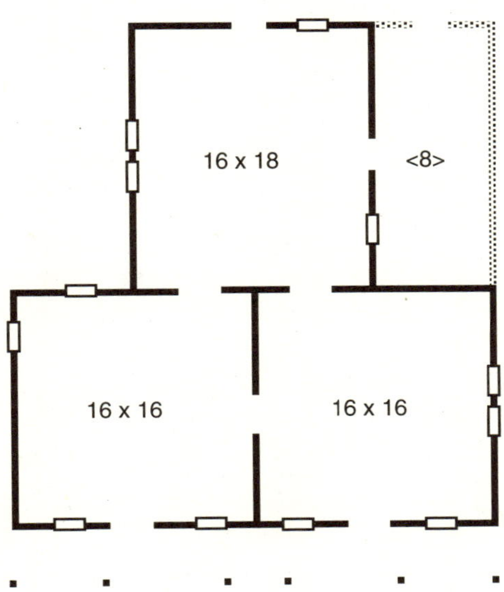

▲ Fig. 4-22. Double Pen House Plan: Daisy and Albert Blair House (1926), Pleasant Grove, Stone County. *Drawing by Stacy Rennhoff*

Fig. 4-23. Henry Copeland House (c. 1900), Pleasant Grove, Stone County. This simple house is typical of the many double pen houses with two front doors that were popular in the early 1900s through the 1920s. In the Ozarks they seem to have been the rural alternative to the small urban bungalows. This house has a large two-room ell with its own full-length porch (visible in the photograph). The facade has six openings as many double houses do, but it has a somewhat unusual window-window-door/door-window-window arrangement. The substitution of a single exterior stone chimney instead of the traditional pair is common in twentieth-century small houses. (The plan is seen in fig. 4-21.)

Fig. 4-25. Agnes and Harrison Pierce House (1928), Cove Creek, Washington County. Located in isolated, mountainous terrain in southern Washington County, this cheerful double pen house with two front doors was occupied until recently by the widow of its original builder, Harrison Pierce. Mr. Pierce, with the help of a neighbor, constructed the house from oak lumber cut on his farm. The popular blue-and-white exterior paint scheme is intact, with the doors and window frames outlined in blue and the middle sections of the chamfered porch posts (which Mr. Pierce chamfered by hand, using a draw knife) also painted blue. This dwelling differs from the standard double pen plan in having two full-sized rooms at the rear and a hipped gable roof. The Pierces exemplify the many Ozark farmers who practiced general farming on a small scale. They grew a variety of vegetables and oats and kept small herds of cattle and pigs that grazed on the open range, all of which could be sold for cash. Rather than transporting these to the county seat at Fayetteville, the Pierces descended thirty miles down the Boston Mountains to Fort Smith in their farm wagon, where they would stay overnight in the wagon yards furnished by each town. They could obtain additional cash or credit at the local general store by selling their milk, cream, and butter. The full array of outbuildings is outlined in the farm layout sketches. (See Figure 5-2.)

◀ Fig. 4-24. Daisy and Albert Blair House (1926), Pleasant Grove, Stone County. This plain double pen house with its bilaterally symmetrical facade openings replaced the Blairs' single pen log house, which is shown and discussed in figs. 4-15, 8-18, and 8-19. Albert Blair was a farmer who operated a sorghum mill; like most other Ozark farmers, he constructed this house himself from lumber on his own farm, which was sawn at a nearby sawmill. The Blairs' choice of this old plan and its means of construction testify to the durability of traditional house plans and construction practices well into the twentieth century in the less populous areas of the Ozarks. The Blairs' daughter, Mrs. Novelle Blair Baumert, continues to live in this house. The sturdy outhouse, one of the few remaining, was constructed by the Blairs in the early 1930s with one of the first federal farm home loans. Before this, they simply did without, as many others did.

Saddlebag Houses

The saddlebag house is a double pen house with a large central chimney serving the room on either side; it is generally one room deep and one story tall (fig. 4-3). Because of its heat retention qualities, it was a common floor plan for seventeenth-century New England houses of braced frame construction. Like the dogtrot house, saddlebag construction provided an easy solution to enlarging single pen log houses; the addition was made on the chimney end, creating a central chimney. The pens could be built a few feet apart, with the space on either side of the chimney occupied by storage or by narrow stairs to upper lofts.

Saddlebag houses appear widely throughout the eastern United States, but rarely are a dominant type. Because of its heat retention, the saddlebag house is considered primarily a northern type. It is frequently found in West Virginia, Indiana, Kentucky, and southern Illinois.[27] Scholars agree that the central fireplace arrangement is an ancient one common to many parts of Europe, but disagree on the New World origin and dissemination of the type.

Whatever its origin, the log saddlebag house proved to be the rarest in the study area with only one documented in Stone County (fig. 4-26). Two two-story log structures were documented in Washington County, which had one-story frame additions in a saddlebag arrangement.

Fig. 4-26. Taylor-Stokes House (now barn) (1876), Marcella, Stone County. This is the only log saddlebag house documented in Stone County. Like many log houses, it now serves as a barn and the casual passerby could miss it entirely. The names of both Thomas Stokes and J. W. Taylor, two early owners of the house, are scratched into one of the stone mantels, along with the date of construction, 1876.

Dogtrot Houses

Surely the most picturesque house, both in name and appearance, is the dogtrot type. The term is somewhat loosely used; Henry Glassie defines it as a house with two equal one-story units joined by a common gable roof over an open central, floored hall from which the rooms are entered.[28] It is my contention, however, that the open hallway and the living patterns it dictated were so distinctive that a house that originally had an open hallway separating units of equal size and a symmetrical relationship is a dogtrot house whether it has one story or two. Given this criterion, what is perhaps the oldest extant dwelling in the Ozarks, the Jacob Wolf log house in Norfork, Baxter County, constructed around 1820, is one of the now rare two-story dogtrot houses. Two others were documented in the fieldwork (figs. 4-27 and 4-35).

Since the open passageway provides maximum ventilation, the dogtrot house is especially suited to warm climates. According to Terry Jordan, dogtrots are a common but minor type throughout the Upper South and are especially numerous across the inner coastal plain of the Deep South.[29] Henry Glassie has cited the common presence of dogtrot houses in the Arkansas Ozarks as indicative of an architectural heritage from the Lowland South, as well as from the southern mountains. "The dogtrot house, for example, rare and late in the Blue Ridge, is not unusual in the Ozarks."[30] Dogtrot houses extend as far north as Indiana and Iowa, although not as a major type.[31] Since it is associated with the Lowland South, it is a common house type in central and southern Arkansas. Fieldwork for this study indicates that the dogtrot house is not simply "not unusual in the Ozarks," in Glassie's words, but is a predominant type, especially in mountainous areas.

Scholarly debate over the American origin and the European prototype for the dogtrot house has been heated, with different scholars asserting that the type has German, Swedish, English, or Scotch-Irish origins. Terry Jordan, in his definitive study of Texas log structures, presents a comprehensive overview of the debate, concluding, "Whatever their origin, many early American dogtrot houses seem linked to eighteenth-century central and southwestern Virginia as well as Tennessee."[32] The important point to the debate seems to be that because the dogtrot house so conveniently solved the difficulty of constructing two log pens adjacent to one another, it not only spread rapidly through climatic zones in which it was appropriate, but also it could well have had multiple origins.

Dogtrot Houses in the Arkansas Ozarks

It should be noted that the term dogtrot house is not often used by people who inhabit them. Inhabitants usually refer to the type as a hallway house, a house with a hallway, or as a house with a breezeway. If the structure is log, the term often used is double log house or double house.

Further fieldwork is necessary to clarify patterns of distribution, but based upon this study, the following hypothesis can be made: although the type is fairly common throughout the Ozarks, it predominates only in the more mountainous and isolated areas.[33] Although, as just noted, two extraordinary log dogtrot houses with two stories were documented, the typical dogtrot, whether log or frame, was one story with a full-length front porch, twin gable-end stone chimneys, and a third smaller room behind one of the front pens, forming a rear ell. The overall configuration, then, is an "L-shaped" house when viewed from the rear. Full-length porches also forming an "L" were usually present at the rear as seen in the Chaney house (fig. 4-35). Less often, each front pen had a small rear shed addition and no rear porches, as in the Zachariah Ford house (fig. 4-31).

Like the single pen house, most of the room dimensions were square or approximately square, with the most common measurements being sixteen by sixteen feet or eighteen by eighteen feet. Hallways ranged from eight- to ten-feet wide. The only house with truly rectangular pens was also one of the oldest, the 1858 log two-story house called Parks Station because it functioned as a stop on the Butterfield Overland Mail Route through Washington County. Its pens measured fifteen by nineteen feet with an eleven-foot-wide breezeway (figs. 4-27 and 4-40).

Dimensions did not seem to correlate with age, but one consistency was noted: newer houses were more likely to have doors opening only into the breezeway, while the oldest houses often had doors that opened onto the front porch as well, but there were exceptions. Representative floor plans of dogtrot houses are illustrated in figs. 4-27 to 4-30.

The dogtrot is unique among the house types in having a public quality to its use of space—the open breezeway so distinctive it gives the house its name. Every person who has ever lived in a dogtrot house comments upon the marvelous breeze-catching quality of the open hallway. Thus, besides functioning as a storage area, this breezeway functioned as an outdoor room in good weather. Here one might perform chores, eat, sit, or sleep in the summertime. A double bed, for instance, was moved onto the breezeway of the Zachariah Ford house (fig. 4-31) in summer because even on the hottest nights a breeze would be stirring there.

It is partly the public quality (in addition to being difficult to heat) of this space that renders the dogtrot house a vanishing species and thus a barometer of social and economic change. A dogtrot house, through the simple carpentry involved in enclosing the open hallway, vanished in its old uses and its rural, quaint associations and was transformed immediately into the more fashionable central hall cottage type. This remodeling may have been due not so much to "putting on airs" as to the fact that increased road travel rendered the public aspects of the open hallway increasingly undesirable. (For the same reason, one rarely sees a dogtrot house in town, and, significantly, most of the documented dogtrot houses that retained an open hallway were located on lesser-traveled dirt roads.)[34] A variety of dogtrot houses are shown in figs. 4-31 to 4-35.

The dogtrot house type relates to the single pen type, then, in that both are vanishing species that are subject to remodeling or abandonment by their inhabitants. Just as families remodeled the dogtrot into a central hall cottage (for whatever motive), families quickly rendered the single pen invisible by adding onto it in the traditional ways shown in figs. 4-3 and 4-4.

It is fairly easy to identify those dogtrot houses that were built of frame construction originally and had their breezeways enclosed at a later date (fig. 4-37). On the other hand, log dogtrots that were both covered with weatherboard and enclosed simultaneously often successfully masquerade as central hall cottages; close structural examination, oral history, or old photographs are needed to penetrate the disguise. Examples of dogtrot houses with enclosed breezeways are seen in figs. 4-36 to 4-40.

The Pruitt-Campbell house in Stone County (fig. 4-38) is an excellent example of the transformation a typical Ozark house underwent as its owners prospered. Thought to have been constructed around 1870, the original form was a single log pen with a gable-end stone chimney on the east that has since been removed. In the late nineteenth century, a second pen of frame construction was erected, as well as a second stone chimney, to form a dogtrot house. The whole was, at that time, presumably sheathed with weatherboard, and a small pedimented portico was built over the breezeway entrance as illustrated in the old photograph (fig. 4-38). Around 1910, the open hallway was enclosed to form a central hall house and a handsome walnut paneled wainscot was applied throughout the two front rooms and in the now-enclosed hallway.

Judging from old photographs and a few extant houses, constructing a small pedimented portico instead of the more common full-length front porch was a common device for dressing up a dogtrot house. The 1894 photograph of the Benjamin Franklin Henley house in Searcy County (fig. 4-32) illustrates a house of this type in all its unremodeled charm. As this and other photographs indicate, the dogtrot house could be a rather stylish dwelling, despite its associations with rural life.

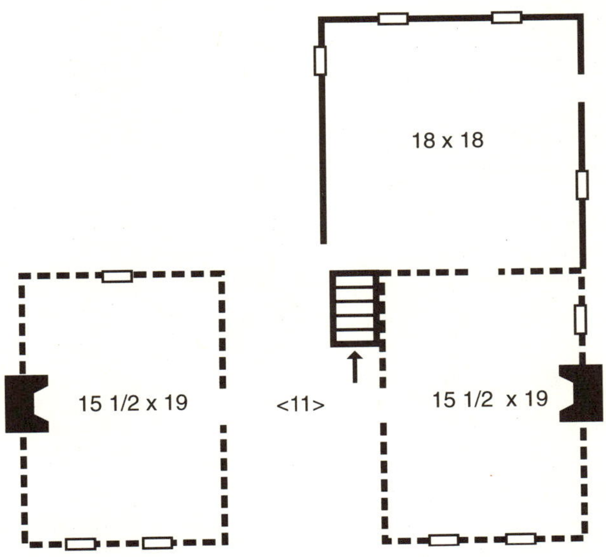

Fig. 4-27. Log Dogtrot House Plan: Parks Station (1858), Hogeye, Washington County. *Drawing by Stacy Rennhoff*

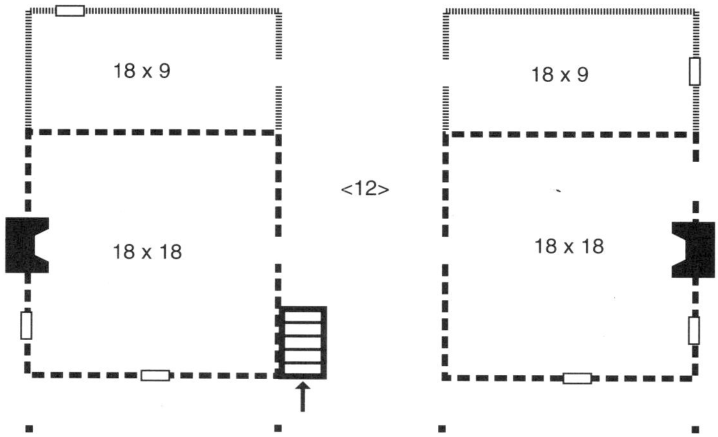

◀ Fig. 4-28. Log Dogtrot House Plan: Wesley Copeland House (1858), Timbo, Stone County. *Drawing by Stacy Rennhoff*

▶ Fig. 4-29. Dogtrot House Plan: Noah McCarn House (1920), Bickles Cove, Stone County. *Drawing by Stacy Rennhoff*

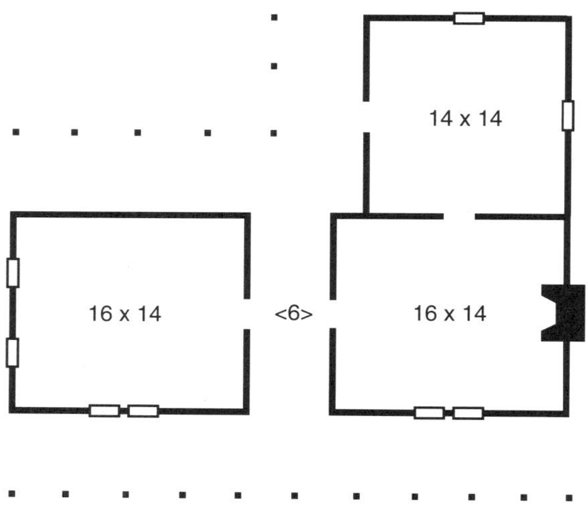

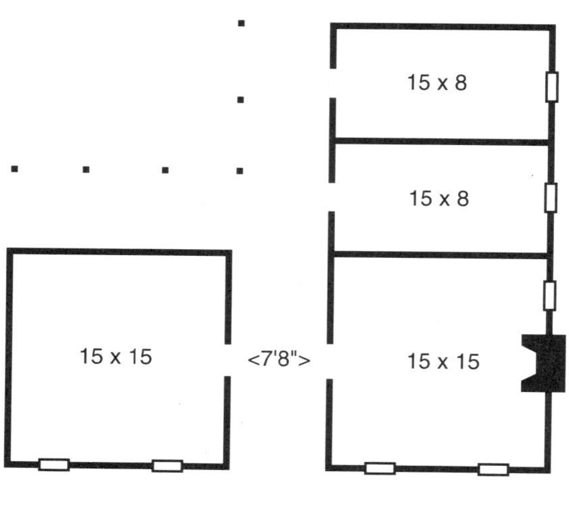

◀ Fig 4-30. Dogtrot House Plan: Walter Gray House (1909), Melrose, Stone County. *Drawing by Stacy Rennhoff*

Fig. 4-31. Zachariah Ford Log House (1856, 1885), St. James, Stone County. This fascinating log house demonstrates a typical method of adding on to a single pen log structure as well as the log and stone craftsmanship of two successive generations. In 1856 Zachariah Ford received land here for his service in the Mexican War. Near a bluff over the White River he built a single pen log house with an exterior stone chimney. The interior had a loft with a ladder providing access to it. The cabin's rough-hewn logs were joined with square notching. About thirty years later, around 1885, Zachariah's son George constructed a second log pen, joining it by an open breezeway to the older pen to form a dogtrot house. The newer log pen differs from the old one in its finely crafted half-dovetail notching at the corners and rather wide interstices, which were apparently never chinked because sealing boards were added to the interior at the time of construction. The newer pen has the usual door opening onto the breezeway and a window at the front. The chimneys differ both in proportion and in craftsmanship. The older chimney is made of rough-hewn stone and is wider at its firebox and shaft than the later one. The 1885 chimney displays finer craftsmanship in stone cutting and overall proportions. Each of the log pens has a rear shed room addition, one dating from the 1885 construction period, the other an early twentieth-century addition. The open breezeway is a spacious ten-feet wide, allowing room for the family to sleep there in the summertime. (Floor plan is seen in fig. 4-19.)

Fig. 4-33. Eric Bodine House (c. 1900, nonextant), Maguiretown Vicinity, Washington County. This dogtrot house, probably of box construction because of its board-and-batten exterior, is atypical in that its pens differ in size. The background of its owner was atypical, too; Eric Bodine and his wife were Swedish immigrants who arrived in Washington County in 1885. He was a farmer who became a self-taught carpenter and worked for many years in the Elkins and Maguire's Store area. The unique cellar with its stone barrel vault interior is visible through the open breezeway of the house and is still used by his son, Ernest Bodine, who, along with his family, occupies a second house on the site. (The cellar is seen in fig. 5-14.) *Courtesy of Ernest Bodine*

◀ Fig. 4-32. Benjamin Franklin Henley House (1870, 1876), St. Joe, Searcy County. This dogtrot house represents a typical enlargement of an Ozark single pen house to reflect the post–Civil War era of rebuilding and increased prosperity. Henley was a Union veteran from Missouri who settled after the Civil War in the St. Joe Valley with his wife, Martha McNair. They first lived in a log cabin until the east portion of their house was complete around 1870. In 1876 they added the west portion, connecting it to the original pen with an open breezeway to form a dogtrot house. A hint of Greek Revival influence can be detected in the simple gable-roofed portico. Choosing a small portico such as this rather than the traditional full-length Ozark front porch apparently was a common way of making dogtrot houses appear more stylish. Mr. Henley's prosperity stemmed from his varied roles as farmer, cotton factor, storekeeper, and banker in the St. Joe area. This 1896 photograph pictures Mrs. Henley (in the dark dress) seated in the breezeway with several of her children and grandchildren. *Courtesy of the Arkansas Historic Preservation Program*

Fig. 4-34. Noah McCarn House (1920), Bickles Cove, Stone County. This balloon frame dogtrot house has the latest construction date, 1920, of any of this type documented. It is also the only dogtrot house with an open breezeway that is still occupied. As in many dogtrot houses, the kitchen extends as a room to the rear of the pen on the right, and there is an L-shaped rear porch. This is one of the few houses documented that displayed Craftsman-style trim, seen in the exposed rafters at the eaves. A smokehouse located just a few feet from the kitchen has been torn down, but the unusually decorative lattice wellhouse remains, visible in the photograph on the left. Noah McCarn Jr. still occupies this house built by his father and runs the 116-acre farm that accompanies it. (Plan is seen in Fig. 4-29.)

Fig. 4-35. Rear of Chaney House Showing Typical Rear Ell Addition with Porches, Chaney House (1841), Osage, Carroll County. Two typical features of dogtrot houses are seen here: the rear ell addition (rather than a rear shed), which retains the open breezeway, and the full-length porches along the L-shaped rear, which provide shady places to perform chores.

Fig. 4-36. Samuel Brown House (1848), West Richwoods, Stone County. Samuel Brown, a farmer from North Carolina, arrived in Stone County in 1840 and began amassing land. In 1848 he built this log dogtrot house with twin stone chimneys. It is thought that about the time of the Civil War, Brown added the weatherboard covering, enclosed the central hall, and installed unusually handsome paneled doors and paneled wainscoting in the interior. The house is noteworthy because it represents the upgrading of a log dogtrot house to a more finely detailed central hall house and because it has unusually finely crafted interior woodwork.

Fig. 4-37. William Lancaster House (1895), Round Bottom, Stone County. Its picturesque setting lends this simple house a dramatic air. In a typical location of an Ozark house in mountainous terrain, it is situated on the first bench of a mountain overlooking the White River. The front porch overlooks broad meadows leading down to the river and the bluffs along it. The house was built in 1895 by William Lancaster, who owned the Round Bottom Ferry and a cotton gin and store. The house, which features a small front porch with chamfered posts, was originally a dogtrot. At some time in the early twentieth century, the hallway was enclosed. It has a rear ell with a combined kitchen and dining area and a rear shed as well. In a lingering touch of the Greek Revival style, a wide frieze board outlines each gable end. At some distance down the hill is Mr. Lancaster's impressive six crib log barn, built in a community effort; it housed horses, mules, and feed. (Fig. 6-2 shows the view from the front porch; Fig. 5-17 shows the well.)

Fig. 4-39. Jacob Wolf House (1830), Norfork, Baxter County. This two-story log structure is the oldest house in the Ozarks. Using the open hallway as the determining factor in designating type, this is a rare two-story dogtrot house. *Courtesy of the Arkansas Historic Preservation Program*

◀ Fig. 4-38. Pruitt-Campbell House (1870, 1895), St. James, Stone County. The evolution of this house demonstrates the typical way many Ozark houses were enlarged and embellished. Around 1870 Pinkney Pruitt built the single pen log house (measuring sixteen by eighteen feet) that forms the core of the larger house in the photograph. The log pen is the room on the right (east) of the entrance. Around 1895 Walter and Emma Campbell bought the house and added a frame single pen addition the same size as the original room. Connecting the two was an open breezeway eight feet wide, forming a typical dogtrot house. It is thought that at this time the original log pen was sheathed with weatherboard to match the new addition and that the gable-roofed portico with latticework panels was added. The wide frieze boards, the gable returns, and the square columns of the porch are all lingering hints of the the Greek Revival style. At some time in the early twentieth century, the Campbells enclosed the open breezeway with flush boards (visible in the photograph) and added a door with sidelights and transom, thereby creating a central hall house. They also added a paneled wainscot in the hall and the two front rooms; this was grained, along with the doors. The photo dates to around 1906; it shows the familiar practice in central hall houses of leaving the front and back doors open to form a breezeway. *Courtesy of Ed Luther*

Fig. 4-40. Parks Station or John P. A. Parks House (1857), Hogeye, Washington County. Hidden beneath the weatherboard exterior with its picturesque steep front gable and Craftsman style porch is one of the largest and most noteworthy log houses in the entire Ozarks. It is made of finely crafted half-dovetail log construction and has two chimneys made from on-site bricks at each gable end. The two principal front rooms measure nineteen by nineteen feet, and the hall is a spacious eleven-feet wide, making this a large house for the region, even if it were constructed in balloon frame, much less in log. Before the house was sheathed in weatherboard (probably in the late nineteenth century), it would have resembled the Jacob Wolf house seen in fig. 4-39. It was built by John P. A. Parks and his wife, Mary, around 1857 and was used as a station stop on the route of the Butterfield Overland Mail from St. Louis to San Francisco that began in 1858. A newspaper man, Waterman Ormsby from the *New York Herald*, was aboard the first run, and in his account he mentions Parks Station.

I-Houses

Standing out like a sentinel, the rare two-story house in the Ozark countryside is a picturesque sight. In form, it is invariably an I-house—the most common folk house type in the eastern United States.[35] Whatever its regional variations, its unfailing characteristics are these: it is at least two rooms in length, it is one room deep, and it is two full stories in height (fig. 4-41).[36]

For once there are no scholarly disputes over the origin of this house—its source is from English folk architecture—nor over its "almost exclusive association with economic success in an agricultural society" in the United States.[37] According to Henry Glassie, I-houses were common in England during the American Colonial Period,[38] and Kniffen found the type recorded in the Delaware-Chesapeake area by the late seventeenth century.[39]

In his pioneering 1936 study of Louisiana house types, Fred Kniffen first identified and named the I-house type, calling it the Midwest House or the I-house in recognition of the Indiana, Illinois, or Iowa origin of many of its builders in Louisiana. In part because of this name, the type has been closely identified with the Midwest. But in an important and often overlooked footnote in this study, Kniffen stated, "It is not intended to imply that this house type is restricted to, or originated in, the three states named."[40] As architectural historian Michael Southern has asserted, the I-house has also been identified as the "dominant folk house type throughout the Upland South from the late eighteenth century to the early twentieth century."[41] Perhaps the reason for its popularity as a symbol of agrarian prosperity is because, as Southern explained, "It presents to the viewer on the road, the largest, most impressive facade possible for a house of only four rooms. In addition, its good ventilation properties make it especially suitable for a hot, humid Southern climate."[42]

Owing to their widespread diffusion and their long duration (from the late seventeenth century in the Delaware-Chesapeake area through the early decades of the twentieth century in many rural areas of the Upland South) several features of I-houses vary, including floor plans. Regional variations exist in construction

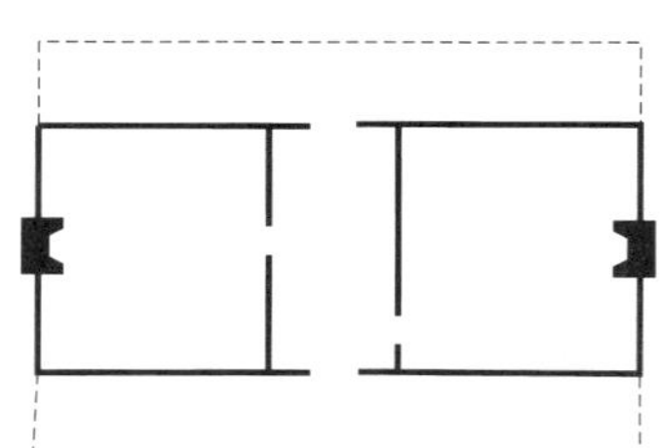

Fig. 4-41. Typical North Carolina I-House with Three-Bay Facade and Full-Length Front Porch. *Adapted from Doug Swaim, "North Carolina Folk Housing,"* Carolina Dwelling, *figure 17*

Fig. 4-42. Comparison of a High Style Eighteenth-Century Georgian Colonial House with a Vernacular Central Hallway Plan I-House. The I-house can be thought of as literally half of a Georgian house, both in width of the facade and in plan, as the full Georgian plan was two rooms deep (or double pile), while the I-house type is one room deep (or single pile). *From Doug Swaim, "North Carolina Folk Housing,"* Carolina Dwelling, *figure 18*

material, chimney placement, facade openings, placement of gable-end windows, porches, and rear additions.[43] For example, the symmetrical three-bay facade I-house with a central hall plan, a full-length front porch, and a rear shed addition is so ubiquitous in North Carolina that it has been called "the Carolina I-house" (fig. 4-41). On the other hand, a typical midwestern I-house (as illustrated in Kniffen's study of folk-housing diffusion) has a small entrance porch, a rear ell, and an asymmetrical door and window arrangement. Variations can also occur within a single state; Robert Bastian, for example, noted that I-houses of three, four, and five facade openings appeared in all parts of Indiana.[44]

Scholars writing about I-houses in various regions often note that the earliest versions of this type had asymmetrical floor plans, usually in the old hall-and-parlor English folk house type.[45] However, the impact of Georgian architecture and its strict symmetrical facades dramatically changed the plan, so that by the mid-nineteenth century, the symmetrical central hall plan was the predominant type; this is true in the Arkansas Ozarks. In fact, as Doug Swaim has pointed out, the vernacular I-house of the Upland South is almost literally "half" a high style Georgian house in both width of facade and depth of plan, the I-house being one room (single pile) deep and the high-style Georgian plan two rooms (double pile) deep (fig. 4-42).[46]

One mid- to late nineteenth-century version of this type represents the "high style" rural I-house in many sections of at least three states in the Upland South: Tennessee, North Carolina, and Arkansas. This is the frame (sometimes brick) I-house with a central hall plan and two-story portico that is often embellished with sawnwork (fig. 4-43). The decorative portico is often a narrow one (figs. 4-50, 4-51, 4-52, 4-53), but in the Arkansas Ozarks, the full-length two-story porch was also popular (figs. 4-55, 4-56).

Fig. 4-43. James Waddell House (1889), Prathers Creek, Alleghany County, North Carolina. The I-house with a decorative narrow two-story portico is the folk equivalent of a "high style" dwelling in farming areas throughout the entire Upland South. *Courtesy of North Carolina Division of Archives and History*

Because the I-house is closely associated with agrarian prosperity, in many parts of the country it displays exterior ornamentation and architectural details derived from high style architecture. It is for this reason that Michael Southern, in a study of North Carolina vernacular houses, termed the I-house a "carrier of style," and illustrated examples in which details of period styles like Greek Revival, Gothic Revival, and Italianate were grafted onto the basic I-house form.[47] To a lesser extent, this appears in Ozark I-houses as well.

I-Houses in the Arkansas Ozarks

The range of dates for I-houses documented in the fieldwork was from 1855 to 1912. With regard to geographical distribution, the fieldwork for this study revealed a surprisingly close correlation between the Arkansas Ozark subregions and the I-house type. For instance, only one example of a full two-story I-house was documented in the entire Stone County architectural survey (fig. 4-57). On the other hand, in Washington County two-story I houses were common in all areas and were a dominant type in the prosperous farmlands around Prairie Grove and Cane Hill. This distribution, in which I-houses are common only in Springfield Plain good farming areas and are rare in the Boston Mountains, underscores the association of this type with agricultural prosperity. Diane Tebbetts' analysis of Independence County's traditional houses contains similar findings; she concluded that the I-house made up only 2.5 percent of the total number of traditional houses in that county. She further observed that they were rarely seen in the countryside and were clustered in towns instead.[48] Most I-houses throughout the country are frame or brick with frame predominating, but nearly all brick houses are of I-house type.

Two extraordinary log houses documented have the requisite two full stories to qualify as I-houses, but because both have the open hallway of the dogtrot house, they have been classified as dogtrot houses. All the other I-houses were of frame or brick, with frame predominating. In considering the entire stock of brick houses documented, it should be noted that most were the I-house type.

I-houses that depart from the central plan are scattered throughout the region. Instead, these examples have the familiar double pen plan with two front doors that make up a four-bay facade arrangement. These houses lack the formality and imposing quality of the central hall variations; like the double pen houses they emulate, they are usually quite plain and often have smaller room dimensions than the full-blown central hall I-house type. The plan of the S. E. Crouch house, a double door I-house, is shown in fig. 4-47.

The most common Arkansas Ozark I-house facade variation displays the full five bays and a central hall plan derived from the English eighteenth-century Georgian high style house, which so beautifully captured classical formality and symmetry. Without exception, these five-bay facade houses had (at least originally) a two-story porch, ranging from narrow to full size, although the full-length two-story porch was perhaps most favored. Somewhat surprisingly, few I-houses of the three-bay facade plan with a central hall, like the typical North Carolina type, were documented. Variations of I-house floor plans are illustrated in figs. 4-44 to 4-49 and variations of houses are illustrated in figs. 4-50 to 4-58.

While most I-houses, like most Ozark houses in general, had exterior-end chimneys, I-houses, more than any other traditional type, sometimes featured internal-end chimneys, which are more commonly found in the northern United

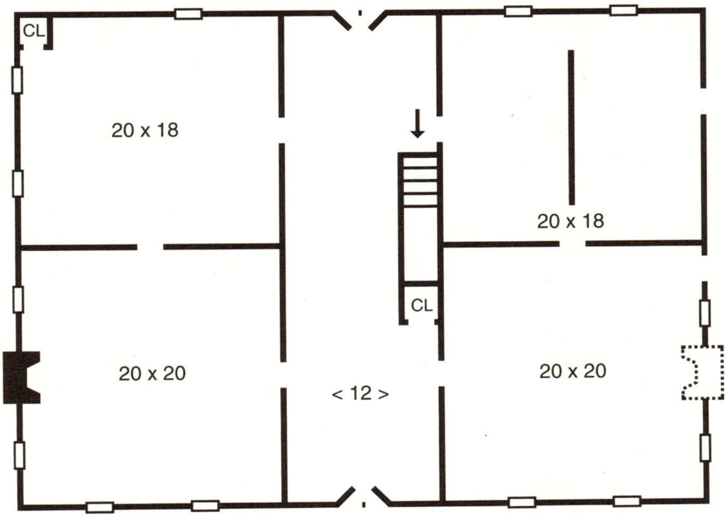

Fig. 4-44. Eliza and William Wilson I-House Plan (1857), Rhea's Mill, Washington County. *Drawing by Vicki Francoeur*

States than in the Upland South. These usually appeared in brick I-houses of relatively early construction. All the I-houses had a rear ell of one or two stories. This contrasts markedly with the rear shed addition commonly found in North Carolina I-houses.

Another consistency appeared in the room and hallway dimensions of measured examples. All the rooms had square or nearly square proportions with the most common central hall measurement being eight feet in width. Similar to the other house types, common dimensions of the two principal first-floor rooms were sixteen by sixteen feet, sixteen by eighteen feet, fifteen by fifteen feet, and eighteen by eighteen feet. The largest I-house, the 1857 William Wilson I-house near Prairie Grove in Washington County (fig. 4-51), had twenty-by-twenty-foot rooms and a twelve-foot-wide central hall; it will be discussed at length in the subsequent chapter on interiors.

Consistent with the Ozark preference for architectural simplicity and the disinclination to "put on airs," few of these types proved to be carriers of high style details like those documented in North Carolina. One notable exception, however, is the Homsley-Shofner I-house with its grand Greek Revival portico and dentil moldings; constructed in fertile farmland in western Madison County in 1845, it burned in 1911 (fig. 4-50). Two existing I-houses in Washington County are good examples of the use of high style details: the 1866 E. W. McClellan house in Cane Hill, which displays Greek Revival details (fig. 4-52), and the Benjamin Franklin Johnson house of 1878 in the Middle Fork Valley near Elkins, which displays sophisticated Italianate style features (fig. 4-54). The Johnson house is by far the most stylish house documented. Sited atop a knoll among rolling meadows, it is a testament both to market-oriented farm prosperity—made possible by the fertile river valley and by access to a nearby railroad—and to the capital-acquiring talents of its builder. B. F. Johnson served in the Union army during the Civil War; upon returning to Washington County, he began developing a major hog and cattle operation in the 1870s. Johnson drove his hogs and cattle to a nearby railroad spur, loaded them onto a train, accompanied them to St. Louis, and then saved half and invested half of the livestock proceeds upon his return.[49] The Johnson house's unusual hipped (instead of gabled) roof, round-arched windows and fanlight, chamfered porch columns, and paired brackets lining a paneled frieze are all features Johnson could have seen on his trips to St. Louis. Or he could have seen such details in a nineteenth-century pattern book, such as *Palliser's American Architecture* of 1870 or Cummings and Miller's *Victorian Architectural Details: Two Pattern Books* of 1865 and 1873. Most pattern-book Italianate houses, however, display much more complex massing than Johnson's house, which is simply an old-fashioned boxy I-house with an overlay of stylish details. Both the two-story narrow portico and its fancy jigsawn balustrade in a cloverleaf pattern reflect local taste, rather than pattern-book details. The abundance of stone details on this house, including the porch floor, window sills, porch column bases, and exterior stairway testify to the high quality of the stone craftsmanship available in the area; moreover, these details are some of the most impressive features of the house.

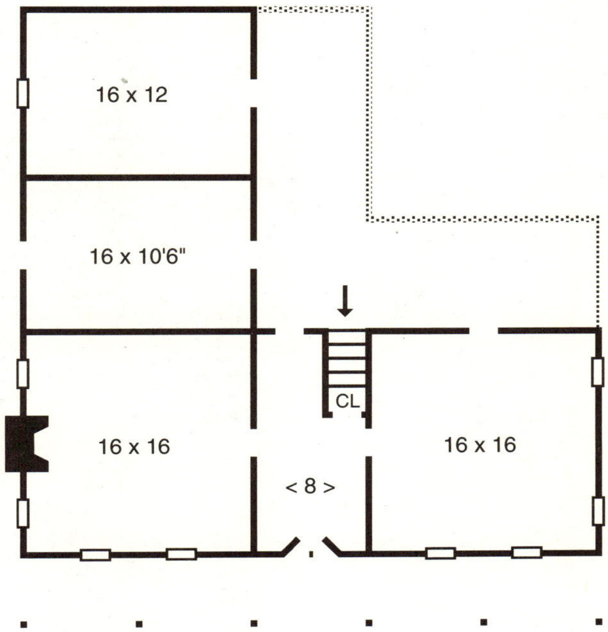

◀ Fig. 4-45. Lawson-Johnson I-House Plan (1867), Wesley Vicinity, Madison County. *Drawing by Vicki Francoeur*

▶ Fig. 4-46. Benjamin Franklin Johnson I-House Plan (1878), Middle Fork Valley, Washington County. *Drawing by Vicki Francoeur*

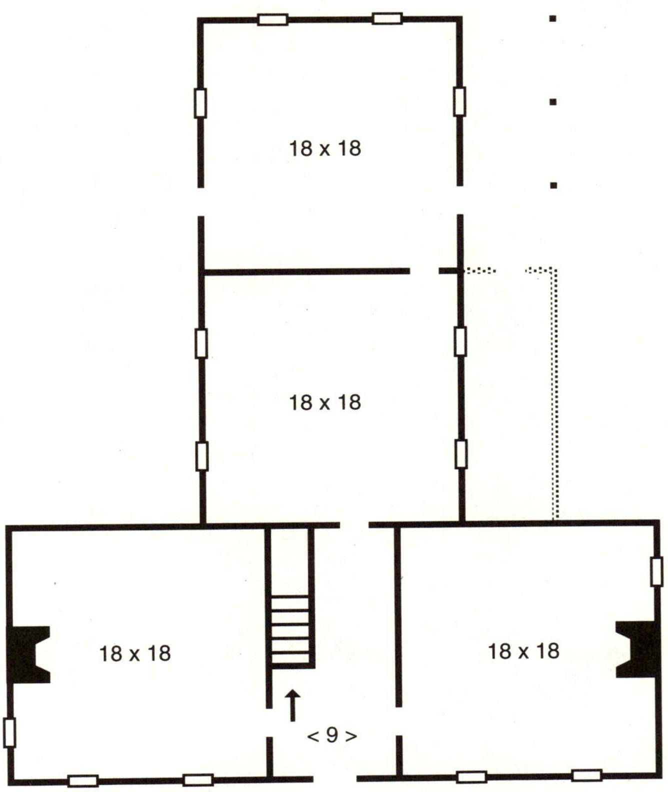

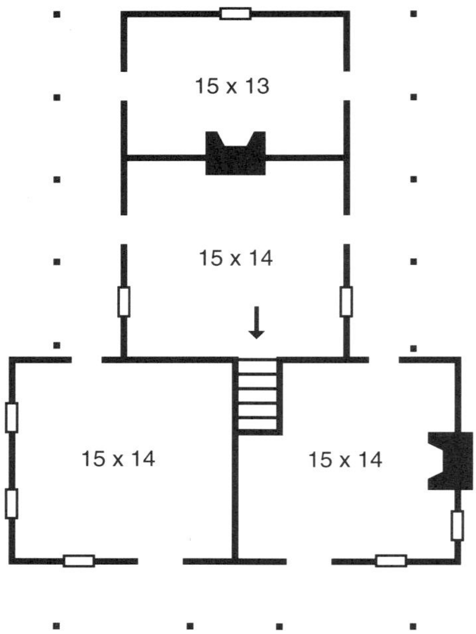

▲Fig 4-47. S. E. Crouch I-House Plan (1883), Center Point, Washington County. *Drawing by Vicki Francoeur*

▼Fig. 4-48. McBrien-Bellamy I-House Plan (1896), Old Greersburg Vicinity, Washington County. *Drawing by Vicki Francoeur*

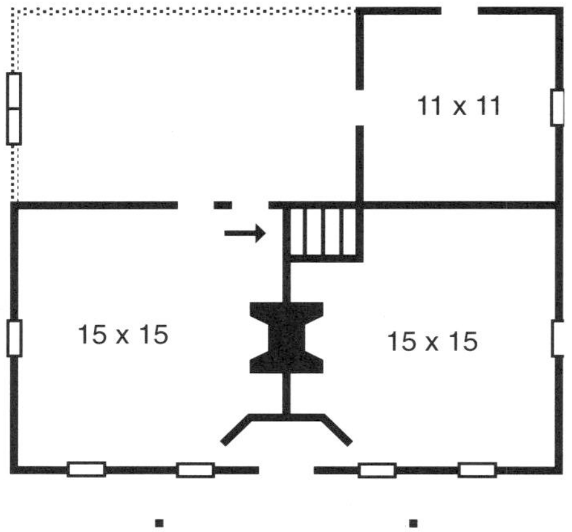

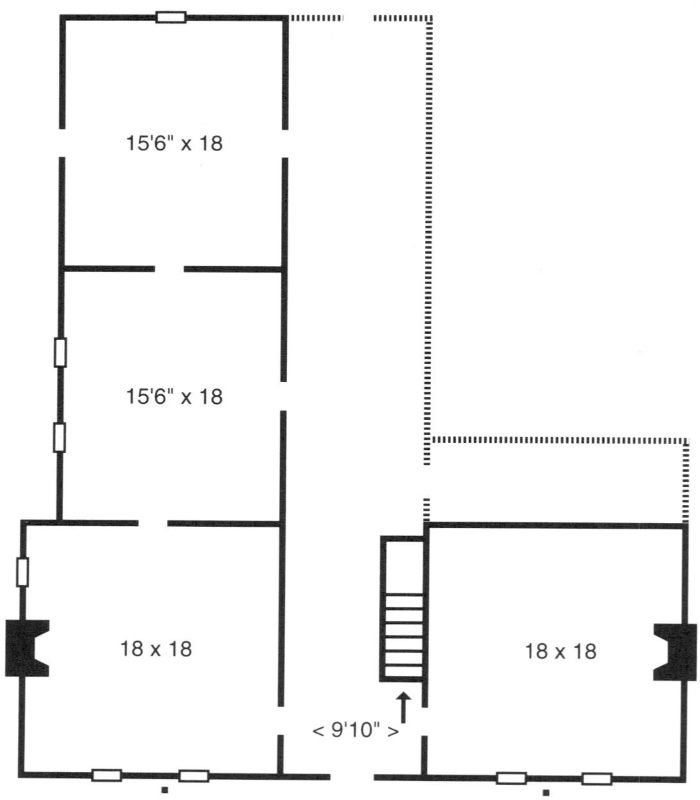

►Fig. 4-49. Thomas E. Hess I-House Plan (1900), Marcella, Stone County. *Drawing by Vicki Francoeur*

Fig. 4-50. Homsley-Shofner I-House (1845), Tuttle Vicinity, Madison County. This brick Greek Revival I-house was surely one of the most outstanding rural vernacular houses ever constructed in the Arkansas Ozarks; no other extant house documented in field work or found in old photograph collections had such a grand two-story portico, featuring dentil molding that outlines the pedimented gable and the cornice and monumental Tuscan columns that uphold a simple entablature. The fanlight over the door is an uncommonly elegant feature as well. Nine-over-six light sash and the internal-end chimneys are typical antebellum elements, however. Few examples survive of the latticework balustrade on the rear ell kitchen porch; judging from old photographs, however, this was a popular decorative element before being replaced in the late nineteenth century with Victorian spindlework, which was commercially available. Burl Homsley built this imposing house in 1845 on a rise overlooking the rich meadowlands of this area. Just a few years later, in the early 1850s, Newton King Shofner purchased the house for $3,600. According to family tradition, Mr. Shofner bought the house at the insistence of his wife, who had seen it as the family passed it on their way from Shelbyville, Tennessee, to settle in Washington County. Reportedly Mrs. Shofner remarked, "I must have that house." This 1902 photograph shows the second and third generations of Shofners to live in the house, which unfortunately burned to the ground in 1911. *Courtesy of University of Arkansas Library, Special Collections*

Fig. 4-51. Eliza and William Wilson House (1857–59), Rhea's Mill, Washington County. The importance of this house can hardly be overestimated. This is one of the few antebellum houses left standing in Washington County. It was built by William Wilson (1807–1886), a native of Georgia, and reflects not only his astute business sense, but also the fertile farmland in the Springfield Plain area near Prairie Grove where Wilson amassed a holding of some 2,400 acres. The Wilson family continues to own the house, and Rollans Wilson, the child on the rocking horse in the photograph, occupied the house until his death just a few years ago. All the family records are intact, including Wilson's daybook of materials, costs, and names of carpenters who constructed his house of braced frame construction in 1858–59. The house was not completely finished when the Civil War erupted. One brick chimney is visible on the east, but the one on the west was never built. The I-house form with double doors front and rear, the five-bay facade, and the central hall plan are typical of larger I-houses in the region. Atypical are the large windows with nine-over-six-light sash and the spaciousness of the house; the two front rooms measure twenty by twenty feet and the hall is twelve-by-eighteen-feet wide. The rear arrangement is unique; instead of being the customary rear ell or shed, there are two gable-roofed rear rooms immediately behind the front ones and almost all of the same dimensions (twenty by eighteen feet), so that the effect is of a double-pile plan on the ground floor. With its unusually shallow pitched roof and its long five-bay facade, this house harks back to the old-fashioned high style Georgian rectangular block house popular in eastern seaboard houses of the eighteenth century. A few details, such as the wide frieze board, the square porch columns, the sidelights, the transom, and the general severity of the facade lend it a slightly more up-to-date vernacular Greek Revival flair. The simplicity of the exterior is echoed on the interior. The two front rooms have been wallpapered, but the moldings and staircase are simple; the walls in the hallway are the customary horizontal board walls and are unpapered. The stairway is utilitarian instead of impressive and, in an unusual orientation, rises from the rear of the hallway to accommodate the many hired hands who worked for the Wilsons and lived upstairs. The house plan appears in fig. 4-44 and furnishings plans of both the first and second floor are shown in figs. 8-20 and 8-21, and daily life in this house is discussed in chapter 8. *Courtesy of Caswell Wilson*

Fig. 4-52. E. W. McClellan House (1866), Cane Hill Vicinity, Washington County. When it is finally glimpsed at the end of a long winding lane, atop a picturesque wooded knoll, this finely detailed I-house is a commanding sight. Like several other large rural houses in Washington County, this one was planned before the Civil War, but its actual construction was postponed until the hostilities ceased. Its rather sophisticated details and the two internal-end chimneys bespeak its early date. A Greek Revival high style influence is apparent in the handsome box columns of the portico, in the pedimented gable ends of the house, and in the pedimented gable crowning the portico. This dwelling reflects the lingering popularity in the Ozarks of the Greek Revival style, a popularity that peaked before the Civil War in the East and in parts of the Midwest. It is important to note that the Greek Revival style did not usher in new house types to the Ozarks, but simply applied classical details to traditional houses, as seen in this I-house. The house is also a reflection of the fertile farmland in the Cane Hill vicinity, one of the earliest settlements in the county.

Fig. 4-53. Sarah Louisa and Hosea Marmaduke Maguire House (1850), Maguiretown, Washington County. Born in Kentucky in 1813, Hosea Marmaduke Maguire immigrated with his parents to this White River Valley in 1828. In 1850 he married Sarah Louise Trammel, and it is thought that around this time he constructed this I-house across the road from his parents' large log dogtrot house. Like the three preceding I-houses (figs. 4-50, 4-51, and 4-52) this one displays Greek Revival style–influenced details in the portico with its box columns and wide board simulating a frieze and the raking cornices in the portico's gable. Contrasting Victorian touches (which might have been added at a later date) are the brackets with pendants grouped in threes along the cornice and in the portico gable. A long rear ell containing a kitchen and separate dining room extends at the end of the pen on the right. In contrast to the rather decorative exterior, the interior is quite plain, beginning with the simple narrow stairway in the central hall. This plainness is characteristic of many of the I-houses documented, demonstrating that in Ozark farmhouses, the owner's prosperity is demonstrated primarily in the large size of the house (which, after all, is functional) rather than in ornamentation.

Hosea Maguire was a farmer and outstanding merchant; in 1867 he established Maguire's Store (near this house), which became a popular trading center as well as mercantile store. In fact, the post office was officially named "Maguire's Store" for many years. Maguire and his brother bought cattle and other livestock and drove them to Pierce City, Missouri, where they could take the train to St. Louis, sell the livestock, and buy goods for their store. *Shiloh Museum of Ozark History*

Fig. 4-54. Lydia and Benjamin Franklin Johnson House (1878), Middle Fork Valley, Washington County. This large I-house is one of several constructed from on-site hand-molded bricks in Washington County in the 1870s and early 1880s. Situated atop a small knoll in the Middle Ford Valley, this is one of the most impressive I-houses in the entire region. At first glance it resembles many Arkansas Ozark I-houses with typical features, such as a five-bay facade with central hall plan, a one-story rear ell, and a two-story front portico. Its roof, however, is the low-hipped type instead of the usual gabled roof. Upon closer inspection, the sophisticated Italianate details and excellent stone craftsmanship become apparent. The eight-foot-long windows and the front door and fanlight all have unusual round-arch openings. Paired scroll brackets decorate the paneled frieze and the porch. The two-story portico is supported by unusually decorative square columns and the porch is embellished with a striking balustrade of jigsawn cloverleaf pattern. C. Allen Brown has noted the similarity in these details to those in 1870s pattern books, such as Marcus Cummings and Charles Miller's *Victorian Architectural Details: Two Pattern Books,* published in New York in 1865 and 1873. In his flourishing hog and cattle business, Mr. Johnson traveled by train to St. Louis frequently and while there he could have seen many houses with the Italianate details then in vogue. The outstanding stone craftsmanship exhibited in this house is described in chapter 7 and details appear in figs. 7-22 and 7-23.

Fig. 4-55. Lawson-Johnson House (1867), Wesley Vicinity, Madison County. Recently meticulously restored, sited atop a steep hill and sheltered by large trees, this dwelling seems the quintessential Ozark I-house with its five-bay facade, double front and rear doors, two-story full-length porch, and twin stone chimneys at the gable ends. It is especially noteworthy for the beauty of its well-proportioned, utter simplicity, both on the exterior and the interior. The house was built adjacent to the Richland River by the William Lawson family around 1867. The family farmed 332 acres of fertile land. In 1927 the house and farmland were purchased by Edyth and Ezra Johnson and E. M. and O. M. Johnson, brothers of Ezra, all of whom lived there for many years. (The plan is seen in fig. 4-45 and the interior stairway in fig. 8-9.)

Fig. 4-57. Thomas E. Hess House (1900), Marcella, Stone County. Owing to the poor agricultural conditions of land outside the Springfield Plain areas, this house was probably the only full two-story I-house ever constructed in Stone County. The Hess family was among the earliest settlers in the county, founding the community of Marcella (which was originally known as "Hesstown"). The Hesses operated a steamboat landing on the nearby White River and were prosperous farmers. Both the three-bay width of the porch (instead of a full-length or one-bay porch) and the degree of embellishment of the porch with its jigsawn brackets and spindlework balustrades are unusual. Otherwise, the five-bay facade, the stone gable-end chimney, and the rear ell containing a kitchen and a dining room are all typical I-house features. The interior of this house, like those of most other I-houses, is extremely simple, save for the wood graining on all interior doors. Several outbuildings remain, including a one-room log schoolhouse, which was moved to serve as a barn. (The floor plan is shown in fig. 4-49; the elder Mr. Hess's house is shown in fig. 4-59.)

◀ Fig. 4-56. Luke Kantz House (1880), Fayetteville Vicinity, Washington County. Although it has been moved from its original location a few miles northeast of Fayetteville, this farmhouse was once surrounded by acres of apple orchards and reflected the prosperity that fruit growing brought to northwest Arkansas for several decades. With its five-bay facade and its full-length two-story front porch, it typifies the Ozark frame I-house, except that its interior brick chimneys substitute for the more common exterior stone ones. The square balusters, the porch columns with simple capitals, and the transom and sidelights at the door are late reflections of the Greek Revival style. The plan features the typical rear ell containing a kitchen and dining room. Simplicity is the keynote for this house, both on the exterior and interior. Most interior walls are the old-fashioned wood-sheathed type; only the parlor had plaster walls with wallpaper. (The stairway is seen in Figure 8-8.) Luke Kantz rose from raising a small orchard with ten to fifteen varieties of apples to becoming a commercial grower, working with the University of Arkansas Horticulture Department to improve the quality of fruit in the region. *Courtesy of the Arkansas Historic Preservation Program*

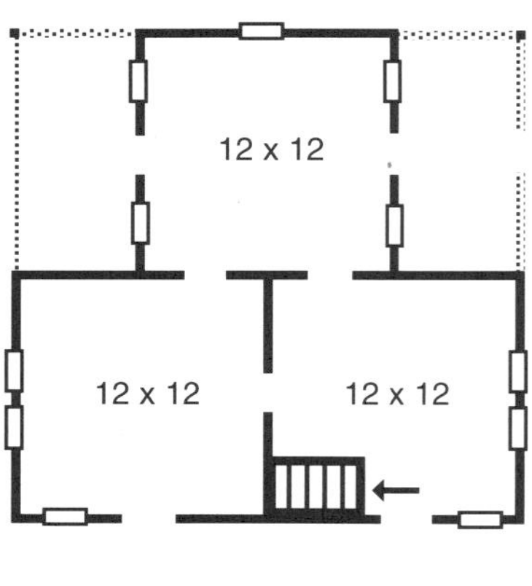

Fig. 4-58. Grubbs-Hamilton House (c. 1900), Old Alabam, Madison County. Lee Grubbs, a farmer and blacksmith, built this unusual house around 1900. Nestled among rocky hillsides, it has a full array of outbuildings, a layout of which is shown in fig. 5-3. (Other outbuildings are shown in figs. 5-13 and 5-16.) This is an unusual one-and-one-half-story I-house with two front doors, rather than a central hall plan. The exterior details are unusual as well. The three steep, prominent front gables and the little "wings" of shed roofs at either side of the portico at the second floor level are all outsized and lend this house a whimsical, eccentric air. These qualities, combined with its attractive hilltop setting and its interesting outbuildings, make it an often-photographed house. The porch and large gables belie the small size of this house; the two front rooms and rear kitchen measure only ten feet by twelve feet each. Geraldine and Pat Hamilton purchased the house in the 1940s and have preserved it in its original condition; this is still an old-fashioned Ozark farm complete with well and outhouse and contentedly scratching chickens.

Central Hall Cottages

Central hall houses were common in Europe and were introduced to the colonies by various groups, most notably the English and the Scotch-Irish in the Chesapeake Tidewater region.

The central hall cottage in the Arkansas Ozarks is a single-pile (or one room deep) one-story house with two rooms of equal size separated by a central hall. Like other traditional houses, it has a gable-end roof and exterior chimneys, but it differs in having an enclosed hall with a single central door.

It is a commonplace among vernacular architecture scholars that the central hall type (like the central hall I-house) is a response to the far-reaching symmetry introduced by the Georgian architectural style. As introduced to the English colonies during the late seventeenth century, the prototypical high style Georgian house had a five-bay facade and a double-pile or two-room deep plan with a central hallway providing a strong symmetrical axis; other common features were paired internal-end chimneys and a hipped roof (fig. 4-42). This symmetrical form, whether one story or two, replaced the old asymmetrical folk house types, such as the hall-and-parlor house. Doug Swaim, in his illuminating study of North Carolina folk houses—which parallel Ozark houses to a great degree—finds the impact of Georgian symmetry to be so profound that he distinguishes between the categories of the older pre-Georgian asymmetrical types, which he calls "Old World types," and the newer "Georgian plan types." By 1850, Swaim observes, "American folk Georgian had all but replaced the Old World building traditions that the earliest settlers had brought over from a Europe less affected by the Renaissance wave."[50] The Georgian-influenced plan types Swaim designated include all the symmetrically arranged central hall houses, i.e., the two-story single-pile I-house and the one-story central hall house, both single and double pile (that is, one and two rooms deep).

Henry Glassie has also written at length about the profound attraction the Anglo-American folk builder felt for the symmetry of the Georgian model. Observing that "bilaterally symmetrical, tripartite structures mark Western quests for control,"[51] Glassie views Georgian architecture with its hallmark of symmetry as "the perfect end to the builder's search for architectural order."[52]

All the central hall cottages documented were one story high and one room deep, sharing the latter characteristic with I-houses.[53] From all indications it has never been a common type. Moreover, like the I-house, its geographical distribution is clearly tied to the more prosperous areas of the Springfield Plain. The date range, from 1851 to 1895, is narrow compared to other types. It seems, then, that families who could afford the "formality" and the "wasted" space of an enclosed central hall preferred to build a two-story I-house instead. Central hall cottage plans are seen in figs. 4-60 to 4-62 and the houses in figs. 4-59 and 4-63 to 4-65.

No log central hall houses were found. Most were either balloon or braced frame, depending on their ages. Significantly, the one stone house documented was the central hall cottage type (fig. 4-65). A few had simple Greek Revival

Fig. 4-59. Thomas M. Hess House (1868), Marcella, Stone County. Although by Stone County standards this is an unusually large and imposing house, it is typically Ozarkian in its quiet, unassuming air. Its several fine details include the well-proportioned facade, the continuous fieldstone foundation, large stone steps, and stone sidewalk. Two aspects of this house are, however, retardataire for 1868: its braced frame (instead of balloon frame construction) and its Greek Revival details visible in the broad pedimented portico, the wide six-over-six light sash windows, the box cornice, and the plain frieze board and square columns of the portico. It is important to note that these Greek Revival details were well within the expertise of the local carpenter and did not necessitate the use of carpenters' handbooks, which had helped spread the Greek Revival style across the country. The portico is unique in its folk-painting decoration, which appears to be a garland of leaves or perhaps long cornstalks that outline the raking cornice, while in the center appears an upright plant, perhaps a cotton plant. The unusually decorative interior featured a simple paneled wainscot below and wallpaper above in the two large front rooms. (See fig. 8-11.) The furnishings, which according to the family were shipped upriver from New Orleans, included the unusual decorative window shades visible in the photograph. Thomas M. Hess, one of the earliest settlers in Stone County, operated a flourishing steamboat landing on the nearby White River and farmed in the rich bottomlands. The plan for this house is shown in fig. 4-60; fig. 4-57 is the house Mr. Hess built for his son Thomas E. "Turk" Hess. *Courtesy of Ed Luther*

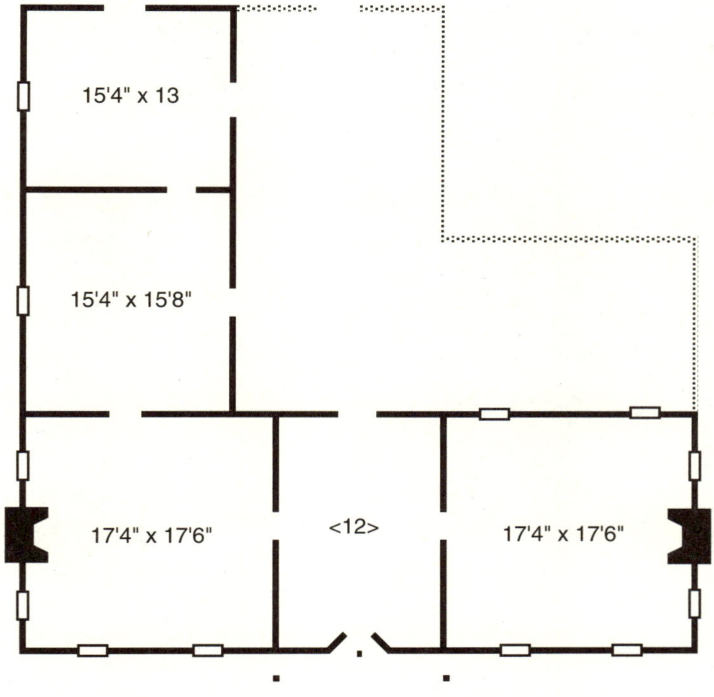

◄Fig. 4-60. Central Hall Cottage Plan, Thomas M. Hess House (1868), Marcella, Stone County. *Drawing by Stacy Rennhoff*

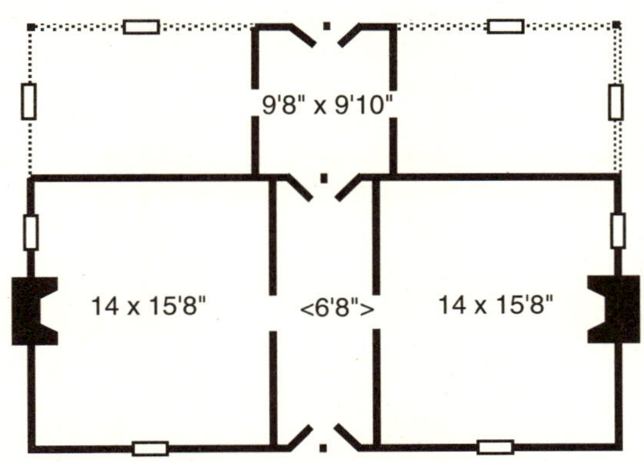

►Fig. 4-61. Central Hall Cottage Plan, Preston Jarnigan Lea House (1882), Fayetteville, Washington County. *Drawing by Stacy Rennhoff*

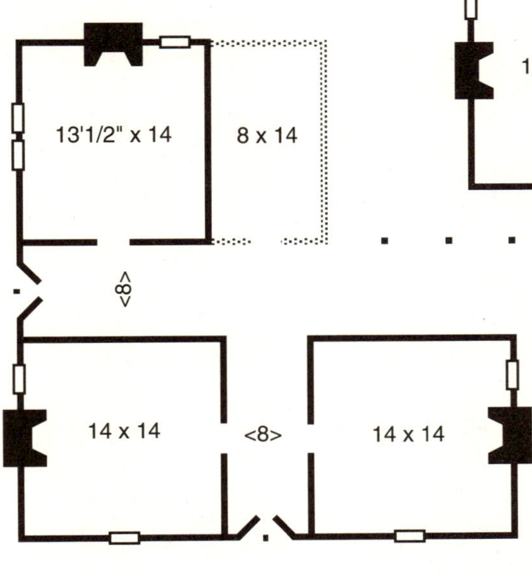

◄Fig. 4-62. Central Hall Cottage Plan, Sam Younger House (1870), St. James Vicinity, Stone County. *Drawing by Stacy Rennhoff*

Fig. 4-63. Troy Gordon House (1851), Fayetteville, Washington County. Although it is now located in a bustling area of Fayetteville, this was originally a farmhouse. Constructed for Troy Gordon around 1851, this handsomely proportioned and finely detailed one-story central hall cottage is one of the oldest houses in the county. Its somewhat horizontal proportions, strict symmetry, and prominent gable returns at the gable ends and on the central portico set a Greek Revival tone. This style is echoed in such details as Doric columns and pilasters and the simple, wide frieze board on both the portico and the facade, the little moldings atop each window, and the pilaster cornerboards. As is often the case in antebellum houses, the chimneys are brick internal ones. Inside, the two original mantels and interior moldings remain; they are shown in fig. 8-12.

details that were too plain to have been derived from the many carpenters' handbooks available in the era of Greek Revival style popularity, usually cited as from about 1820 to 1860.[54] Two examples are the Troy Gordon house (fig. 4-63) and the P. J. Lea House (fig. 4-64).

A notable similarity is that most have a five-bay facade, a close link with the high style Georgian tradition. Porches were also similar in that they generally featured small pedimented porticoes with a somewhat formal air, contrasting markedly with the popular full front porches of other house types. Rear additions are fairly equally divided between rear ells and shed rooms, with the larger houses featuring rear ells (like the Thomas M. Hess house, fig. 4-60, and the smaller houses having rear shed rooms, like the P. J. Lea house, fig. 4-61.

Finally, it is illuminating to compare the dogtrot and the central hall type since, morphologically, they both consist of "two pens and a passage." Although similar in form, these two types differ significantly in their associations with economic and social status. The key distinguishing element, the enclosed central hallway of the central hall type, immediately renders the house more closed, private, and formal than the dogtrot. Accordingly, the central hall cottage is invariably associated with more prosperous families, is much more likely to display some high style Greek Revival touches, and, unlike the dogtrot, is often located in towns. The dogtrot is also closely linked to log construction, however, as noted, no central hall houses appeared in log.

In sum, then, the dogtrot is more rural, more open, more informal, and less sophisticated than the central hall type; the dogtrot is a true "country cousin." Despite the differences between them, the bilaterally symmetrical tripartite form the two house types share is so deeply ingrained that it was employed for both of these two very different kinds of houses. As the owners of dogtrot houses prospered, they could signal their increasing prosperity by simply transforming their house into the central hall type.

Fig. 4-64. Mary and Preston Jarnigan Lea House (1882), Fayetteville, Washington County. Suburban subdivisions have replaced the acreage of apple orchards that once surrounded this farmhouse. Tax records indicate a construction date of 1882; if this is accurate, it testifies to an exceptionally long post–Civil War period in which the Greek Revival style remained popular in the Arkansas Ozarks. A Greek Revival flair is manifested in the wide frieze board-and-box cornice at the eaves, the gently sloping roof, the overall horizontal proportions, and pilaster cornerboards. The double-leaf front doors are matched with identical doors at the center of the rear ell; it was customary practice to open all these doors to form a breezeway in hot weather. A large fieldstone apple house is still standing near the main house. (A close-up of the exterior box cornice and frieze is shown in fig. 8-5.)

Fig. 4-65. Peter Smyth House (1886), Fayetteville, Washington County. Nineteenth-century stone houses are extremely rare in rural areas of the Arkansas Ozarks. This central hall cottage was constructed for an Irish immigrant, Peter Smyth, who settled near Fayetteville in the 1840s with several other Irish families. It is constructed of coursed sandstone with handsomely chiseled stone window lintels and ledges. The two internal end chimneys are more common in houses of earlier construction dates. *Shiloh Museum of Ozark History*

The One-and-One-Half-Story House

Although not numerous enough to constitute a major type, several houses share characteristics of both the I-house and the double pen, thus presenting a classification problem. Like the I-house they are vertical in proportion, two rooms wide, and one room deep. Instead of two stories, however, they are only one-and-one-half story in height. Like the double pen house, the plan usually features the favored two adjoining front rooms with two front doors, rather than a central hallway.

In some regions this house appears to be a dominant type. In Indiana, for example, Robert Bastian observes that they compete with the I-house for the dominant position among folk dwellings.[55] In the Ozarks, however, as noted earlier, it is not common enough to be classified as a major type. The Ozark one-and-one-half story house does share one important characteristic with the Indiana houses described by Bastian; within the scale of rural affluence, it represents an intermediate dwelling between the modest double pen type and the I-house type.

Popular House Types

Three house types—the bent house, the prow house, and the one-story pyramid roof house with a square plan—are categorized as popular types, not as traditional types, for three reasons: (l) their forms do not fit any of the well-established categories of the traditional house types; (2) they are not found in log construction and appear only in balloon frame, a fact that helps substantiate the contention that the traditional house forms emerged from solutions to the problem of adding on to single log pens; (3) they do not appear in the periods of early settlement, but date instead from the late nineteenth and early twentieth century.

There are several other ways these houses depart from the folk architectural tradition. Two of them, the bent house and the prow house, leave behind the simple square or rectangular facade of the traditional houses and exhibit an irregularity—the "variety of prospects" referred to in nineteenth-century pattern books—typical of the Victorian picturesque architectural aesthetic. The third type, the one-story pyramid roof house with its square plan, seems to relate more to the popular bungalow than to the Victorian architectural tradition because of its simplification, its compact plan, and its dating (primarily from 1900 to 1915). All three of these house types depart from the strict Ozark folk tradition of one-room-deep massing. All three display variations in roof lines that depart from the deeply entrenched traditional side-gabled roof with the entrance in the long side.

It would be a mistake, however, to overemphasize the atypical qualities of these houses, for like all rural dwellings in this area, they shun display and eccentricity. By late Victorian standards even their irregularity is of a quiet sort. Moreover, considering the availability of reasonably priced, mass-produced "gingerbread" or sawnwork decoration, they are modestly ornamented, if at all.

Since these houses represent a degree of sophistication and influence from beyond the local tradition, it is not surprising that they are more widespread in areas like Washington County, with its open countryside and highly developed travel networks, rather than in the Boston Mountain region.

In the conceptual spectrum of a strict folk architectural tradition at one pole and high style architecture at the opposite end of the spectrum, these houses appear to represent a middle ground, exhibiting elements from both traditional and popular sources. The following discussions of each of the three types will clarify these similarities and differences.

The Bent House

There are at least five other terms commonly used to describe the bent house type. The "T" house and the "L" house are the most common terms. In different regions, the house might be termed a cross-wing, an upright-and-wing, or a gable-front-and-wing house.[56]

The term bent house has been chosen because of its descriptive clarity and in deference to architectural historian Dell Upton, who has most cogently employed the term to identify houses of different periods and styles in a coherent manner based on form, not on decorative stylistic elements. As Upton describes it, "The bent house was a house whose exterior effect depended upon the juxtaposition of two (gabled) perpindicular wings."[57] In the Ozarks these houses are generally, but not always, one story, and they have one wing with the gable end facing the road and the other wing is a traditional side-gabled wing lying parallel to the road. An entrance porch always appears in the angle between the two wings. Both wings are of the same height. Since the houses are of varying sizes, the plans are irregular and varied; however, they generally do not incorporate a central hallway that separates the two wings (as they often do in pattern books), but simply add a third room forward of the traditional double pen plan or enlarge one of the two principal rooms to form a projecting block. In the Ozarks region, the small one-story bent house is the most common nontraditional house type.

The bent house has its visual roots in the picturesque cottage, an important house in American architectural history, introduced by architect A. J. Davis in his 1836 architectural handbook, *Rural Residences*.[58] The breakthrough in architectural form that the picturesque cottage introduced can only be grasped by understanding the conservatism of American domestic architecture of that period. In both high style and vernacular streams, the principal American architectural vocabulary consisted of only two house types. Architectural historian William F. Pierson, Jr., has explained the two building types that dominated American domestic architecture: "The first was the rectangular block of the late colonial and early Neoclassical years, which was always oriented length-wise to the street and had its principal door in the center of the long side. . . . The second type was the classical temple of the Greek Revival. Oriented short end toward the street, (it) was always crowned by a pediment. . . ."[59] As has been discussed at length in an earlier chapter, the first house Pierson refers to seems to have been an essential part of the "house in the mind's eye" of the Anglo Americans who moved westward through the Upland South to settle the Arkansas Ozarks. Such a form without a central pavilion—its plainest version—can be seen as the fully developed prototype of all the Ozark traditional house types, readily adaptable to both log and braced or balloon frames and retaining the favored bilateral symmetry of the facade. The single pen, the double pen, the saddlebag, the dogtrot, the central hall cottage, and the I-house are all indebted to this basic type (fig. 4-3). The second house type that Pierson cites, the classical temple oriented with the short end toward the road, seems to have had little if any impact in the rural Arkansas Ozarks. Instead, buildings with the short gabled end facing the road were invariably schools, churches, stores, or outbuildings.

The picturesque cottage was, in effect, "A combination of these two earlier forms . . . in which the two blocks interpenetrated one another to form a two-directional system. . . . It was a lively picturesque concept which rejected the single rectangular block of the classical tradition in favor of the dynamic opposition of strongly directional units."[60] Pierson further noted that this new type became "as ubiquitous in rural and suburban America during the 1840s and 1850s as the classical type had been in the early part of the century."[61]

Variations of this picturesque cottage with its two-directional block system spread throughout the country through the influence of architectural pattern books. It is to these that Dell Upton applies the term "bent house" because of its new picturesque effect of the "juxtaposition of two perpindicular wings."[62] After citing the tremendous impact of the bent house upon nineteenth-century pattern books and upon vernacular builders who were influenced by these books, Upton termed the bent house "the single most important nineteenth-century innovation in American domestic architecture" and cited it, in its smaller versions, as the house that American vernacular builders "learned most thoroughly from books. . . . The bent house was introduced by pattern-book writers in two related forms in the 1840s: as the cross-wing house, usually with Gothic decoration and as the Italianate house with a tower."[63] Neither the cross-wing house with Gothic decoration nor the Italianate house with a tower (fig. 4-66) appear in the Arkansas Ozark architectural tradition, but the bent house, the most common popular, nontraditional house type, can be seen as a drastically simplified version of these two picturesque houses.

a

Fig. 4-66. Nineteenth-Century Pattern Book Prototypes for Vernacular Bent Houses. (a) Waldwic Cottage from William Ranlett, *The Architect,* 1849; (b) a bracketed villa in the Italian style from A. J. Downing, *Cottage Residences,* 1842. *From Dell Upton, "Pattern Books and Professionalism: Aspects of Domestic Architecture in America, 1800–1860."*

b

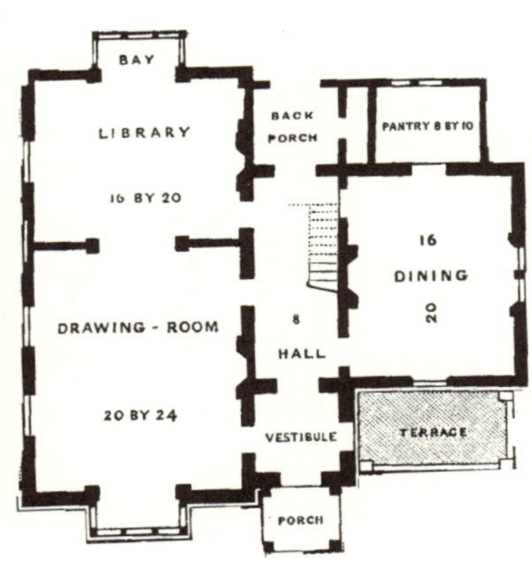

Grasping the process by which vernacular builders used forms from nineteenth-century pattern books is essential for our understanding of the bent house as it appears in the Ozarks. Houses that were copied directly from pattern books are rare, Upton argued, because the vernacular builders were actually using a quite different aproach to building from that taken by the pattern-book writers. As Upton explains it,

> Architectural writers increasingly thought of their designs as cohesive artistic productions. . . . If the writers' architectural theory was an integrated one, in which every part was intricately related, the vernacular process was an additive one, in which the whole was literally the sum of its accumulated parts. . . . American vernacular builders reduced the integrated designs of the pattern-book writers to distinctive essences, abstracting from them key architectural elements that could be grafted onto their own buildings.[64]

The form that bent houses most commonly take in the Ozark countryside is that of a one-story cottage with two perpendicular wings. These became commonplace in rural America. Upton terms these houses a "colossal feat of abstraction" because the vernacular builders "cut through the miasma of styles with which nineteenth-century architects strove for picturesqueness and reduced that quality to its minimal expression. They achieved 'variety of prospect' through the simple contrast of two gables set at right angles to one another."[65]

Once again, it is important to note that Ozark vernacular builders of bent houses were not copying from pattern books, but simply that the pattern books introduced new building forms into the building repertoire in all parts of the country, so that by the late nineteenth and early twentieth century, when most of the Ozark bent houses were being built, the vernacular builders were drawing from "a familiar image rather than a published source," but always in terms of abstraction and simplification.[66]

Bent Houses in the Arkansas Ozarks

Most of the bent houses are located in the more open, well-traveled, and fertile areas of the Springfield Plain, and most adhere to the common Ozark norm of being rather small one-story dwellings; most of the small bent house cottages dated from around 1900 to 1917 (figs. 4-67, 4-68, 4-70). A rare example of a Boston Mountain area bent house is the John Avey house of 1906, located at Big Spring in Stone County (fig. 4-69).

As we shall see in the subsequent discussions of the two other nontraditional house types (the prow house and the one-story pyramid roof house), the vernacular builder, even though incorporating new forms, retained favorite, reassuring features of the older traditional dwellings. In the case of the bent house, for example, Upton describes the plan of pattern-book bent houses as having two areas of public spaces separated by a formal hallway.[67] As will be discussed in more detail in the chapter on Ozark interiors, owners of Ozark houses generally eschewed "public" and "formal" spaces and entries, thus the hallway rarely appeared in any of the Ozark bent houses, whether they had one story or two. Instead, the common Ozark tradition of having one entry that opens directly into a front room was retained. Moreover, in several of the bent houses, each of the perpindicular wings had its own front door with the doors set at right angles adjacent to one another—again retaining a favored Ozark feature, two front doors. Thus, even in the construction of the modest one-story bent house, we see the process by which Ozark vernacular builders incorporated popular pattern-book images into traditional building practice: they simply extracted the novel, picturesque essence of the pattern-book prototype—in this case, the juxtaposition of the two perpindicular wings—and grafted it onto traditional Ozark features.

In fact, only one house of all those documented departed so radically from the traditional arrangements underlying even the nontraditional house types that it appears to have been directly inspired by a pattern book with no adaptation. This is the fashionable Allen Sea King house of 1906 (fig. 4-71).

Fig. 4-67. Herman F. "Ute" Stokenbury House (1898), Elkins Vicinity, Washington County. This bent house, with its gables decorated with lacey jigsawn bargeboards and shingles, its porch ornamented with turned porch supports, jigsawn brackets, and spindlework, was quite ornate by Ozark standards. (All of these elements were commercially available at the time.) Besides the ornamentation, other elements that set this dwelling apart from its traditional house type counterpart, the one-story double pen house, are the high pyramid roof with picturesque cross gables and the corbelled brick chimney tops, typical of late nineteenth-century taste. The old photograph depicts Mr. and Mrs. Stokenbury and their family, who built the house in 1898 on fertile White River area land that was given to "Ute" by his father Herman Stokenbury, Sr. The elder Mr. Stokenbury emigrated from Germany to Washington County in 1846 and became a prosperous farmer with large landholdings. This bent house represents not only the prosperity of the Stokenbury family but also the style consciousness of the younger sons, Roedolphus, John P., and Ute, who all chose for their dwellings the newer popular house types, the prow house or the bent house, as seen here. The father and the eldest son, however, built the old-fashioned I-houses for their residences. (John P. Stokenbury's prow house is shown in fig. 4-75.) *Courtesy of Verd Shofner*

Fig. 4-68. McAtee-Winsted House (1905), Evansville Vicinity, Washington County. Rev. W. B. McAtee, a farmer and Baptist preacher, built this frame house in 1905 on his 173-acre farm. It is an unusually decorative bent house with its chamfered projecting block and decorative shingles in the gable front, reflecting Victorian taste for the picturesque Queen Anne style. The 1930s remodeled porch is a somewhat jarring note, but the fieldstone steps and a low stone wall along which old-fashioned flowers abound add to the traditional appeal of this house. Both the house and the large, sturdy barn with a stone lower story that stands just across the road attest to the prosperity of this farming and orchard area in the Springfield Plain. Corn, wheat, oats, and apples were grown on this farm; the apples were hauled in wagons to Fort Smith.

Fig. 4-69. Edna Jane and John Avey House (1906), Big Spring, Stone County. In the photograph are Edna Jane and John Avey (along with their six children), who in 1906 built this large two-story bent house with a two-story portico in the angle of the two front wings. This is one of the few two-story houses of any type to be constructed in rural Stone County. Although the bent house type has its roots in Victorian architectural pattern books, the Avey house is severely plain, resisting Victorian ornamentation, which was commercially available from millwork catalogues. The wide frieze boards outlining the gables are reflections of a long-forgotten Greek Revival style. The Avey family operated a gristmill near this house at Big Spring on Panther Creek for generations. Note the ubiquitous cane-bottom chairs on the front porch and the spinning wheel on the rear kitchen porch. Fig. 6-6 shows this house (now drastically remodeled) in its setting and fig. 5-12 shows the unusual bank barn that still stands near the house. *Courtesy of Harman Avey*

◀ Fig. 4-70. H. W. Lower House (1917), Fayetteville Vicinity, Washington County. This bent house is typical of its type in the Arkansas Ozarks—small, frame, one story, and quite plain. It was built for the Lower family in 1917 by carpenter Tom Bryant. In typical Ozark recycling practice, a one-room house was moved from another location and attached to form a rear ell. Although they are necessarily set perpendicular to one another rather than side by side—as in the traditional double pen house—the favored two front doors are present. Picturesque rolling hills and a pond surround this house. The Lowers have always grown fruit on their ninety-six acres: the elder Mr. Lower had extensive apple orchards; the younger Mr. Lower (who now occupies the house) grew strawberries and currently grows grapes.

Fig. 4-71. Mary and Allen Sea King House (1895), Lincoln Vicinity, Washington County. Of all the houses documented in the field work, this triple-gabled house most reflects the popularity of the late nineteenth-century Queen Anne style and seems likely to have been inspired by a pattern book. This conjecture is given credence by family members' assertions that "Aunt Mary King" designed the house herself. The highly irregular plan can only be described as Y-shaped; narrow stairs arise from the center of the house to an unfinished upper story, which according to family members was used as a sleeping area nonetheless, in typical Ozark fashion. The most traditional features are the presence of the popular two front doors and the side porches on either side of the rear room. Otherwise, the plan's irregularity and the profuse decorations all depart from the predictable rectilinear construction and plainness of most Ozark vernacular houses. The Lincoln area is prime orchard country, and the Kings owned extensive orchards of apples and peaches. Thus, this house exemplifies the transition to Victorian-inspired house types that seemed to accompany the transition from subsistence to specialized farming, especially in Washington and Benton counties. *Shiloh Museum of Ozark History*

The Prow House

The prow house retains the traditional rectangular block of the double pen house but adds a third room extending to the front from the exact center of the block so that this one-room extension, under a front-gabled roof, is visually balanced by the two lateral wings of the rooms behind. Thus, the composition retains the bilateral symmetry of the traditional types and the additive quality (an essential aspect of the vernacular process as has been noted) of the third pen as well. Prow houses, like all Ozark dwellings, are generally one story, but there are one-and-one-half and two-story versions as well (figs. 4-75 to 4-77). Generally, the whole is unified by a wrap-around front porch that encircles the projecting room and also extends across the lateral wings. When this porch is present, and especially when the projecting room has chamfered corners, the effect is of a ship's prow; this type was named the prow house by Cyrus Sutherland of the University of Arkansas School of Architecture, an authority on Arkansas's vernacular architecture.

The prow house unquestionably demonstrates the far-flung influence of the decorative Queen Anne architectural style, popular from about 1880 to 1900 (and longer in rural areas) and of late nineteenth-century pattern books as well. The prow house appeared in at least one of the pattern books that promulgated the Queen Anne style. Bicknell and Comstock's 1881 *Modern Architectural Designs and Details* featured two versions of the prow house (fig. 4-72). One is a one-and-one-half-story cottage and the other is a full two-story house (see fig. 4-73); both have encircling porches, but only the two-story version has the ornamental chamfered corners on the projecting block. Both are labeled "Sea or Lake Shore Cottages," undoubtedly because of the breeze-catching qualities of the projecting rooms and the informality of the large encircling porches.[68]

Although these images do appear in the Bicknell and Comstock pattern book (and perhaps others as well), it is not being contended that the Ozark vernacular

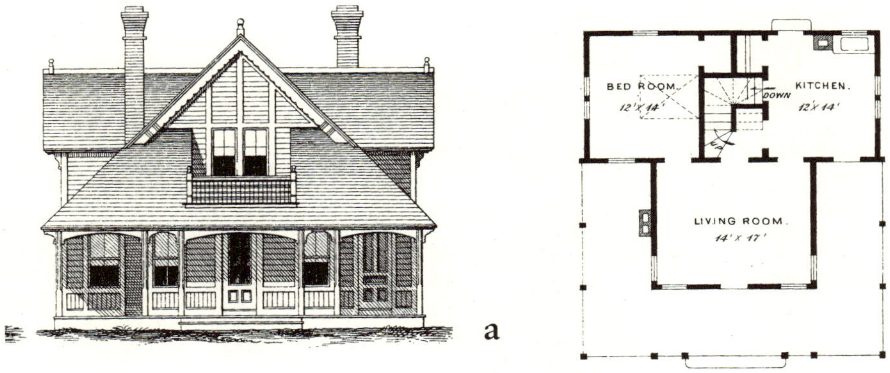

a

Fig. 4-72. Two Pattern-Book Prow Houses. (a) One-story prow house and plan from Bicknell and Comstock's *Modern Architectural Designs and Details*, 1881. (b) Two-story prow house from the same volume.

b

builder actually copied from this pattern book; instead, the builder drew upon what had become a familiar image, as was the case with the bent house. It is easy to see the appeal of this house to vernacular builders; the builder had only to extract the picturesque projecting chamfered bay, which is a staple element in Queen Anne style houses, and graft it onto the old double pen house. In so doing, the builder achieved the picturesque quality of having the two gables perpendicular to each other (as seen in the bent house) but modified the house in the direction of traditional houses by balancing the projecting room with a second lateral wing which retained the old bilateral symmetry of traditional Ozark facades. When the prow house appears without the encircling porch as in the J. S. Jones house (fig. 4-77) and the Fitzgerald house (fig. 4-78), the additive thinking of the vernacular builder is unmistakable in the three blocky sections; in the prow house, even more than in the bent house, the old familiar symmetrical facade of the "house in the mind's eye" appears to win out over picturesque asymmetry.

Another traditional feature the prow house retains is two front doors. One door opening into the side of the prow and one into each of the lateral rooms is the standard arrangement. It is noteworthy that in the documented houses, only one prow-house builder chose the arrangement of placing the front door at the

Fig. 4-73. Hugh Rogers House (c. 1900), Prairie Grove, Washington County. Built by a prominent citizen, this large, two-story prow house with Queen Anne decorative details must have influenced local taste, for both in this small town and in surrounding rural areas several smaller, plainer prow houses were constructed.

front of the projecting room; this would have had the entrance at the gable end, and such an arrangement, as we have repeatedly seen, went against the strict Ozark vernacular building orientation of placing doors for houses in the long side-gabled facade, reserving doors under the front gable for schools, churches, and outbuildings, such as smokehouses and stores.

The front or "prow" room has excellent ventilation and is used as a bedroom, a parlor, or a sitting room. In reflecting the decorative, picturesque roots of this type, one of the larger prow houses, the two-story Charlie Williams house (fig. 4-76) features imbricated shingles that decorate the upper story in typical Queen Anne style fashion.

The prow house, consistent with its pattern-book origins, appears in small towns in several parts of Arkansas, in Missouri, in Iowa, and no doubt in many other states as well. It did not appear in Stone County or in the surveyed areas of Madison County. In Washington County, it was clustered principally around the communities of Prairie Grove and Elkins. The clustering of this type in certain communities leads to the conjecture that the prow house was in the repertoire of one or two local carpenters. In the small town of Prairie Grove, for instance, there is an imposing full two-story version of a prow house (fig. 4-73). Its rural counterparts are much smaller and less exuberant (figs. 4-74 to 4-78). Most dated from 1900 to 1920.

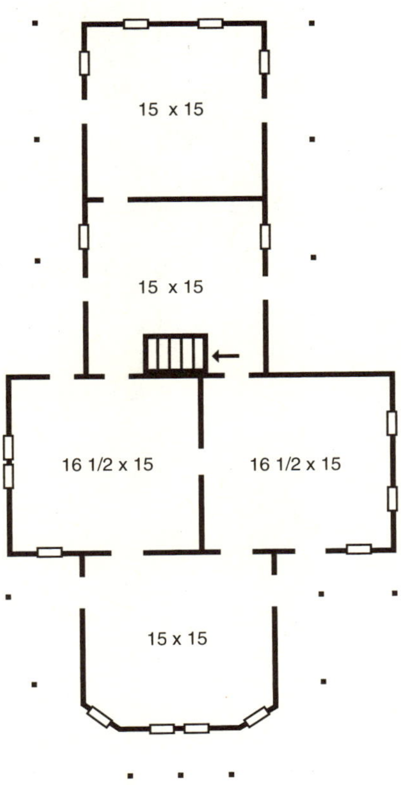

Fig. 4-74. Prow House Plan of John P. and Pearl Stokenbury House (1900), Elkins Vicinity, Washington County. *Drawn by Stacy Rennhoff*

Fig. 4-76. Charlie Williams House (1912), Elkins Vicinity, Washington County. Built by a prosperous farm family in 1912, this two-story house exemplifies the prow house type with its front bay projecting from the traditional double pen block to form a "prow" with chamfered corners. The whole structure is surrounded by a polygonal wrap-around porch with two front doors symmetrically arranged on either side of the prow. This prow room was used as a bedroom, and two exterior doors open into it for ventilation.

◀ Fig. 4-75. Pearl and John P. Stokenbury House (1895, nonextant), Elkins Vicinity, Washington County. This house was built by Pearl and John P. Stokenbury around 1900 on good farmland given to the couple by Mr. Stokenbury's father, Herman, who had emigrated from Germany to Washington County as a young man and who had become a prosperous farmer and landowner. (Another Stokenbury son's house is shown in fig. 4-67.) This one-and-one-half-story prow house was one of the most decoratively detailed houses documented in the fieldwork. Its chamfered, projecting front was ornamented by a large wrap-around porch with turned porch supports and jigsawn brackets. The front door was a decorative glazed one available through millwork catalogues, as were many other of the exterior ornaments. The prow house plan reveals the typical Ozark approach to a Victorian architectural pattern book–influenced design, in that the projecting front is merely grafted onto the old double pen plan with two rooms set side by side with the customary two front doors. The rear of his house overlooked the lush green meadows of the White River bottomland. A stone fruit cellar, a smokehouse, and a large barn remained at the time the photograph was made; since then, the house has been demolished.

Fig. 4-77. Ella and J. S. Jones House (1904), Springdale Vicinity, Washington County. The severity and the perfect balance of this one-story prow house without the customary encircling front porch create a striking image. The turned porch supports are the only hint of the Victorian architectural roots of this house type, and in typical Ozark fashion a vestige remains of the old Greek Revival style in the wide frieze board outlining the gable ends. This house differs from the typical prow house in that the projection of the front room is too shallow to allow for the front doors, which typically open into the sides of the prow. The plan here is, instead, a modified Greek cross plan with three rooms across the main block with a kitchen forming a third block at the rear. This design shows the desire for more specialized functions, such as private bedrooms. Apple orchards and vineyards provided the principal farm livelihood for the J. S. Jones family, who built the house in 1904. Both the date and type of farming underscore the supposition that new, popular house types, such as the prow house, appear primarily in good farming areas and coincide with the advent of specialized farming.

Fig. 4-78. Mirtie and L. B. Fitzgerald House (c. 1900, nonextant), Winslow, Washington County. This prow house without the chamfered projecting block and the encircling porch (and like the Jones house just discussed) clearly reflects the additive thinking that created this popular house type by simply adding a third projecting block to the old rectangular double pen house and retaining its symmetry. *Shiloh Museum of Ozark History*

The One-Story Pyramid Roof House

Like the other nontraditional house types of the Arkansas Ozarks, the one-story pyramid roof house is located primarily in Springfield Plain areas. It appears fairly infrequently before 1930. It has simple, boxy massing with a square (or relatively square) floor plan that consists of four rooms without a central passageway, all under a pyramid roof. Other than the steep, centered gables that sometimes break the monotony of the square shape—as in the Tom Dye house (fig. 4-79)—this house type eschews the picturesque details and irregular massing of the prow house and the bent house. Most pyramid roof houses seem to date from around 1910 to 1930. Thus, in its dating, its simplicity, and its compact plan, it relates much more to the American bungalow than to the nineteenth-century picturesque pattern-book tradition as the two previous popular house types do. Sometimes this house type retains the favored two-front-door arrangement; the Tom Dye house is an example (fig. 4-79). This house features identical double-door facades on two sides of the house. Another variation retains the old-fashioned wrap-around porch.

Fig. 4-79. Tom Dye House (1920, nonextant), West Fork Vicinity, Washington County. In 1920 carpenter George Latham built this square one-story frame house for Tom Dye. It has the pyramid roof and the four-room square plan that became popular in the Ozarks in the 1920s. Although the pyramid roof with cross gables and the two-room-deep plan depart from Arkansas Ozarks building tradition, the customary two front door facade is present here in not just one but in two sides of the house, presenting a striking view on its corner lot. Tom Dye farmed 250 acres of good White River bottom land nearby. The house was recently demolished.

True to its origins in popular culture, the pyramid roof house type can be seen in all regions of the country, and it is always a modest dwelling. It is scattered throughout both small towns and the countryside and in Arkansas Delta cotton-growing areas where it sometimes clusters around cotton fields, serving as tenant farmer houses.

It is important not to confuse this compact, modest twentieth-century house with what some scholars have called the "Southern Pyramidal House," a nineteenth-century type in the Lowland South that has a double-pile plan with a central hall, a prosperous farm house comparable to the I-house in the Upland South.[69]

Conclusion

Six house types are identified as traditional types, representative of old, communally sanctioned Arkansas Ozark building traditions with the least influence from the larger popular culture. These six types are: the single pen, the double pen, the saddlebag, the dogtrot, the central hall cottage, and the I-house. (A seventh type, the one-and-one-half-story house, is classified as a subtype of the I-house.) They share the following characteristics: all appear in the early settlement period or by the mid-nineteenth century at the latest; all appear either in log or braced frame construction; in massing, all are either simple square or rectangular, boxy shapes that could have emerged as forms created in the process of expanding single pen log houses; all are oriented with a side-gabled roof and with the entrance location on the long side parallel with the road; all are one room deep with either a rear ell or a rear shed addition. The fact that these houses are also typical of vernacular dwellings in North Carolina, Kentucky, and Tennessee reenforces the speculation that this simple, boxy form, which conceptually originated with the square (or nearly square) single pen unit and was always added onto in prescribed ways, constituted the shared house model, or the "house in the mind's eye," that the Upland South people moving west brought to the Arkansas Ozarks.

Of these traditional types, the I-house is the most widespread in the eastern United States, and it exhibits regional variations. The I-house with a narrow two-story portico (often embellished with either Greek Revival details or Victorian sawnwork) is popular throughout the Upland South and in the Arkansas Ozarks as well. A second Ozark version, however, seems almost as popular: the I-house with a full-length two-story portico and a five-bay facade. Since the I-house in the Ozarks, as elsewhere, is associated with agricultural prosperity, it often carries details from period styles fashionable within the larger popular culture. For example, the B. F. Johnson house of 1878 (fig. 4-54) features Italianate details, and the E. W. McClellan House of 1866 reveals Greek Revival touches (fig. 4-52). The one-story central hall cottage is second only to the I-house in association with prosperous farm families; it sometimes has Greek Revival details, like those in the Troy Gordon house of 1851 (fig. 4-63).

The location of the house types most closely associated with prosperity—the I-house and the central hall cottage—correlated with geography to a much greater degree than was anticipated when this study began. Both were found predominantly within the relatively prosperous countryside of the Springfield Plain. Two more modest house types—the dogtrot house and the double pen house—appear, on the contrary, with greater frequency in the mountainous, less prosperous areas.

Three types are considered nontraditional and have been classified as popular house types: the bent house, the prow house, and the one-story pyramid roof house. These are so classified for the following reasons: they do not appear in log or braced frame, nor in times of early settlement; they depart from the Ozark tradition of being one room (or single pile) deep, a trait deemed to be representative of English rural folk building; and they reflect influences from beyond Ozark architectural traditions to the larger popular culture.

The bent house and the prow house exhibit unequivocally the influence of nineteenth-century architectural pattern books. But, even though the prow house is found in at least one Victorian pattern book, it is important to note the process by which the house was translated into the Ozark building tradition. As Dell Upton has noted, vernacular builders in all parts of the country simply extracted distinctive essences from pattern-book designs and grafted them onto familiar building elements. In the prow house and the bent house, a key element from the popular Queen Anne architectural style, the projecting block or room (forming two angles overall with gable ends perpendicular to each other), was simply added to the front of the traditional rectangular block. In the bent house, this added block forms an L-shaped asymmetrical facade. In the prow house, the projecting room is placed at the center of the double pen rectangle and retains the balance and bilateral symmetry of traditional Ozark facades. Both these houses reflect the continuing additive method of composing house forms, a method that is inherent in the vernacular building process. The bent house, with its L-shaped facade and its two perpendicular wings, is found in several variations and in one or two stories. The small one-story bent house is the most common of the popular types.

The third popular house type, the one-story pyramid roof house, has a compact four-room square plan without a passageway. Its inexpensive compactness and absence of stylish details place it in the sphere of influence of the ubiquitous bungalow, rather than under the influence of the nineteenth-century pattern book.

In sum, if a hypothetical architectural spectrum is imagined with the convention-bound traditional houses (or folk houses) at one end and high style houses (representing dwellings designed by architects who attempted to set or follow national and international architectural design trends) at the opposite end, the houses classified as traditional would cluster at the folk architecture end of the spectrum; the houses classified as nontraditional and popular would fall in the middle, exhibiting influences from both traditional Ozark building practices and from popular culture. No houses were documented that fall into the high style end of the spectrum, thus all the dwellings reflect to some degree, the familiar architectural vocabulary cherished by the common people of the Arkansas Ozarks and, indeed, of the entire Upland South.

Chapter 5

Barns and Outbuildings

The Ozark farmstead is made up of a house and a cluster of what appear to be randomly arranged outbuildings. Consistency appears only in the invariable siting of the dwelling near the road, and in the relative location to the house of two common outbuildings, barns and smokehouses. Because the smokehouse served as a pantry, it was located nearest the house, often just a few feet away from the rear kitchen door. The barn was much farther away from the house, because in the mild winters long treks to the barn were not too unpleasant. If the farm was laid out on a hillside, the barn was almost always on the same level as the house or below it, but it was rarely placed above the house, as is often the arrangement in Blue Ridge Mountain farms.[1] A barn was placed in front of a house only when a road separated them.

Figs. 5-1 to 5-4 depict both sketched layouts of outbuildings and photographs of individual outbuildings on three typical Ozark farms: the Walter Ford farm (fig. 5-1, 5-4) near St. James in Stone County; the Agnes and Harrison Pierce farm at Cove Creek (fig. 5-2) in Washington County; and the Grubbs-Hamilton farm (fig. 5-3) at Old Alabam in Madison County. While the log barns at the Ford and Pierce farms predate 1930, the entire ensemble of outbuildings in all three sketches dates from about 1930. All of the outbuildings on these working farms are still being used, although not all for their original functions. All the farms are located in somewhat remote areas.

Many outbuildings that now appear on farms are probably of fairly recent vintage (around 1910 to 1930). They were, in the main, unnecessary until the advent of farm equipment. Moreover, they were dependent upon the availability of scrap milled lumber for affordability and ease of construction.[2] Earlier farmsteads had fewer outbuildings, and these were made of log, not milled lumber construction. The varieties of newer outbuildings are discussed in the last section of this chapter and are visible in the three farm layout sketches.

After the barn and the smokehouse, the chicken house is probably the most common of the older structures. Protection of chickens from predators was a vital concern because eggs and chickens were staple foods; moreover, both could be bartered at local stores. Single-purpose structures, such as apple houses or granaries, are less common since such crops were usually stored in a multipurpose barn.

Fig. 5-1. Layout of Outbuildings at Walter Ford Farm, St. James Vicinity, Stone County. *Drawing by Laura Richens*

Fig. 5-2. Layout of Agnes and Harrison Pierce Farm, Cove Creek, Washington County.
Drawing by Laura Richens

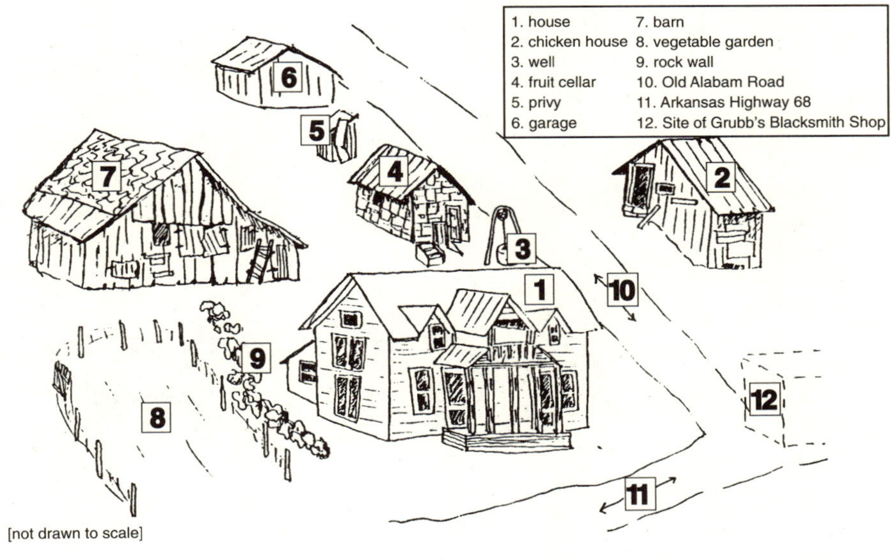

Fig. 5-3. Layout of Outbuildings at Grubbs-Hamilton Farm, Old Alabam, Madison County.
Drawing by Laura Richens

Smokehouses

Because pork, cured in the form of hams and sausage, was an important part of the Ozark diet, the preservation of pork after hog slaughtering in the late fall was important, so smokehouses were essential components of farmsteads. (As noted, chicken was the other staple meat; Ozarkians rarely ate beef.) Smokehouses were generally well crafted and seemed to have survived on many farms after all other outbuildings had vanished. Although frame versions predominate, log smokehouses are still common sights. Only a few stone and brick ones were documented in the fieldwork. All are slightly rectangular structures, with the average size being about twelve by fourteen feet, the largest fourteen by twenty feet, and the smallest ten by ten feet. Unlike dwellings, smokehouses are oriented with a front gable roof over the door, often sheltered by a roof overhang (fig. 5-5). Invariably located close to the back door of the house, smokehouses served as outdoor pantries. A common practice was for the housewife to slice off just enough ham for the day's use every morning.

Inside the smokehouse slabs of pork were rubbed with salt and placed on benches that lined the sides or on a large wooden table. This curing process took about six weeks, after which the salt was washed off and the pork was peppered (to keep out insects called "kippers") and then rubbed with sage and

Fig. 5-4. Outbuildings and Fences at Walter Ford Farm, St. James Vicinity, Stone County. Some of the outbuildings sketched in fig. 5-1 are visible, including the double-crib log barn and corn crib at the rear, and in the foreground, a smokehouse and doghouse.

Fig. 5-5. Log Smokehouse at Sam Brown Farm, West Richwoods, Stone County. Note the typical roof overhang on a smokehouse and its close proximity to the house.

perhaps other spices as well. Finally, the slabs were hung on hooks from the rafters. Since the meat was already cured through the salt-absorption process, it did not actually require smoking for its preservation. When smoking was desired, fires were built in an old stove, a kettle, or a tin box placed in the smokehouse. The fires burned hickory chips and corncobs and were kept banked for several days.[3] Other foodstuffs were stored here as well; for example, bunches of onions were hung from the rafters or walls, and sacks of flour and meal were sometimes placed on boards that were suspended by wires from the rafters.[4]

Barns

The largest of the outbuildings in the farm complex is, of course, the barn. All those documented in the fieldwork are of wood construction, although a few of the more substantial ones have stone lower portions. The size and soundness of construction of barns vary with age and with the relative prosperity of the farms. The earliest barns were invariably log, and log construction persisted in barns and outbuildings well into the twentieth century, long after it was abandoned for houses. The later barns were the largest, most specialized, and most solidly constructed, reflecting the transition from subsistence to more profitable market-oriented farming. Some of the largest barns documented, for example, are the barns for mules and horses—which represented a specialized enterprise themselves—that were built in the 1910s and 1920s.

Ozark barns are generally multipurpose structures, used for storing hay and grain and for feeding and sheltering the "work stock," horses and mules. Reportedly, sheep sometimes were also penned in the barn. Cattle usually foraged on the open range along with the hogs. All barns, even the smallest, have upper and lower levels, with room for hay storage above and stalls and sometimes grain bins located below. Side sheds offered shelter for animals, wagons, farm machinery, and nowadays automobiles as well.

Hundreds of log barns and outbuildings remain in the Ozarks, and most of them are still in use. They are generally crude structures with the logs left round and saddle-notched at the corners. As in traditional houses, their form consists of single- or multiple-log units, except that, in references to barns and outbuildings, the term for the unit is crib rather than pen. An essential difference in orientation exists, however, since barns have front gables, whereas traditional houses have side gables. Fieldwork showed that barns could have one, two, three, four, or six log cribs. Single-crib barns were, however, the most common log type (figs. 5-6, 5-7, 5-8, 5-9).

Fig. 5-6. Pinkney Pruitt Single Crib Log Barn, St. James Vicinity, Stone County. There is little distinction between a generous-sized corn crib and a small, single crib log barn, except that the barn characteristically has side sheds, as seen here. *Courtesy of the Arkansas Historic Preservation Program*

With rare exceptions, all the frame barns documented were the transverse crib type that "occur throughout the Upland South and periphery as easily the dominant barn . . . ," as Fred Kniffen has observed.[5] This type has a gable front, a central (or end-to-end) driveway, and is flanked by cribs serving both as stabling and storage areas that are arranged transverse to the ridgepole. As illustrated in fig. 5-10, the roofs of transverse crib barns generally swoop down to create side sheds; less often, they have gambrel roofs or breaks in the roofline.

A second and much rarer type of barn is the English barn, a frame structure with gable ends and a central passage resembling the form of a dogtrot house (fig. 5-11). The English barn type was common in the British Isles and in parts of central Europe, and it is believed to have originated in this country in New England with English settlers, who practiced braced frame construction rather than log construction.[6] Rarer still is the Pennsylvania Bank Barn type, which is conveniently built against a hillside to provide easy wagon access to the loft area. The only such barn documented is the John Avey barn of 1906 (fig. 5-12).

Fig. 5-7. William Dillard Double Crib Log Barn, Round Bottom, Stone County. Here the two cribs were subdivided to make a four-chambered structure; the central passage was recently enclosed.

Fig. 5-8. Thellitha, Annie, and Bob Light Pitching Hay from a Wagon into the Loft of a Double Crib Log Barn. The location of this barn is unknown. *Shiloh Museum of Ozark History (Cora Humble Collection)*

Fig. 5-10. Transverse Crib Barn at John Carter Farm, Stone County. Although large by Ozark standards, this transverse crib barn with enclosed side sheds is the most common type of the Upland South and the Arkansas Ozarks.

◀ Fig. 5-9. Fred Lancaster Four Crib Log Barn, Round Bottom, Stone County. This 1918 log barn originally had two drives separating the four log cribs; later, the side-to-side drive was closed, creating the familiar gable-front configuration. This alteration illustrates what most scholars accept as the morphological evolution of the frame transverse crib barn, the typical barn of the Upland South.

Fig. 5-11. Okey Davis English Type Barn, Pleasant Grove Vicinity, Stone County. The English barn obviously resembles a dogtrot house, but unlike the dogtrot, it is uncommon in the Ozark countryside.

Fig. 5-12. Bank Barn at Edna and John Avey Farm, Big Spring, Stone County. The bank barn, built into a hillside with its stone lower story and its easy wagon access to the loft area, is a common barn in the eastern United States. Rare in the Arkansas Ozarks, this bank barn was the only one documented in the field survey. According to family history, Mr. Avey got the idea for this barn after a trip "up north" to visit relatives.

Corn Cribs and Granaries

Several small log or frame structures called corn cribs or granaries (the terms seem to have been used virtually interchangeably) were documented. These structures measured around six by eight feet or eight by ten feet, and they were usually rickety constructions. In fact, there is little distinction between a generous-sized corn crib and a small single crib log barn, except that the latter characteristically had side sheds, while the corn cribs did not (fig. 5-6). Since cattle and hogs foraged on the open range for most of the year, and only fodder for horses and mules needed to be stored, there was little necessity for large cribs or granaries in earlier subsistence farming. The grain needing storage was primarily for the family's use rather than being a cash crop. As the larger twentieth-century multipurpose barns were built, even the small corn cribs became unnecessary because these newer barns always contained special bins for grain storage.

Fruit Cellars

Among the outbuildings of recent vintage, stone fruit cellars (which also served as storm cellars when the need arose) were popular. Most were constructed around the 1920s and early 1930s because home canning on a large scale was introduced at that time.[7] Generally made of poured concrete, the lower walls and floors vary to the degree that they are below ground. Fruit cellars functioned as root cellars and as storage areas for the mason jars of home-canned vegetables and meat. Occasionally, early cellars without poured concrete were dug into hillsides (fig. 5-14). In some cases, they were dug under the floor of one room of a house with the entrance always on the exterior of the house. Some smokehouses have small cellars dug beneath them (fig. 5-13). On farms without cellars, vegetables were stored in earth mounds over the winter or hung in cloth sacks in the often unfinished upper stories of houses.[8]

In the prime orchard areas of Washington and Madison counties, apple dryers, specifically constructed for that purpose, were documented. They measure around fifteen by twenty-two feet with a stone lower section, a frame upper section, and a slatted wooden floor in between (fig. 5-15). In the apple-drying process, apples were sliced in rings and spread out on the slatted floor in frames while a fire in the stove on the lower level was kept burning continuously for about twenty-four hours. The fruit was stored in cloth sacks and either sold or stored for the family's use. These small, individually owned apple dryers were not common, however, because in the major apple-growing areas each community operated a large commercial dryer. Commercial dryers provided welcome seasonal work for local people, especially women.

Fig. 5-13. Smokehouse with Fruit Cellar at Grubbs-Hamilton Farm, Old Alabam, Madison County. Smokehouse-fruit cellar combinations are fairly common in the Ozark countryside and are located near the house as seen here. The farm layout for this largely unchanged farmstead is shown in fig. 5-3. (Note the well in the foreground and the outhouse in the rear in the photograph.)

Outdoor Toilets

Outdoor toilets are becoming rare sights. By the 1950s even houses in the remote areas generally had indoor plumbing, rendering the "privy" obsolete, since, unlike the smokehouse, it did not serve as a useful storage facility. Several families in remote areas reported that outhouses were considered an unnecessary "nicety," given the availability of woods and brush for privacy. Some reported that their families did not construct outdoor toilets until the availability of FHA loans in the 1930s (fig. 5-16).

Springhouses and Well Houses

Contrary to reports of local people that springhouses were once common, scarcely any remain. Many people remember that their families kept milk and butter cool simply by suspending them in the well or by placing them outdoors in large crocks in which well water was replenished several times a day in hot weather. Wells are never elaborate structures; picturesque lattice well houses, of the sort one sees in town, are rare. Sometimes the well had a little roof covering it, but most often it did not (fig. 5-17).

Other Outbuildings

As the farm layout diagrams in figs. 5-1 through 5-3 indicate, from about 1910 to 1950 various kinds of outbuildings and sheds were constructed to accommodate new machinery and appliances. Pump houses, wash houses (which first housed washing machines with gasoline motors), tool sheds, storage sheds, and small garages are all commonly seen (fig. 5-18). These varied small structures are sometimes "recycled" buildings moved from abandoned farms or from other sites on the owner's farm.

◀ Fig. 5-14. Barrel Vaulted Stone Fruit Cellar Built into Hillside at Eric Bodine Farm, Maguiretown Vicinity, Washington County. Swedish immigrant Eric Bodine built this unique stone fruit cellar into the hillside behind his dogtrot house; the house has been replaced but the cellar is still in use. (The Bodine house is shown in fig. 4-33.)

Fig. 5-15. Apple Dryer at Clara and Lester Neal Farm, Drakestown Vicinity, Madison County. In prime apple orchard areas, community apple dryers were common, but individual farmers built them as well. Apple rings were spread out on the slatted floor above while a fire in the stove on the lower level was kept burning for about twenty-four hours in the apple-drying process.

Fig. 5-16. Outhouse at Grubbs-Hamilton Farm, Old Alabam, Madison County. Outhouses are rapidly vanishing structures. (See Grubbs-Hamilton house in fig. 4-58 and farm layout in fig. 5-3.)

Fig. 5-17. Well at William Lancaster Farm, Round Bottom, Stone County. Wells are nearly always simple and straightforward, as this one is. (See Lancaster house in fig. 4-37.)

Fig. 5-18. Wash House at Will Ford Farm, St. James Vicinity, Stone County. Most outbuildings for specialized functions such as this one are of fairly recent vintage. (See Will Ford house in figs. 6-7 and 6-8.)

Chapter 6

The House and the Ozark Landscape

Every dwelling is only a fragment of a larger whole: a neighborhood, a town, a farmstead, a landscape. This chapter moves beyond individual houses to describe and interpret the Ozark landscape and the place of houses within it. It draws heavily upon the recently established field of landscape studies, especially the writings of John B. Jackson. The term *landscape* in this context means much more than scenery or natural setting. It includes both natural and cultural elements, and is, in fact, the product of interaction between humans and the land. As geographer Douglas Crary explained it, "Landscape is in geography what Gestalt is in psychology . . . the totality of aspect of a given area, just as in Gestalt psychology a melody is the totality of a series of tones, not a sum of separate tones."[1]

In this ceaseless, ever-changing relation of life and land, then, certain landscapes develop, grow old, and die. So it has been in the Ozarks. There are two Ozark landscapes, one is the traditional landscape that can only be glimpsed in its totality in old photographs, the other is the landscape that is presently experienced. In some aspects these two merge, and vestiges of the old seem reassuringly and quaintly the same; in other aspects the traditional landscape has irrevocably vanished.

In his perceptive and thought-provoking book, *Discovering the Vernacular Landscape,* John B. Jackson helped clarify our understanding of the Ozark landscape, past and present, by contrasting two archetypal landscapes with opposite characters, the political and the vernacular. The political landscape is "designed to impose or preserve a unity and order on the land in keeping with a long-range, large-scale plan." It is characterized by "the visibility and sanctity of boundaries, the importance of monuments and centrifugal highways, the close relationship between status and enclosed space."[2] Boundaries around individual properties are a clue to the vivid imprint of a political landscape. In Jackson's words, "It is when we find ourselves in a landscape of well-built, well-maintained fences and hedges and walls whether in New England . . . or Mexico, that we realize we are in a landscape where political identity is a matter of importance, a landscape where lawyers make a good living and everyone knows how much land he owns."[3] The vernacular landscape, on the other hand, is characterized in this manner:

> . . . Its spaces are usually small, irregular in shape, subject to rapid change in use, in ownership, in dimensions; . . . the houses, even the villages themselves grow, shrink, change morphology, change location; . . . there is always a vast amount of "common land"—waste, pasturage, forest, areas where natural resources are exploited in a piecemeal manner; . . . its roads are little more than paths and lanes . . . finally, . . . the vernacular landscape is a scattering of hamlets and clusters of fields, islands in a sea of waste or wilderness changing from generation to generation, leaving no monuments, only abandonment or signs of renewal. Mobility and change are the key to the vernacular landscape, but of an involuntary reluctant sort; not the expression of restlessness and search for improvement, but an unending, patient adjustment to circumstances.[4]

These words could hardly be more descriptive of the Arkansas Ozarks landscape, past and present.

Three interconnected natural elements have determined the character of this setting: topography, vegetation, and the quality of the soil. Of paramount importance is the varied and irregular topography; it has dictated settlement patterns and the location of farms, roads, and untouched forests. In his classic study of the geography of this region, Carl O. Sauer noted the marked contrasts in topography, concluding that the Ozarks are characterized by "an unusual wealth of geographic responses." Owing to the variety of both the kinds and the formation of rocks and the region's "complicated erosion history," such diverse formations as caves, glades, knobs, benches, balds, gorges, sinkholes, and slip-off slopes make the area a paradise for vacationers and photographers, but not, obviously, for farmers.[5] While maps present deceptively neat subregions of the Boston Mountains and the Springfield Plain (fig. 1-2), in reality the traveler experiences a constant interplay between uplands and valleys; between moun-

Fig. 6-1. View of Meadows from E. W. McClellan House in Springfield Plain Area, Cane Hill Vicinity, Washington County. (See also fig. 4-52.)

tains, rolling hills and meadows; between swift-flowing streams with limestone bluffs and lazy creeks that are dry much of the year. Lush meadows are contrasted with fields of rocky outcroppings (figs. 6-1 to 6-3).

A close correlation exists between topography and soil fertility. According to Sauer, "In general, the most desirable soil types are those which are associated with gentle slopes, the undesirable ones those found for the most part in regions of greatest relief."[6] As a determining factor for this entire study, Sauer's conclusion that "Except on the plateau of the western border, a preponderance of cheap, poor land exists in all parts of the region"[7] is of immense importance.

Because of the widespread infertility of the land, much of it has always been uncultivated, or cultivated only on a rotating basis. Accordingly, the abundance of brush and forest is still an outstanding characteristic. A constantly changing pattern of ground cover exists, from scrub timber and brush that choke areas that once were clearings, to the prevalent oak-pine and oak-hickory forests, with much that is in between.[8] Sauer summarizes, "The greater part of the Ozark highland consists of unimproved, so-called wild land, covered with forest or brush. This land either has steep slopes, or is so removed from lines of transportation that it has not been profitable to clear it."[9] Certainly the landscape viewed from almost any point is dominated by trees.

Vegetation, including trees, is a powerful presence in the Ozarks; abandoned fields, farm implements, and houses alike are quickly engulfed by it. According to folklorist E. Joan Wilson Miller, local speech vividly reflects this reality by

Fig. 6-2. View of White River Bluffs and Bottom Land in Boston Mountain Area, William Lancaster House, Round Bottom, Stone County.

Fig. 6-3. Rocky Field and Pastures, Allie and Neal Morris Farm, South Richwoods, Stone County, Boston Mountain Area.

differentiating between three kinds of ground cover: "woods," "timber," and "brush."

> There were shacks in the "woods", but the inhabitants of such dwellings were truly backwoods in attitude according to settlement people. The impression gained . . . is that the "woods" existed but were traversable and there was considerable coming and going through them. This may be an indirect comment on the absence of good roads. By contrast "timber" implied a wilder, denser, more lonely setting. People moved at the edge of the "big timber" or were lost in it. The lawless and the fugitive knew security in its trackless extent. The frequence of the use of the words "timber" and "woods" implies a great impact on folk activity and there is a sense of the vegetation being the master. "Brush" meaning bushes, was nearer home and was obviously the result of seedling trees establishing themselves faster than the settler could destroy them by burning, cutting or grazing by livestock. The "brush" served as a cover for rabbits, as open-air privy, and as a source of privacy for members of big families who were often being raised in one-room cabins.[10]

The overall sensation, then, created by this rough, timbered terrain is in decided contrast to the unfolding spaciousness of the flat Mississippi Delta lands to the east and the Oklahoma plains to the west where the presence of the earth itself is seen and felt. In contrast, in the Arkansas Ozarks one generally experiences limited visibility and a sense of enclosure by woodlands, hills, mountains, and above all, ever-encroaching vegetation (figs. 6-5, 6-6).

Settlement Patterns and Sitings of Houses

Settlement is generally thinly dispersed throughout the Ozarks area. Topography links with personal inclination in this regard. For, while the Anglo-American pioneer's desire for "elbow room," both psychological and physical, is well known, such dispersion was also necessary in an area where patch farming, in which only one-third of a farmer's land was cultivated at a time, and open range herding of livestock was the rule.[11] Topography also influenced settlement patterns. In the plateaus, settlements are rather evenly distributed, but in the mountainous sections, they occur only in certain areas. In his study of the geography of the Boston Mountains, O. O. Maxfield analyzes three possibilities for settlement within that rough terrain: flat ridge tops, valley walls, and valley bottoms.[12] Because of the difficulty in ascending them and because of their limited level land and steep drop-offs, the ridge tops are not major settlement areas. Valley walls are also sparsely populated: farmsteads are located only on those of gradual ascent where natural terraces (or "benches") afford good building sites. The steeper valley walls are left alone. As Maxfield observed—referring to the problem of erosion and the difficulty of using agricultural machinery—"It is advisable to leave the valley walls forested, and either from wisdom or lack of initiative, man has done so."[13]

Several benefits, such as preservation of wildlife habitats, protection against erosion, and provision of forage for livestock accrued from the practice of leaving forested areas. The locales that attracted most of the settlement in the Boston Mountains were the major valleys, which opened onto lower and less rugged areas; soon a network of dirt roads was developed, along which churches, grist mills, lumber mills, and crossroads stores as well as farmsteads appeared. Fieldwork for this study verified Maxfield's observations about patterns of siting houses. In the plateaus and prairies, the preferred site was atop a knoll (fig. 6-4). In mountainous sections, the houses were located either in valleys or on the first bench of a mountainside of gradual ascent; no dwellings were found on the steeper mountainsides.

But other considerations were brought to bear when an Ozarkian chose a home site. According to oral history and published reminiscences, two issues were paramount. Because of the universal dread of chills and fevers, it was essential to choose a site high enough to avoid flooding streams and swampy land. An 1831 guide for immigrants explains the danger:

> Physicians and philosophers have not yet determined what the thing is, called miasma, which invariably produces yellow, bilious, intermittent and other summer and autumnal fevers; but if it is a species of carbonic gas, as some think, it is heavier than the surrounding atmosphere, is more dense on

Fig. 6-4. Unidentified Farmhouse atop Knoll in Norwood Prairie, Benton County. In rolling terrain and in prairies, the preferred house site is atop a knoll; in more mountainous areas, houses are sited on the first bench. Steep mountainsides are avoided as house sites.

> low grounds and bottoms, and in ravines, and naturally concentrates in confined places. . . . It is enough for practical purposes to know that any spot where the air is confined, as in a cove, in the timber or bluff, or where it is forced through a passage, as the head of a ravine, is always less healthy than a spot freely ventilated, or on elevated ground.[14]

The second compelling factor was to locate the house near a good water source, usually a spring. Since springs are plentiful in the Ozarks, presumably this presented little problem. An Ozark anecdote about choosing a house site underscores the concerns for elevated ground and proximity to water. "The house site was selected by husband and wife going to the spring. The wife was given two large buckets of water and told to carry the water up the hill as far as she could without resting. The place where she had to rest was selected as the building site."[15] Nevertheless, wells were dug as soon as possible and only "shiftless" people continued carrying water from a spring or stream after the farmstead was established.[16]

Perhaps the anecdote just cited refers to only the earliest, temporary houses, or perhaps it has no grounding in reality, for it certainly belies the present visual evidence—Ozark houses are invariably at the roadside and face the road. Ozark farmers apparently never heeded the advice published in midwestern and northern farm journals aimed at "progressive" farmers. Since they envisioned the farmhouse as a base for business operations, these journals specifically advised the wise farmer to locate the farmhouse at the center of the farm to reduce travel to distant parts of the farm. Another concern was that proximity to public roads would foster inevitable social encounters, thus wasting precious time. One writer advised farmers to let "the traveled highway go where it may" and attend "solely to his own domestic affairs."[17] Based upon this philosophy, Ozark farmers, in contrast, seemed to be incorrigibly social creatures, because their dwellings not only faced the road but also were usually located near it, as if it were a lifeline or an umbilical cord to a larger world. Such a social orientation was commonplace in American nineteenth-century vernacular houses, but it contrasted with farmhouses in colder climates, which were likely to be oriented in relation to the prevailing winds.[18]

A vivid example of the tenacity of the desire for one's house to face the road is the Will Ford house of 1905 (figs. 6-7, 6-8). In 1951 when the road in front of their double pen house was rerouted to the rear, the Fords rearranged the house to make what were formerly the two back doors into the front doors. Mrs. Ford said, "Our living room used to be a bedroom; what used to be the living room is now our kitchen."

The Traditional Ozark Landscape

Old photographs provide only partial glimpses of the traditional landscape. They rarely depict the larger view, but instead show families grouped in front of their houses or people engaged in specific activities. One of the few photographs

Fig. 6-5. Unidentified Community in Washington County. Rarely does an old photograph depict a view of the landscape; in this one, a mill, a single-pen log house, two I-houses, various outbuildings, pastures, garden patches, and fences are visible. It is instructive to compare this view with a recent photograph of the Big Spring community in Stone County (fig. 6-6). *Courtesy of the Washington County Historical Society*

Fig. 6-6. Distant View of Big Spring Community, Stone County. This view shows an old mill site (a gristmill long gone) and two large houses that reflect the prosperity of the mill owner's sons. (The house on the far upper left is the Edna and John Avey house, fig. 4-69.) Here, too, the road meanders, the clusters of buildings seem randomly placed, and engulfing everything is the ever-present brush and timber, all typical of the vernacular landscape described by J. B. Jackson. ▶

depicting a rural settlement is of an unknown location in Washington County, probably at the turn of the century (fig. 6-5). The photo shows a building that may be a mill, a single pen log house, two I-houses, various outbuildings, garden patches, pastures, fences, and both brush and woodlands. It is instructive to compare this view with a recent photograph of the Big Spring community in Stone County (fig. 6-6). This scene, too, contains an old mill site (a gristmill long since gone) with two large houses which reflect the prosperity of the mill owner's sons. Here, too, the road meanders, the clusters of buildings seem randomly placed, and ever-present brush and timber seem to engulf everything. Both photographs recall Jackson's description of the vernacular landscape with its "vast amounts of common land—waste, pasturage, forest . . . the roads being little more than paths or lanes . . . the clusters of hamlets in a sea of waste or wilderness . . . leaving no monuments, only abandonment or signs of renewal."[19] In this instance, the concrete-block auto mechanic's garage (the building nearest the foreground in the photograph of Big Spring, fig. 6-6) represents the "sign of renewal," for this enterprise replaces the vanished mill, as it commonly has throughout rural areas, in providing a much-needed service in the community.

What cannot be detected in the photographs, but is obvious to the traveler throughout rural areas, is the isolation of most dwellings and the paucity of signs that mark social affiliations. It is obvious, then and now, that this is no domesticated landscape, but rather one that reflects the "patient, unending

Fig. 6-7. Will Ford House (1905), St. James Vicinity, Stone County. This house demonstrates the Ozark penchant for recycling houses and the tenacity of the desire to have one's house face the road. This frame double pen house with a rear ell, constructed in 1905, became a triple pen house around 1920 when the Ford family tore down an empty one-room house on a nearby farm, marked the lumber, and rebuilt it to adjoin their original double pen house. Then, in 1951, when the road in front of the house was rerouted to the rear, they rearranged the entire house to make the former two back doors (seen here) into front doors. As Mrs. Ford said, "Our living room used to be a bedroom; what used to be the living room is now our kitchen." A full array of outbuildings is still in use on this farm. The wash house is shown in fig. 5-18. Mr. Ford has maintained his great-grandfather's log house, the Zachariah Ford House (fig. 4-31), located nearby, for years.

adjustment to circumstances," to borrow Jackson's words again. To phrase it another way: this is a landscape that reflects an accommodation to circumstances with the least adjustment possible.

An important element in the traditional landscape is visible only in the earlier photograph of the pair just compared. It shows the ubiquitous wooden fences that are recorded in hundreds of old photographs of families posed in front of their houses. In a fascinating variety of post-and-rail, picket, or log "snake" or "worm" styles, these fences enclosed the yards of houses, garden patches, and the small fields and pastures. They were prominent features in the landscape, creating an enlivening patchwork effect on the land by establishing definite boundaries and enclosures.[20] The reason for their existence, and their disappearance, is quite simple: from the time of earliest settlement to the mid-twentieth century, livestock, including both hogs and cattle, were allowed

Fig. 6-8. Front Porch Detail, Will Ford House (1905), St. James Vicinity, Stone County.

to graze at will in woodlands, and the rural folk were obliged to fence themselves in from the animals, rather than the other way around. It is important to note, however, that these little boundaries are the fluid ones typical of the archetypal vernacular landscape. Instead of marking permanent boundary lines, they created temporary enclosures for patches and fields; they were boundary lines that changed shape and function from time to time.[21] These little enclosures left room for the larger acreages of woodland to be used in common. This arrangement, as J. B. Jackson observed, is similar to the medieval agricultural arrangement with its tripartite division of lands in which every farmer had arable land for farming, pasturage for grazing (in the Ozarks this was reserved for milk cows and work animals), and woodlands for both pasturage held in common and for hunting.[22] "Only a Southern farmer can really understand the concept of woodland as grazing land. To this day we can observe in the rural parts of the South cows and hogs and even horses wandering and grazing at will in what used to be called waste: abandoned fields . . . the margins of roads and highways, much as animals did in northern Europe more than a thousand years ago."[23]

When the law prohibiting this open range system finally was enacted in the Ozarks in the 1950s, it not only ended a time-honored agricultural practice (and thus met with opposition from Ozark farmers who blamed it on city folks who were in too big a hurry to slow down) but changed the look of the landscape as well. Since the mid-1950s animals have been enclosed within wire fences that are invisible from a distance. The old wooden log, rail, or picket fences were recycled into other uses or simply allowed to rot away, and now, instead of the patchwork aspect of enclosures, the spaces around the house and farmstead appear more open and undefined than they do in old photographs (figs. 6-9, 6-10). An even more drastic transformation of spatial organization was wrought by mechanized farming. As late as 1929, geographer W. A. Browne noted that Ozark farms (at least those located in mountainous areas) retained the traditional multipurpose use of farmlands in the tripartite division among arable land, pasture, and woodlands discussed earlier: a variety of crops were grown for the family's own use in small patches, but most of the land in wooded ranges was used in common.[24] Since the 1940s, however, most Ozark farms have become specialized, and the visual effect has been further eradication of the old-fashioned patchwork aspect. Instead, around the typical Ozark farms one now sees extensive cleared areas occupied by huge chicken houses or serving as grazing pastures for livestock (fig. 6-10).

Other transformations of the traditional landscape have taken place in this "ceaseless and patient adjustment to circumstances." Several decades ago, a blight eradicated almost all of the old Ozark orchards, which had once brought a modicum of prosperity to some areas. Automobiles and paved roads rendered the little crossroads general stores obsolete, along with the sawmills and gristmills. With school consolidation, many country schoolhouses were abandoned or turned into churches. Even the meandering dirt roads, although still following the paths of least resistance in hilly terrains, are occasionally and mystifyingly rerouted, as anyone following a United States Geological Survey map

Fig. 6-9. Postcard entitled "Arkansaw Homestead," Winslow, Washington County. Again, a small log house is used as a symbol of rusticity. This photograph depicts the ubiquitous wooden fences that created an enlivening patchwork effect on the land. Visible in most old photographs, the fences always surrounded the house and yard because stock roamed on the open range. Today one sees, instead, extensive areas of cleared land occupied by large commercial chicken houses or serving as grazing pasture for livestock as in fig. 6-10. *Courtesy of the University of Arkansas at Little Rock Library, Special Collections*

more than a few years old soon discovers. As discussed earlier, modern agriculture transformed both the types and numbers of outbuildings on farms. Finally, the many abandoned houses bear witness to the steady population decreases that until only recently have characterized most of this region.

Despite these far-reaching changes, however, the traveler on the remote dirt roads in the Ozarks experiences a vivid sense of going backward in time. For now, as in the nineteenth century, settlement is thinly dispersed in the land, and the wilderness is present to a remarkable degree. The back-roads trek from one farmstead to another is often lonely, and the wilderness seems to be waiting to regain the upper hand as thickets of vines and underbrush engulf the abandoned houses, the stone fences, and the old farm implements left standing in the fields. Since the countryside does not usually afford long vistas, often the arrival at a farmstead over the next hill or around the next curve is sudden.

As is typical of the vernacular landscape, most of the man-made features in the Ozarks appear puny and transitory, especially when contrasted with the prosperous midwestern farms just a few hours away to the north. In the liberating and spacious landscape of the Midwest, under a full arch of sky, one can see mile after mile of orderly crops, fields, and fences. The farmlands lie within the straight ribbons of roads that reflect the long-range grid plan west of the Alleghenies dictated by the Land Ordinance of 1785. Farm layouts are punctuated by the vertical accents of windbreaks, silos, two-story farmhouses, and the massive silhouettes of barns. In the kindlier midwestern terrain with its more generous soil, prosperity has kept at bay "the sea of waste and wilderness" that characterizes the Ozarks; in the landscape of the Midwest, everything seems more reassuringly substantial, straight, and true.

In the Ozarks, on the other hand, one still sees the kind of landscape that European visitors to rural America complained about as seeming "vast, wild, empty, formless and unfinished."[25] It is precisely these qualities that recent changes, like the disappearance of patchwork fields and fences, have exacerbated.

It is not just the natural setting—the sense of vegetation being the master—that produces this "formlessness" the Europeans complained of. It is also the way in which the Ozark house adjusts to the natural setting and is in a sense lost within it. The arrival at a farmstead, for instance, brings into view only a low cluster of ramshackle, often unpainted, buildings, with no discernible pat-

Fig 6-10. Area Surrounding Typical Ozark Farmhouse Today. Instead of old patchwork fences, one now sees extensive cleared areas around Ozark farmhouses. Barely visible in the photograph are the large commercial chicken houses located at the rear.

tern in layout whatsoever. Indeed, there is often a temporary and formless quality to these farmsteads themselves. The small wooden houses appear to be flimsy, and, perched on their rock pier foundations, they sit lightly, as Reyner Banham once observed, "barely engaged with the ground and the landscape."[26] The seemingly random placement of outbuildings, the meandering dirt roads, and the ever-encroaching brush and woodlands add to this formless quality. The disappearance of the wooden fences that once created enclosures and the small units of gardens and fields intensifies this impression of diffusiveness, of an extremely vague separation between what is "there" and what is "here," that bothered the European visitors so.[27]

Chapter 7

Construction Methods and Materials

As American material culture has historically been dominated by wood, so the vast majority of houses documented for this study were constructed of wood. Indeed, in Stone County apparently no rural houses other than wooden ones were built during the period the study covers. Although stone was commonly used for chimneys and foundation piers, nineteenth-century stone houses in the rural Ozarks are extremely rare. Because brick was expensive to purchase and labor intensive to make, brick houses are not common; when they do appear, they cluster in more open, prosperous areas. Apparently the cheapness, the availability, and the rapid construction possible with wood offset its lack of durability and insulating qualities.

Wood Construction

Four types of wood construction methods were documented. Listed in the order of frequency from the most common to the least common, they are as follows:

(1) balloon frame construction, (2) log construction, (3) box construction, and (4) braced frame construction.

Balloon Frame Construction

Balloon frame construction, or conventional stud wall construction (fig. 7-1), awaited two technological developments: cheap, mass-produced nails and light lumber sawed into standardized sizes. Balloon framed construction was so named because it "went up with the speed of balloons," and it replaced earlier, more laborious methods of log construction or braced frame building using heavy framing members that had to be mortised and pegged together. The balloon frame brought about a whole new order of speed and economy; even relatively unskilled workmen could construct these buildings soundly and quickly.

Its inventor was George Washington Snow, a carpenter who first used it in the erection of a warehouse in Chicago in 1832.[1] Fully exploited in Chicago's phenomenal growth in the 1830s, the technique was transported to San Francisco during the California Gold Rush of 1849.[2] The method was first publicized in Gervase Wheeler's *Homes for the People in Suburb and Country,* published in 1855. In 1858, William E. Bell provided clear construction diagrams for the balloon frame in his book called *Carpentry Made Easy.*[3]

By the 1870s, balloon frame construction seems to have been the predominant mode of construction in vernacular architecture in the United States and in the Ozarks as well.[4] Gristmills began appearing in the 1830s, and by the 1870s their machinery seems to have been readily adapted for sawmills too. Additionally, new mills were constructed solely as sawmills, and portable sawmills could be brought to building sites. In keeping with their tradition of self-sufficiency, however, most Ozark people would furnish the logs from timber off their own land whether they were using the local sawmill or a portable mill, just as they would bring their own corn and wheat to be ground at a gristmill.

The balloon frame did not suddenly make log construction obsolete in the Ozarks, however; it represented a gradual replacement as shall be seen.

Log Construction

Images and lore of the pioneer log cabin abound in the American imagination, and much of it is mistaken. Scholarly consensus brings to light four aspects of log construction that debunk the log cabin myth.[5] (1) A "cabin" is technically a single pen dwelling; hence, by no means is every log house a cabin. (2) The log construction envisioned in the popular imagination is the type seen in toy Lincoln Logs; this is not the technique carried westward by American pioneers. (3) Early English settlers had no knowledge of log construction, despite the popular association of log cabins with English settlers. (4) While a log house can be a crude dwelling constructed rapidly and with only a few tools, it can also be sophisticated and well crafted, requiring as many as seventy-six tools to construct.[6] Briefly summarized, the voluminous scholarly literature on the history and techniques of American horizontal log construction is as follows.

Although as ancient as the Mesolithic era, by the time of New World settlement log construction had receded to a few still heavily forested areas in northern and central Europe.[7] Thus, log construction was unknown to English, Dutch, and French emigrants. Two possible source areas for American log construction have been identified: New Sweden on the Delaware, where Swedes first built horizontal log houses in 1638, and southeastern Pennsylvania, where log construction originated with German emigrants in the eighteenth century. While the Swedish log work seems not to have spread beyond New Sweden, the Germans' log technology, on the other hand, was quickly adopted by the Scotch-Irish who began arriving in that area in the late seventeenth century.[8] German techniques were then carried from the southeastern Pennsylvania source area in all directions by both the Germans and the Scotch-Irish in the period from 1730 to 1750.[9] Because this technology was so wonderfully suited to a forest-rich environment, various British groups, including the Scotch-Irish, adopted it in the "melting pot" of the Middle Atlantic colonies, taking it westward as part of their "cultural baggage." But its use remained confined largely to the peoples of these Middle Atlantic colonies and their descendants. The English in New England and the Tidewater South, for example, never adopted it.[10]

American log work obviously resembles German, not Swedish, techniques. These techniques differed considerably both in log preparation and in methods of corner notching, which is all-important, for the rigidity and solidity of a log wall depends upon the joints at the corners, and it is in the corners where rain can collect to cause rot. The Germans used hewn logs, while the Swedes left them round (fig. 7-2). Other attractive features of German work that the Scotch-

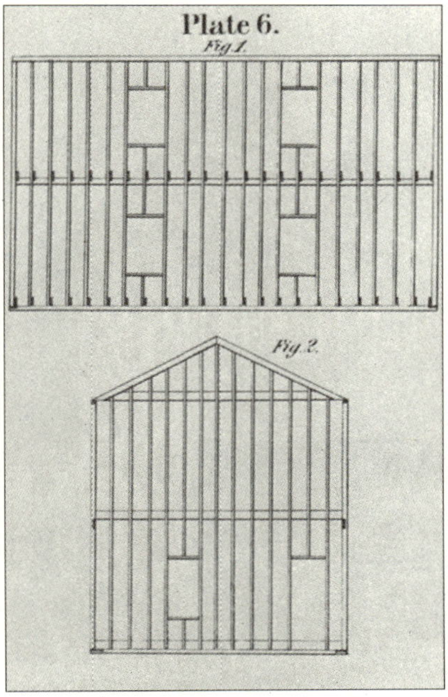

Fig. 7-1. Diagram of Balloon Frame Construction. *From William E. Bell,* Carpentry Made Easy, *1858.*

Irish and English groups found superior for New World conditions have been summarized by Richard Pillsbury and Andrew Kardos:

> The traditional German methods of corner timbering relied on several types of notches which were cut so that any moisture that collected in the corner splice would automatically drain away from the house, preventing rot. These notches were also cut so that the logs' ends were flush with the sides of the building. In contrast, the Swedes used less sophisticated corner notchings which relied on an intentional overhang of the logs at the corners, much like children's toy Lincoln logs. In these corner splices, the protruding log ends protected the corners, rather than the notching, from the weather.[11]

In the Pennsylvania source area, three "parent types" of corner notching have been identified: V-notching, full-dovetailing, and saddle notching (fig. 7-5). Saddle notching was generally used only for outbuildings, because the logs were left round (fig. 7-3). The notch was on the bottom of the log only and as close to the end as possible, unlike the Swedish type of saddle notch, which left overhanging log ends.[12] This construction method characterizes log outbuilding construction all over the Ozarks, indeed all over Arkansas. In the course of diffusion from the source area, other notching types were developed: the diamond notch, the square notch, and the half-dovetail notch, the latter two being the predominant types used in the Ozarks (figs. 7-4, 7-5, 7-6).

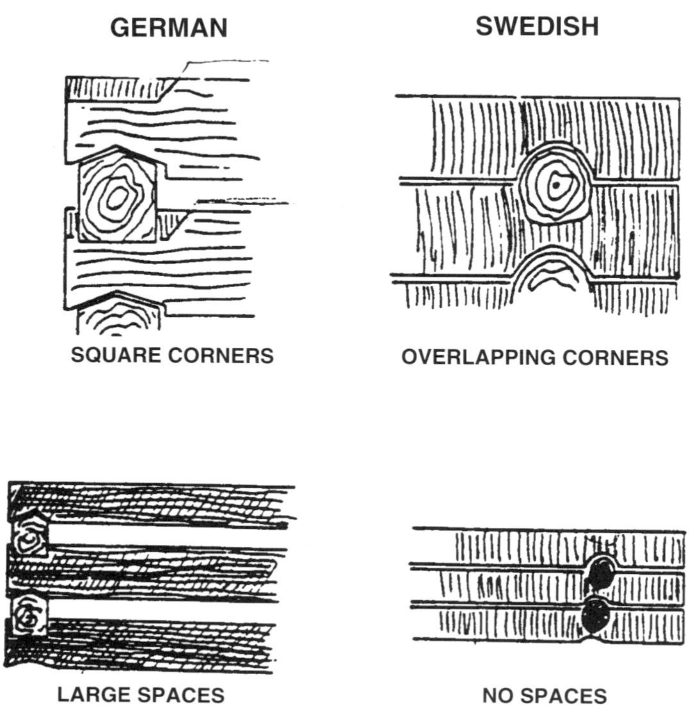

Fig. 7-2. Comparison of German and Swedish Log Construction. *Drawn by Vicki Francoeur, adapted from Richard Pillsbury and Andrew Kardos, "A Field Guide to the Folk Architecture of the Northeastern United States."*

◀ Fig. 7-3. Saddle V-Notch with Logs Left Round, Fred Lancaster Log Barn, Round Bottom, Stone County.

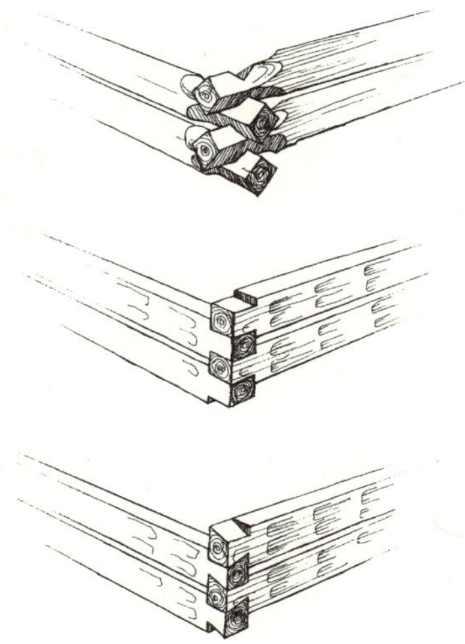

▲ Fig. 7-4. Log Notching Types Developed in the Diffusion Westward: Diamond Notch, Square Notch, and Half-Dovetail Notch. *Drawing by Vicki Francoeur*

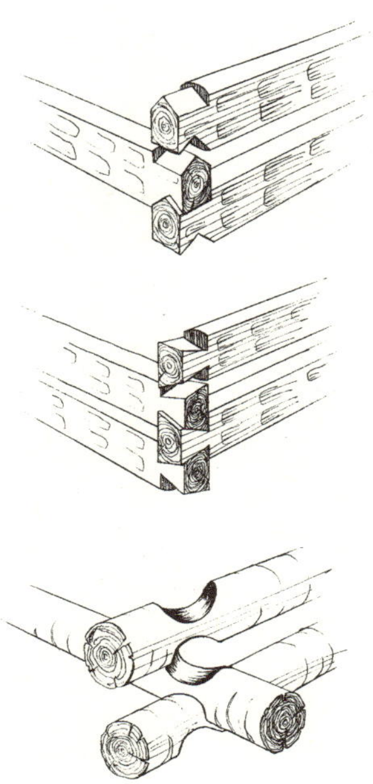

◀ Fig. 7-5. Three Parent Types of Log Notching in the Pennsylvania Source Area: V-Notch, Full Dovetail Notch, and Saddle Notch. *Drawing by Vicki Francoeur*

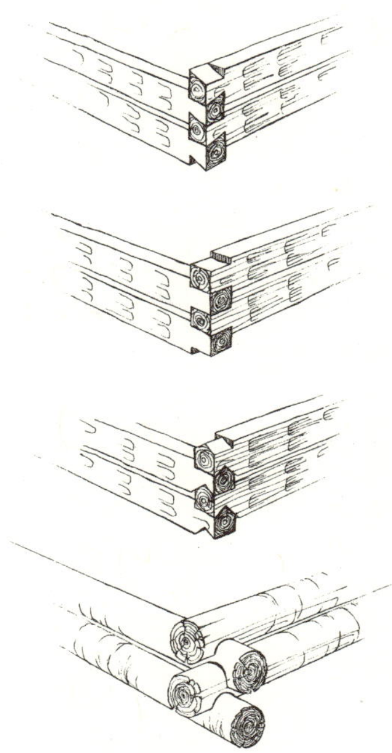

▶ Fig. 7-6. Common Log Notching Types in the Arkansas Ozarks: Half-Dovetail Notch, Square Notch, V-Notch, Saddle Notch. *Drawing by Vicki Francoeur*

Log Houses in the Ozarks

General Observations

Definitive answers concerning log construction in the Arkansas Ozarks await more fieldwork and analysis. Nevertheless, some generalizations can be made based upon the fieldwork for this study and upon analysis of architectural surveys of the Arkansas State Historic Preservation Program.

First, in the Arkansas Ozarks a fairly high degree of log craftsmanship was evident, based upon overall sturdiness of the houses, the prevalence of a superior type of corner notching (half dovetail), and careful log preparation. Log technology here did not undergo as rapid a deterioration as it moved away from the source area as, for instance, log construction in Texas did. In his comprehensive book on Texas log buildings, Terry Jordan, a leading scholar of log construction, stated unequivocally that all the well-built log houses in Texas "were constructed by professional or semi-professional carpenters working for hire."[13] Jordan based his judgment of inferior quality partially on the prevalence of the "degenerate" square notch and of round logs, the simplest log preparation method. If further fieldwork confirms a positive assessment of Ozark log construction, it will verify preeminent folklorists Fred Kniffen and Henry Glassie's observation that, "Although log work of the mountainous areas of Arkansas and Missouri is comparable in quality with that of the Tennessee Valley, in the Deep South the quality declined with distance."[14] Secondly, as the foregoing remark indicates, Ozark log techniques in log preparation and corner timbering are typical of those of the Upland South.

Ozark Log Construction Techniques

With few exceptions, the Ozark log house builder chose oak logs for his house because of their durability and accessibility. In a manner deemed typical of the Upland South, he usually chose a method of log preparation called planking that involved hewing the log on two sides only, creating a flat surface for the inner and outer walls but leaving the bark on the top and bottom of the log.[15] This method may have been desirable simply as a labor-saving device or because the chinking was believed to adhere more firmly to a bark surface than a smooth one (fig. 7-7).

Much less often, he would hew the log on all four sides, forming a rectangular or square-hewn timber. He would then choose one of four types of corner notches: half dovetail (the most widespread in the study area), square notching (fairly commonly seen), V-notching (infrequently seen), or saddle notching, which is primarily used for outbuildings (fig. 7-6).[16]

The predominance of half-dovetail corner notches verifies scholars' observation that this is the predominant type of the upper South.[17] Having evolved from the "parent" full-dovetail notch, the half dovetail is easier to make, yet provides a good slope for water runoff. Its tight interlock provides structural stability as

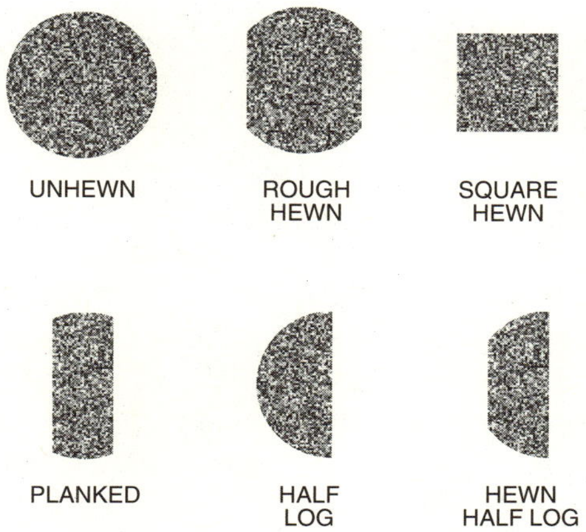

Fig. 7-7. Common Types of American Log Preparation. *Reprinted from* Texas Log Buildings: A Folk Architecture *by Terry Jordan, copyright © 1978. By permission of the author and the University of Texas Press. Adapted by Vicki Francoeur*

well. Its presence signals a high degree of log-working craftsmanship (figs. 7-8, 7-9, 7-10).

The square notch, although fairly common, was less often employed. Thought to be a degenerate type, it is simple to make, but much less desirable because it provides no slant for water runoff and no structural stability unless pegs are inserted through the corners (fig. 7-11).

Infrequently seen in the area, the V-notch forms a solid, locked drain out of the joints. It can be traced directly back to the Pennsylvania source area. Not widely used in the South, it is popular in the Blue Ridge Mountains and in states north of Arkansas, including Missouri, Ohio, Kentucky, Indiana, and Illinois.[18]

After the log walls were completed, the Ozark builder filled the interstices between the logs using one of two methods. The simpler, but less often used method was simply to plaster over the cracks, inside and out, with mud or clay or a mortar of lime mixed with mud, clay, or sand (fig. 7-8). The more common method was to apply one of these mortar mixtures in combination with riven wood shingles that were wedged diagonally in the cracks (fig. 7-11). In a few instances, the interior was sheathed with wood and no chinking appears at all (fig. 7-10).

The original roofs were of split wood shingles, although few of these remain. The rear ell or shed additions commonly found on log houses were constructed of sawn lumber, which is understandable given the difficulty of joining two log walls. These additions were often made sometime after the completion of the log house when sawn lumber was readily available. Many log houses were later covered with horizontal weatherboards. These were nailed to vertical wooden strips that were fastened with nails to the logs.

It should be mentioned that stone was an essential building material in constructing Ozark log houses, for the gable-end chimney was almost always of stone and the log house invariably rested upon stone piers.

▶ Fig. 7-8. Half-Dovetail Log Notch with Hewn Logs and Mud Mortar, Isaac Preston Looney House (1850), Timbo, Stone County.

▼ Fig. 7-10. Half-Dovetail Log Notch with Rough Hewn Logs and Interior Sheathing Instead of Chinking, Zachariah Ford House, 1885 Pen, St. James Vicinity, Stone County. (See figs. 7-11, 4-31.)

◀ Fig. 7-9. Half-Dovetail Log Notch with Planked Logs, Plat House, Sunny Land Community, Stone County.

▼ Fig. 7-11. Square Log Notch with Rough Hewn Logs and Wood Shingle Chinking and Mud Mortar, Zachariah Ford House, 1856 Pen, St. James Vicinity, Stone County. The two log pens on this house provide an intriguing comparison, since the earlier 1856 pen is inferior in craftsmanship to the later 1885 pen (fig. 7-10). Presumably, the Fords were fairly isolated in 1856, but by 1885 when the second pen of their dogtrot house was constructed, there were more expert log-working craftsmen in the community to assist in the traditional communal effort.

While there are no house types uniquely associated with log construction, all the traditional house types were documented in log, although, predictably, the single pen house was the type most frequently found in log, and the I-house least frequently found.

Identity of Ozark Log House Builders

Were Ozark log houses constructed by their owner or by for-hire professionals, as Terry Jordan argued was the custom in Texas? Again, definitive answers await further documentation in the field. It should be noted that recent scholarship tends to refute the log cabin mythology of the broad-shouldered pioneer carving his log house out of the wilderness single-handedly with a few simple tools. Instead, scholars stress the complexity of log structures of even the simplest type and the high degree of technical skill such construction requires. For example, Warren Roberts found that no fewer than seventy-six tools were needed to construct the finely crafted hewn log houses in southern Indiana.[19]

On the other hand, Ozark oral history seems to stress the communal aspects of log construction. Many older Ozarkers can either recall having taken part in communal log house raisings when they were young, or they enjoy passing along a family story about such events.

One of the most credible and detailed accounts of log house construction in the Arkansas Ozarks, especially in its communal aspects, is that provided in Paul Faris's book *Ozark Log Cabin Folks*. In 1950 Faris interviewed Parson Wilson, who recounted in full detail how he constructed his own log house in Newton County in 1893. It was built in the customary manner in which the owner prepared and brought the logs to the site. After felling the logs and hewing them entirely square, the parson hauled them to the house site with the help of two mules. After laying the sills and the floor joists for his sixteen-by-sixteen-foot cabin,

> The Parson was able to build the cabin walls several logs high by himself. When they were as high as the Parson could make them, he sent out the word and six men of the neighborhood came for a day's working. . . . The men leaned poles up against the walls to form skids. Then part of the men climbed upon the walls with chopping axes. Up the skids the men pushed and pulled the square logs as they needed them to build the walls higher. . . . The men notched the ends with their axes to a dovetail fashion that interlocked them and brought them together. To do the job right took a great deal of aptitude; good notchers were always in demand when a cabin was going up. . . . The half-dovetail notch used on the Parson's cabin was a favorite in the Arkansas hills.[20]

The men went home at the end of the day and the parson finished the house himself. The new log house, it should be noted, was sturdy enough to serve as a home for the parson, his wife, and their eight children over the next sixty years.[21]

It seems reasonable to assume that early settlers in the Ozarks came equipped with fairly well-developed wood-working skills, for, as Wilbur Zelinsky observed,

> The log house was only a single element in the log culture complex . . . that characterized the Southern frontier; it may be safely stated that almost the whole of the gross material culture of the pioneer was based on the log. The farmer lived in a log house, built log cribs in which to store his crops and pen his livestock (if they were penned), split logs to arrange in fences, worshipped in log churches, sent his children to log schools and when he paid his taxes, did so in a log courthouse.[22]

From the available evidence it would seem that log-working skills were survival skills, and that most nineteenth-century Ozark settlers possessed at least the fundamental knowledge of how to construct a log building, but Ozark log house building seems to have been a communal effort, like threshing or quilting a bedcover, so that the good craftsmanship evident in the Ozarks depended not so much on the owner's skill, but on a pool of log-working skill available in the community as a whole. As Faris remarked, there were good notchers in every community, and they were in demand.

The Zachariah Ford log house (figs. 4-31, 7-10, 7-11) and its varying log techniques provide an interesting example of the communal nature of log construction. The two pens of this log dogtrot house were built several decades apart, in 1856 and in 1885. The earlier 1856 pen has the "degenerate" square notch, while the later 1885 pen has the superior half-dovetail notch. Perhaps the community was so sparsely settled at the time of the earlier pen's construction that there was not a sufficient pool of talent from which to draw to construct the house using a superior notching technique. Later, however, there evidently was. Echoing a similar remark by Faris, Jimmy Ford, in speaking of this house built by his great-grandfather said, "I can remember when lots of men around here could make a good pigeon-wing [half-dovetail notch]."[23]

A Time Frame for Ozark Log House Construction

Owing to the lack of county-by-county documentation, presenting specific dates to apply to the entire region is impossible. But the generalization can be made that log construction dominated from the earliest settlement period up to the Civil War, remained popular in the 1870s and 1880s, and, except in the most remote areas, decreased in popularity after the 1880s. In Stone County, for example, the last significant log house was dated 1890.[24]

Log houses are good economic indicators in that they signify a persistence of subsistence farming and making a living in which little cash is available. For it was not merely the proximity of a sawmill, but the possession of sufficient cash by a majority of folk to purchase sawn lumber (or pay to have one's own logs sawn) that determined the dates when log construction became obsolete in any given area. Therefore, we would expect log building to remain common for a longer period in the less prosperous areas, like Stone County.

Paul Faris, in his book *Ozark Log Cabin Folks,* supported this assumption. In Newton County, one of the poorest, most rugged, and most highly elevated mountain counties in the entire Ozarks, Faris found that log houses were still commonly constructed in the 1890s.[25] In addition to his interview with Parson Wilson, Faris interviewed two other men who told of regularly supplementing their farm incomes by constructing log cabins for newcomers to Newton County from 1900 to 1912. Faris also described Milas Wishon's log building employment in Newton County:

> Another source of cash was a large flow of homesteaders into the area during 1900–1912. Some were city folks that had never seen a wilderness. The land office in Harrison recommended Milas to show available land to homesteaders. Some of the folks would select 160 acres to homestead, others would return to their homes disgusted, cussing the people and the country. Some of the folks who stayed had no idea how to build a cabin and would hire Milas. His standard price for a one-room house was $50.00. Using only an axe, saw, hammer and froe, he'd have the place ready to move into in a week, he said.[26]

Although falling largely outside the cutoff date for this study, 1930, a second wave of log construction in the 1920s and 1930s should be mentioned. This had two manifestations. First, it is well known that many Ozarkers found it necessary to again build log houses during the Depression (that none of these was documented intact in the fieldwork indicates they were undoubtedly of inferior craftsmanship).[27] A second type of log construction reflected nationwide popular taste. This was the "rustic" or "Adirondack" style, in which the logs were usually stripped of bark, left round, saddle notched, and left with protruding log ends at the corners, similar to children's Lincoln Logs and to Swedish log work. The National Park Service helped to popularize this style with the recreational cabins and lodges they constructed in both state and national parks, often employing Civilian Conservation Corps labor. Many of these picturesque structures, including WPA canning kitchens, American Legion halls, small vacation cabins, and large private homes, are still seen throughout the Ozarks (fig. 7-12).

Box Construction

As vernacular architecture studies increasingly indicate, box construction was very popular as an alternative to balloon framing in many parts of the country. Curiously, however, little has been published on the subject. One of the clearest explanations of box construction is provided by folklorist Diane Tebbetts in her study of traditional houses in Independence County Arkansas.

> In box construction, sills are placed on a foundation, wide boards are nailed on vertically at each corner, and a two-by-four is nailed on horizontally along the tops of these vertical boards. Additional vertical boards are attached to form a single-thickness wall with no framing at all. Ceiling joists

Fig. 7-12. Example of 1930s Log Construction: West Richwoods Canning Kitchen Constructed by Works Progress Administration, Stone County. The "Lincoln Log" look marks this as 1930s log work. In Arkansas state parks, many handsome, durable cabins and recreational buildings, also constructed by the WPA or the Civilian Conservation Corps, were of this type. *Courtesy of the Arkansas Historic Preservation Program*

> tie it together, and doors and windows sit in holes cut in the walls for them, their casings usually projecting into the rooms. In the poorer houses, roll siding is applied on narrow strips of wood which are nailed on outside over the cracks to produce board-and-batten siding. Better versions are covered with horizontal clapboards and are thus indistinguishable from frame on the outside. Inside the walls are usually heavily papered to keep out winter winds. What this manner of construction lacks in durability, it makes up in economy, for it is the least expensive way to enclose a given volume.[28]

The absence of a frame allows the box house to sag, reducing its overall strength; thus, box houses are likely to be small and rarely over one story high (fig. 7-13).[29] In the less prosperous areas of the Ozark countryside, a small one-room house with a board-and-batten exterior, will, upon close inspection, almost surely prove to be a box house. The one-room variety seems to be an early twentieth-century economic equivalent of the single pen log cabin. The Austin Crymes house (1920) (fig. 4-20) and the C. F. Williams house (1910) (fig. 7-14) are prime examples.

Because box construction is most economical when constructed of mass-produced lumber, the box houses recorded in the fieldwork dated from around

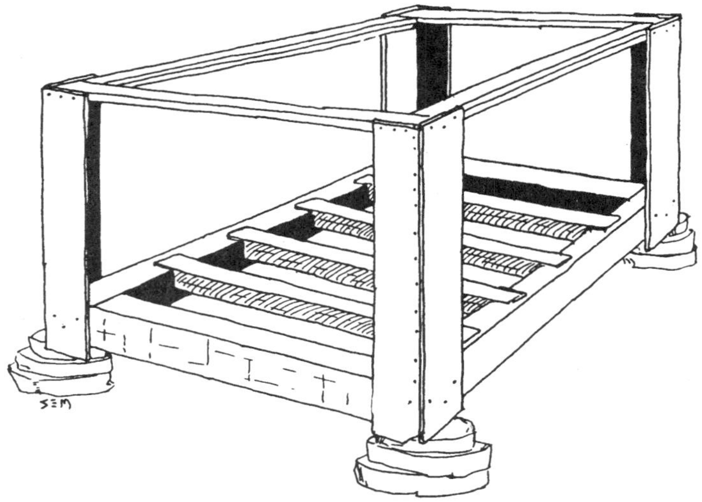

Fig. 7-13. Diagram of Frame for Box Construction onto Which Vertical Boards Could Be Nailed. Box construction depended upon readily available cut lumber and superseded log construction as the cheapest type of construction. Unlike log houses, however, box construction houses, with their single board walls, are extremely flimsy and cold in the winter. *Arkansas Historic Preservation Program*

Fig. 7-14. C. F. Williams House (1910), Herpel, Stone County. Although some box-constructed houses are fairly large, most are the typical single pen houses such as this one.

1880 to 1920. Few box houses were recorded in Washington County. Perhaps in this more prosperous area, box houses were more likely to have been covered with weatherboard, and thus remain undetected, or perhaps very few were built. Architectural surveys conducted by the Arkansas Historic Preservation Program found that in the Stone County survey about 20 percent of the houses were box houses, while studies of both White and Independence counties estimate that box houses make up about 50 percent of the total number.

Box construction throughout the Ozarks is most apparent in the rear shed and rear ell additions to houses, especially log houses, and in chicken houses, garages, and sheds around the farmstead.

In an interesting essay called "The Movable Dwelling," J. B. Jackson conjectured that "there was a time when the box house was one of the commonest types in the United States."[30] According to him, they represent a simpler, cheaper, more rapidly constructed, and more easily moved house than the balloon frame type. As early as 1855, according to Jackson, a book about low-cost American housing noted that workers on railroads and canals lived in settlements of box houses.[31] Throughout the late nineteenth and early twentieth centuries, box houses proliferated in mining communities, lumber company towns, and railroad workers' settlements. Lumber companies, especially, produced box houses in great numbers "for the towns moved from place to place wherever the forest was exhausted, and they needed a mobile dwelling type."[32] Since lumber companies were extremely active in the Ozarks, perhaps box construction was popularized by this means.

Braced Frame Construction

Braced frame construction, which was found among the first group of permanent dwellings at Salem, Massachusetts, around 1630, is a medieval English building method in which heavy, usually hand-hewn timbers form the structural frame (fig. 7-15). The open spaces were filled with clay or mud reinforced with straw, or they were filled with brick. The frame was then covered by weatherboard siding. By the eighteenth century, the brick nogging was abandoned and wood sheathing was used as the nailing base for the exterior clapboards. The timbers were joined by a variety of devices: by simple notches, by dovetailed joints, or by mortise-and-tenon joints. Early in the seventeenth century, handwrought nails were used, and from 1790 to 1830 the hand-wrought nail was replaced by the machine-cut variety. Although this system was common in New England, where wood construction was most popular, it was widely used in all of the English colonies.[33] It was superseded by the balloon frame.

Without close inspection of a house, it is impossible to discern if it is braced frame; hence, possibly the small number of them recorded in the fieldwork for this study will later prove to be erroneous. As it stands, only two examples of braced frame houses were recorded: the William Wilson house of 1857 in

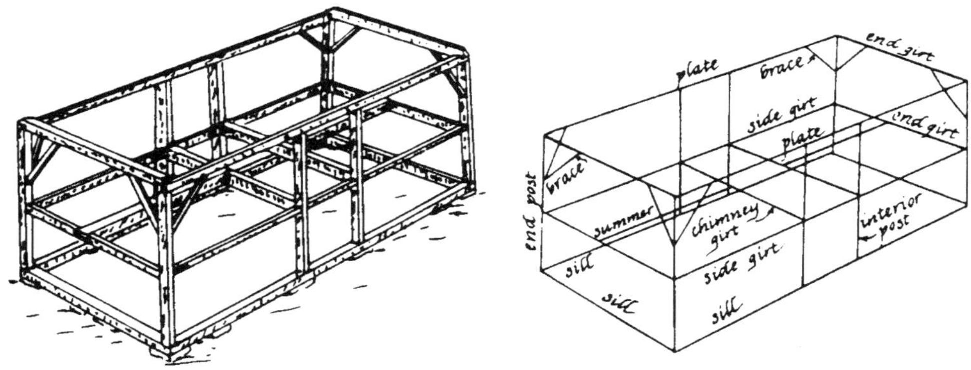

Fig. 7-15. Diagram of Braced Frame Construction. Braced frame construction is a medieval English building method in which heavy, usually hand-hewn timbers form the structural frame. Few houses in the Arkansas Ozarks were of braced frame since log construction was a simpler alternative. One exception is the Thomas M. Hess central hall type house (1868) in Stone County, shown in Fig. 4-59. *Reprinted from* Wood, Brick & Stone: The North American Settlement Landscape, *volume 1, Houses, by Allen G. Noble. Drawings by M. Margaret Geib (Amherst: University of Massachusetts Press, 1984, copyright © 1984 by The University of Massachusetts Press.*

Washington County (figs. 4-44 and 4-51) and the Thomas M. Hess house of 1868 in Stone County (figs. 4-59 and 4-60). Since balloon frame instructions had been published by 1855, the 1868 date of the Hess house makes its construction an anachronism, especially since it is a fashionable central hall type and once had up-to-date furnishings imported from New Orleans. Once again, this house reinforces the notion of the Ozarks as a place of lingering traditions and retarded technology. The apparently small number of houses in braced frame suggests that in the Ozarks the transition was from log construction directly to balloon frame construction in most instances.

Brick Construction

Brick houses are an unusual sight in the Ozark countryside. Stone County has no brick rural dwellings dating from the study period. Unsurprisingly, the brick houses documented were located in good farming areas of Washington County; most were I-houses built by successful farmers with large land holdings. The two houses documented in the field that display the most sophisticated period details are brick houses: the 1845 Homsley-Shofner house (fig. 4-50) and the Benjamin F. Johnson house of 1878 (fig. 4-54), reflecting the Greek Revival and the Italianate styles, respectively. According to a study of brick buildings in Washington County by historian Robert Besom, the bricks for all of these houses, even those of the 1870s, were made in the traditional manner in which bricks were molded by hand and fired at the building site.[34] Two outstanding

1870s brick houses documented in the study area, the Benjamin F. Johnson house (fig. 4-54) and the Herman Stokenbury house (fig. 4-67), are thus anachronisms in this respect, since mass-produced bricks were available in Fayetteville beginning in 1870.[35] These houses were part of the brick-building boom that occurred in Fayetteville and the surrounding countryside during the 1870s in both houses and commercial and public buildings. Several factors stimulated this boom: the availability of mass-produced bricks, the necessity for rebuilding after the Civil War, and people's haunting memories of burning wooden buildings during the Civil War.

Besom found that as late as the turn of the century, some rural houses were still being constructed of hand-molded rather than mass-produced bricks. Victorian taste preferred the more precise, regular lines that machine-made bricks provided, however, so it was not uncommon for the owners to paint precisely ruled white mortar lines on top of the original uneven mortar lines, sometimes even deviating from the original ones.[36] Several of the documented houses reflected this practice.

Since stone was so readily available, it is not surprising that the owners of frame houses rarely constructed brick chimneys. Exceptions are the frame P. J. Lea house (fig. 4-64) and several frame houses in Cane Hill. Two antebellum log houses were recorded with brick chimneys, the John P. A. Parks house, "Parks Station" (fig. 4-40), and the Pleasant and James M. Johnson house in Madison County (not illustrated). In sum, brick chimneys were unusual and were undoubtedly a mark of affluence.

Stone Construction

Since the Ozarks abound in stone it seems somewhat puzzling that it was so rarely used in constructing houses. The time-consuming and labor-intensive nature of masonry construction, especially when compared to the rapid construction possible with log and frame houses, must have been an overriding factor. Moreover, stone houses connote solidity and permanence; they are houses built for generations. Thus, perhaps they were inappropriate in the somewhat transient society of the nineteenth-century Ozarks, where even the oldest families were relative newcomers. If the crops failed, or drought came, or the community became crowded, it was best to have freedom to move on.

The only stone house documented was the Peter Smyth house (fig. 4-65) near Fayetteville, constructed around 1886 of unhewn and roughly coursed sandstone. Significantly, Smyth was a native-born Irishman who had immigrated to Washington County as a child in 1840. Perhaps Old World associations explain his unusual penchant for a stone dwelling. (The house is the central hall type, associated with the upper end of the economic spectrum.)

Although almost never used for entire houses or barns, stone was nevertheless an essential building component for both house and farmstead. While limestone is plentiful, it is not so easily worked as sandstone, which is the usual choice for stone buildings. (Sandstone is often conveniently found in stratas above ground.) The typical Ozark frame house, for example, invariably was set on a stone foundation (usually stone piers, sometimes a continuous foundation in more solidly constructed houses) and had stone exterior chimneys with a stone firebox and hearth and stone doorsteps (fig. 7-19). Both the well and well cover were stone. In the late nineteenth and early twentieth centuries, stone fruit cellars began to appear. In some prosperous orchard areas, substantial barns with stone lower stories were constructed about this time as well.

Among the most picturesque and nostalgic sights in the Ozarks today are the old fieldstone fences or walls that border fields in the countryside, often the sole reminders of vanished farmsteads (figs. 7-16, 7-17). They bordered certain pastures or fields within a farmstead; however, they were seldom extensive enough to enclose an entire farm. Some are more like boundaries than walls, composed of small stones that were probably simply heaped up as farmers cleared the fields. Others are higher, composed of larger stones, and more evenly coursed. None of them contain mortar. Occasionally, as along Knight's Cove Creek in Stone County, one sees a tall, especially imposing wall capped with upright diagonal capping stones (fig. 7-17). Glassie termed limestone walls such as these "bluegrass walls," maintaining they are of English origin; he cited examples in Kentucky, Southern Indiana, upstate New York, and the northeast neck of West Virginia.[37]

Fig. 7-16. Stone Fence at Allie and Neal Morris Farm, South Richwoods, Stone County.

Fig. 7-17. Bluegrass Stone Fence along Knight's Cove Creek, Stone County.

Stone chimneys in the Ozarks generally display a remarkable degree of good craftsmanship, even in remote areas (figs. 7-18, 7-19). They were generally constructed of "dressed" or "hewn" sandstone (not simply stacked, flat stones that are common in the Appalachians); they were laid in courses, sometimes dry, sometimes with mortar. Such stonework was apparently admired because older people can often remember the names of men who built chimneys in their communities. Older chimneys differed from new ones in predictable ways: older chimneys were often larger overall with consistently larger shafts and fireboxes (fig. 7-18). Newer chimneys were often constructed of large, thin stones that were set on end, requiring a substantial amount of mortar to secure the stones, but covering the largest possible area with the least amount of stone (fig. 7-20). This type resembles the stone veneer houses and commercial and public buildings that became popular in the Ozarks in the 1930s. Many of the public buildings with this stone veneer were built by the Works Progress Administration; indeed, throughout Arkansas stone is a hallmark of WPA construction. In Stone County, the old public school complex in Mountain View and many buildings around the courthouse square are of this stone veneer type.

Stone was often used for doorsteps, as the William Lancaster house in Stone County reveals (fig. 7-21). Extensive use of extraordinarily fine stone craftsmanship appears in the 1878 brick Benjamin Franklin Johnson house (fig. 4-54) in Washington County. It boasts five-inch-thick sandstone window sills, a front

Fig. 7-18. Owen Maguire House Stone Chimney (c. 1840), Strain Vicinity, Washington County.

Fig. 7-19. William Acree House Stone Chimney, Inscribed 1874, Marcella, Stone County.

Fig. 7-20. Detail of Wesley Copeland House Stone Chimney (1890), Timbo, Stone County. *Courtesy of the Arkansas Historic Preservation Program.* In the Arkansas Ozarks stone construction (seen primarily in chimneys), like log construction, is generally of fairly good quality, as the first two chimneys demonstrate. Later chimneys sometimes used flat stone slabs set on end, as in the Wesley Copeland house above, requiring much mortar but not as many stones. While the stone craftsmanship seen on the Copeland Chimney is fairly common in later houses, the diamond scoring pattern is unique.

porch floor composed of huge eight-inch-thick stone slabs, stone water table, and front steps framed by two massive, sculpturesque cheek walls (fig. 7-22). Many questions regarding stone construction in the Ozarks await further study. The identity of the fine stonemason responsible for the B. J. Johnson house is unknown, for example, neither do we know whether such craftsmen were itinerant masons or simply farmers in the community with special skills and tools. Interestingly, the Works Progress Administration's *Arkansas: A Guide to the State* cited the abundance of building stone in Stone County: limestone, sandstone, and even marble can be found throughout the state. This source also pointed out that "Little quarrying was done because of lack of transportation."[38]

Fig. 7-21. Stone Foundation Piers, Chamfered Porch Posts, and Stone Porch Steps at William Lancaster House (1895), Round Bottom, Stone County. (See photograph of entire house in Fig. 4-37 and view from porch in Fig. 6-2.) Stone porch steps and stone foundation piers are common; the simple chamfered porch posts are common as well, especially in remote areas like Round Bottom.

Fig. 7-22. Dressed Sandstone Porch Slabs, Steps and Cheek Walls at Benjamin Franklin Johnson House (1878), Middle Fork Valley, Washington County. (See photograph of entire house in Figure 4-54.) This I-house features outstanding stone craftsmanship in keeping with its high style Italianate exterior details.

Exterior Ornamentation

By Victorian standards of taste, even the most richly ornamented houses in the Ozarks are relatively plain. This spareness was due in part to the paucity of cash for luxuries, certainly. But in a deeper sense, display and ostentation went against the psychological grain in these communities where people lived close to the land; where people were physically somewhat isolated from one another, yet dependent upon one another.

The types of houses in the Ozarks that display ornament are predictable. Uncovered log houses, for example, are usually entirely plain. A noteworthy exception is the Wesley Copeland house of Timbo (fig. 7-25), which has a saw-tooth molding outlining the eaves and chamfered porch posts. Most central hall houses and I-houses are, predictably, embellished to some degree (fig. 7-23). Because of the availability of ready-made jigsawn ornament starting in the late nineteenth century, the later nontraditional houses, like the bent and the prow houses, were especially likely to display jigsawn "gingerbread" trim. Of whatever date or type of house, however, ornamentation was concentrated on the front porch and on the gable ends (when they faced the front) and rarely appeared in any other place. Since porches are fragile appendages and were often replaced, much of the original ornamentation has already vanished.

The Greek Revival influence is apparent in some antebellum houses and lingered into the 1870s, well after this style was out of date in eastern urban areas.[39] The Homsley-Shofner house (fig. 4-50), a brick I-house with a two-story portico featuring dentil molding and monumental Tuscan columns, was one of the most outstanding high style houses in the entire Ozarks. Unfortunately, it burned in 1911, but in its day it must have been a uniquely dramatic sight in the countryside.

The Greek Revival influence generally manifested itself in subtler ways, as seen in the pedimented portico, the pedimented gables, and the box columns of the E. W. McClellan house (fig. 4-52), a frame I-house built in 1866. In another section of Washington County, the 1860 H. M. Maguire house (fig. 4-53) features a similar two-story pedimented portico with box columns. Two frame central hall cottages in Cane Hill—the Zeb Edmiston house of 1872 and the William Welch house of 1850—have similar small pedimented porticoes with simple columns capped by a wide board simulating an entablature. The 1851

Fig. 7-23. Upper Porch Sawn Work Balustrade, Benjamin Franklin Johnson House (1878), Middle Fork Valley, Washington County. The handsome balustrade is only part of a decorative ensemble including paired brackets, paneled frieze, and arched windows on this I-house with Italianate style details. (See also fig. 7-22.)

Troy Gordon central hall house (fig. 4-63) has several refinements, including Tuscan columns that support the small portico with a gable return and prominent gable returns at the gable ends of the house and pilaster cornerboards with simple capitals that simulate support of the wide board beneath the cornice, giving the appearance of an entablature. As is visible in an old photograph taken soon after its construction, the 1868 Thomas M. Hess house (fig. 4-59) in Stone County has less finely detailed but still handsome Greek Revival influence apparent in its gracefully proportioned facade featuring a simple portico framed by wide boards and supported by square piers. The portico gable is uniquely decorated with a painting of a garland of leaves and perhaps a cotton plant in the center.

After the Civil War, houses began to display more ornament. The most sophisticated embellishment appears in the previously mentioned 1878 Benjamin Franklin Johnson I-house (fig. 4-54), which has an Italianate flavor. Several details on this house, while commonplace in high style houses in cities and towns, are rarely seen in rural areas; it has round-arched windows, paired brackets on a paneled frieze at the roofline, chamfered columns with capitals and bases along with a charming jigsawn wooden balustrade in a cloverleaf pattern at the second-story portico. These may have been inspired by a Victorian pattern book, such as Marcus Cummings and Charles C. Miller's *Victorian Architectural Details: Two Pattern Books* (1865, 1873).

An old photograph of the Ute Stokenbury house shows ornamentation that may once have commonly appeared on the bent houses of the nineteenth century that turned their backs on the dull, old symmetry of the traditional house types. In a remodeling of this house, all the ornament was removed, but visible in the photograph are lacey bargeboards at the gables, turned spindle railings outlining the porch both above and below (painted in different colors), and a small, stationary diamond-shaped window (fig. 4-67). Old photographs indicate that porches were clearly the focus of decoration. When traveling through the countryside, one sees jigsawn porch ornament infrequently. Often, especially on the traditional houses, turned porch posts, sometimes flanked by spindlework brackets, are the only hint of decoration (fig. 7-24). The folk equivalent of the ready-made turned porch posts is the simple, dignified chamfered post, which often appears on houses in remote areas (figs. 6-2, 7-21). It also seems to appear consistently on log houses covered with weatherboard, and on at least one that was not, the Wesley Copeland house at Timbo (fig. 7-25). These posts often appear to be chamfered by hand.

Prow houses are generally ornamented to some degree, often with variegated shingles in the front gables. Sometimes their porches have turned posts with brackets as seen in the 1895 John P. Stokenbury house (fig. 4-75). The Charlie Williams prow house displays more restrained Tuscan columns (fig. 4-76).

To summarize, with few exceptions Ozark houses were constructed of wood. The chosen methods were the following (from most common to least common): balloon frame, log construction, box construction, and braced frame construction.

Fig. 7-24. Commercially Manufactured Turned Porch Supports and Brackets at Wilson-Collins House (1904), Elkins Vicinity, Washington County. Although readily available from millwork catalogues, Ozarkers used such ornamentation sparingly. These porch supports and brackets form the only exterior decorative elements on this two-story prow house.

Stone houses are extremely rare and the proportionately few brick houses seem to cluster in prosperous, open countryside. Log houses dominated until after the Civil War, after which balloon frame houses became more common; in the mountainous areas, however, log building remained popular at least through the 1890s. Log construction required a generally high degree of craftsmanship. In the area surveyed, half-dovetail notching and planked logs (which are hewn on two sides only) were the favored log-working techniques; scholars have deemed both typical of Upland South log work. Log houses are more common than brick ones. Like the house types, construction materials correlate with geography. Stone County has no traditional brick or stone houses, for example. Brick houses seem, instead, to cluster in prosperous open areas. Similarly, box-constructed houses were more common in Stone County than in Washington County. Everywhere stone was essential in the construction of house foundations, fireplaces, and chimneys. Despite the abundance of limestone, sandstone was almost always chosen.

Fig. 7-25. Hand-Chamfered Porch Posts at the Wesley Copeland Log Dogtrot House (1858), Timbo, Stone County. Simple chamfered porch posts such as these are often the only decorative elements on more modest rural houses, especially log houses. This log house is unusual in that it also has a decorative saw-toothed edging under the eaves. (Note also the diagonally placed wooden shingles with mortar used as infill in the interstices of the front log wall.)

Chapter 8

Living in the Ozark House

Most architectural studies focus on exterior form with its attendant public and concrete aspects. Compared to the exterior, the interior realm is somewhat intimate and ephemeral, subject to frequent rearrangement. It is more likely to be considered the woman's realm, and, as Jean Hess noted, "House interiors are never finished. They are always becoming."[1] Thus, they are rarely examined in detail. Yet, as John B. Jackson noted, the essence of the concept of "dwelling" is the creation of a shelter, a nurturing interior: "The folklore of the house everywhere emphasizes the autonomy and the sanctity, not of the structure itself, but of the inner space. To cross the threshold, to pass through the door of a house . . . is a rite, an initiation into another realm."[2]

This chapter concerns the interiors of Ozark houses—their layout, their appearance, and their relationship to the families', especially the housewives', lifestyle and activities. A tremendous gap exists in the historical record about the arrangements within and the use of interior spaces of vernacular houses. For example, among the several regional photograph collections scrutinized for this study, almost no interiors of vernacular houses were found. An exception is the

Washington County Historical Society's photograph of Mrs. Mary Jane Morton Staples sitting beside her fireplace; its purpose, however, was to portray a well-known elderly woman in the community rather than to document an Ozark interior (fig. 8-1).

The information presented in this chapter was gleaned from observing existing houses and from interviews. Especially important were lengthy interviews with three elderly Ozarkers: Novelle Blair Baumert of Stone County and Rollans and Caswell Wilson of Washington County; furnishings sketches for the two houses in which they grew up were drawn based upon their recollections.[3]

Overall Character of Interiors

In Ozark houses the plain, boxy qualities of the exteriors are echoed throughout the interiors as well. These inner spaces are a series of well-defined square or rectangular rooms punctuated with holes for doors, windows, and fireplaces. Doors are usually aligned so that one walks through the rooms in a straight

Fig. 8-1. Interior Photo of Mrs. Mary Jane Morton Staples' House (c. 1930), Prairie Grove, Washington County. This is one of the rare photographs that document a vernacular interior. Its original purpose was to photograph an important woman in the community. The simple mantelpiece, the hand-woven rag carpet, the rocking chair by the fireplace, and, above all, the two beds in the simple boxy space are all quintessential Ozark vernacular interior features. *Courtesy of the Washington County Historical Society*

line, and doors and windows often open opposite one another for maximum summer ventilation. The simple, straightforward Ozark aesthetic shunned the picturesque irregularities and asymmetries of elevation and floor plan that characterized Victorian high style houses. Thus, the decorative spaces such as bay windows and rooms with chamfered corners, so appealing to Victorian taste, rarely appear in Ozark dwellings.

The strong aesthetic preference for these simple, orderly, and predictable arrangements all seem to go back to the "house in the mind's eye" discussed earlier, in which the overall approach to space involved "additive thinking"—one pen was simply added to another pen in a few basic arrangements. A review of the layouts of traditional house types will underscore and clarify this aesthetic preference for simple, boxy shapes. With the exception of the square single pen house, all have long, rectangular layouts lying parallel to the road because the two principal rooms are invariably arranged side by side. It will be recalled that the entrance may appear between these two rooms (in which case a central hall house or a dogtrot house is formed), or the two pens may each have two front doors (forming a double pen house). The door and window arrangement create a symmetrical or a balanced pattern of openings in the facade. At the rear, one of only two arrangements was chosen: either a shed roof addition (generally about half the width of the front rooms) extended across the back, or the rear was an ell with one or two full-sized rooms (figs. 4-5, 4-6). If the house was enlarged with additional rooms, they were almost invariably added to the rear to avoid disturbing the symmetry of the facade. The two-story I-house did not alter this fundamental layout, but merely stacked the two additional rooms (usually with a hallway in between) on top of the two principal rooms below (fig. 4-41). Two nontraditional houses, the prow house and the bent house, add a third room to the traditional two-rooms-side-by-side configuration, creating interior changes that will be commented upon later.

Windows, Doors, and Moldings

Window size varies with the age of the house; log houses had fewer, smaller windows because of the need to purchase and transport glass from a distance and because structural insecurity could result from too many openings in the walls. Sometimes the small windows in log houses, especially on the gable sides adjacent to the chimneys, are stationary ones. Except for these, all windows were of the ordinary sash variety. Log houses must have been especially dark; Jimmie Ford recalls his grandmother reading the Bible from the light coming through the open door of their log house (fig. 4-31). It is not unusual to see windows in log houses that appear to have been enlarged later. Older houses generally have sashes with more and smaller panes than later houses; for example, large antebellum houses, like the William Wilson house (fig. 4-51) and the Homsley-Shofner house (fig. 4-50) often have rather wide windows with nine-over-six light sash. In reflecting the Victorian high style preference for vertical orientation, however, post–Civil War houses have windows that are longer and narrower than antebellum ones. For example, the Luke Kantz house (fig. 4-56) displays typical long narrow sash of four-over-four lights; two-over-two light sash were also popular, as in the B. F. Johnson house (fig. 4-54). Twentieth-century houses often have plate-glass single panes on top and bottom, as in the Ute Stokenbury house (fig. 4-67). As noted earlier, other than a manifest desire for symmetry or balance, no consistent arrangement of doors and windows on the facade could be determined.

Log house doors are the board-and-batten type with beveled cross bars, as in the I. P. Looney house (fig. 8-2). To counteract the inevitable sagging of such a door are rows of nails, sometimes in decorative arrangements. Some well-made early houses have handcrafted paneled doors, as does the 1838 Col. James M. Johnson house (fig. 8-3). Paneled doors persisted after the Civil War. Some were handcrafted and some were standard millwork doors. In twentieth-century houses, a variety of simple, glazed millwork doors appears.

Except in the unlikely event that they were imported, exterior or interior moldings required specialized skills and tools for manufacture on site; thus, many Ozark houses have no decorative moldings. When they do appear, as on the exterior of the Owen Maguire house and on the P. J. Lea house, they are fairly simple (fig. 8-4, 8-5). An exception is the 1851 Troy Gordon house where elegant molding appears in the mantel and the interior door surrounds (fig. 8-12).

Fig. 8-2. Vertical Board Door with Crossbars at I. P. Looney Single Pen Log House (c. 1850), Timbo, Stone County. Such doors, replete with rows of nails to counteract sagging, are commonly seen on log houses.

Fig. 8-3. Handmade Pegged and Paneled Door at Col. James M. Johnson Log Dogtrot House (1866, now enclosed), Wesley Vicinity, Madison County.

Fig. 8-4. Window Molding and Beaded Board Siding at the Owen Maguire House (c. 1867), Maguiretown, Washington County. The unusual beaded board siding generally indicates an older house. It was used here to cover the logs of a large dogtrot house built by the prominent Maguire family, some of the earliest settlers in this area. When the exterior moldings are used, they are simple, as in this example.

Fig. 8-5. Boxed Cornice and Frieze at the Preston Jarnigan Lea House (1879), Fayetteville Vicinity, Washington County. As in fig. 8-4, simple moldings and box cornices such as these give a Greek Revival flair to this small house, but were not elaborate enough to warrant the use of the many carpenters' manuals that helped spread this style.

Stairways

Space, which was usually scarce in Ozark houses, was begrudgingly allocated to staircases. These are often steep, narrow, tucked out of sight, and predictably located. In log dogtrot houses, stairs generally ascended from the rear of the breezeway, as they do in the John Wesley Copeland house. But a few ascended from the front porch instead, as they do in the antebellum Wesley Copeland house (fig. 4-28). In single pen log houses, interior narrow stairs sometimes led to crudely finished lofts used for storage and sleeping. In smaller one-and-one-half-story or two-story houses, steep boxed-in stairs often rise from an interior wall of a room shut off by a door, as in the 1834 John Latta one-and-one-half-story log house (fig. 8-6). Occasionally, this stair arrangement is found in two-story I-houses as well, such as the McBrien-Bellamy I-house, which is unusual in having no central hall (fig. 4-48). Two large I-houses—the Lawson Johnson house (figs. 4-45, 4-55) and the William Wilson house (figs. 4-44, 4-51)—have unusual arrangements in which simple stairways rise from the rear of the hall, rather than from the front, where a visitor might be immediately impressed. Even stairways ascending in the traditional place near the front door in the central hall are often quite plain, as seen in the photograph of the staircase with its hand-carved newel post of the 1855 Tilley-Buchanan house (fig. 8-7). Houses built in the late nineteenth or early twentieth century, when balustrades, newel posts, and stairs could be purchased from millwork catalogs, were more likely to have decorative stairways.

Fig. 8-6. Interior, John Latta Log House (1834), Prairie Grove Battlefield State Park (relocated from Old Vineyard area), Washington County. The small narrow stairway, with vertical board door and closet tucked beneath, is typical of log houses. *Courtesy of the Arkansas Historic Preservation Program*

Fig. 8-7. Staircase in Central Hall at Tilley-Buchanan House (1855), Rhea's Mill, Washington County. The unusual handmade newel post in this brick antebellum I-house indicates these staircase elements were constructed before the ready availability of mass-produced millwork. *Courtesy of the Arkansas Historic Preservation Program*

Walls, Ceilings, and Floors

Only brick houses have plaster walls and ceilings. Houses constructed of wood, whether large or small, log or balloon frame, were generally sheathed with wood on the interior as well. As the stairways of the Luke Kantz house and the Lawson Johnson house (figs. 8-8, 8-9) show, walls with boards laid horizontally form the typically pleasant, but somewhat austere wall surfaces. Prosperous families might tack patterned wallpaper backed with cheesecloth on the boards, but in most houses, the boards were simply painted and left alone. In log houses the interior walls were finished in one of two ways: either sealing boards were placed over the interstices between the logs, or boarded walls, like the ones just described, were erected to cover the logs. Since the cracks in the log walls created draftiness, most log house interiors were covered with paper of various kinds, and a flour-and-water paste was used as an adhesive. This covering was thought of in terms of insulation, not of decoration. As one man remarked, "the more paper, the warmer the house." Abandoned log houses commonly have layers of paper peeling off the walls like geological strata. In the Cagle Canard house, the layers are of newspaper, corrugated cardboard, advertising circulars, and patterned wallpaper, applied in that order (fig. 8-10). Good housekeepers annually renewed the top layer of paper. In modest houses, newspapers generally form the first layer; the "step up" from newspapers or pages of catalogues was to ordinary patterned wallpaper or to "building paper"—inexpensive,

Fig. 8-8. Central Hall with Staircase at Luke Kantz House (1880), Fayetteville Vicinity, Washington County. In contrast to the newel post at the Tilley-Buchanan House, this one was ready-made and available through millwork catalogues. The horizontal board walls of the hallway of this I-house, however, are of the traditional Ozark type that sheathed the interiors of many frame Ozark houses. (Exterior seen in fig. 4-56.) *Courtesy of the Arkansas Historic Preservation Program*

plain, coarse-grained blue or brown paper, available in thirty-six-inch rolls. This paper was available, in Stone County at least, through the 1950s. The most unusual wall covering consisted of old copies of the *Congressional Record,* which, in the well-refined practice of Ozark recycling, Jimmy Driftwood's family in Stone County received from their congressman and used to paper the walls of their house. Besides being good quality paper, it provided interesting reading material.[4]

In more prosperous families' houses, a simple paneled wainscot might appear in the hallway and in one or two of the principal front rooms, as in the Sam Brown house and the Thomas M. Hess house (fig. 4-60). In the latter house, the paneling and interior doors are decorated with graining (fig. 8-11).

With regard to floors, written accounts of the earliest log houses indicate that rough puncheon floors of split green saplings were used. In all houses documented, the floors were pine boards that good housekeeping practices dictated should be periodically scrubbed with sand and hot water. (See interview in appendix.)

Fig. 8-9. Central Hall with Staircase at Lawson-Johnson House (1867), Wesley Vicinity, Madison County. The simplicity that characterizes Ozark interiors is seen here in this central hall staircase that, as was sometimes the case, rises from the rear rather than from the front of the hall. (Exterior seen in fig. 4-55.)

Fig. 8-10. Cagle Canard House (c. 1884), St. James Vicinity, Stone County. The layers of paper covering the walls of this ruinous log dogtrot house consist of newspaper, corrugated cardboard, advertising circulars, and patterned wallpaper, applied in that order. Most log house interiors were covered with paper of some kind, applied with flour and water as glue. The paper was for insulation, not decoration, and good housekeepers renewed the top layer annually.

Fig. 8-11. Interior of Thomas M. Hess House (1868), Marcella, Stone County. This now ruinous large central hall house was once a fashionable dwelling; its furnishings were shipped upriver from New Orleans. The paneled wainscot and door were grained and, although of the simplest type, were elaborate for a rural Ozark house. (Exterior is seen in fig. 4-59.)

Mantels

Mantels are the most fascinating and variable decorations, and sometimes they are the single decorative architectural component inside the house. Even in the many houses where the fireplace is now boarded up, the mantel is retained as a functional as well as ornamental feature, providing a space on which to display knickknacks, to dry clothes, or simply to form a backdrop for the television (figs. 8-13, 8-15, 8-16). The utterly simple mantel design of the Hash-Langham house was popular in nineteenth-century houses of both log and frame in Washington and Madison counties. Constructed of boards of graduated sizes nailed on top of each other, its profile resembles a molding (fig. 8-15). Mantels were documented in several variations featuring vernacular versions of classical pilasters at the sides, a plain "frieze," and a simple molding supporting the shelf. Two of these (located in Washington County) echoed the simple Greek Revival details on the exterior of the house: The Owen Maguire house mantel simply has a wide molding beneath the shelf (fig. 8-13). The Troy Gordon house features a deep molding outlining the shelf, which is supported in turn by large brackets (fig. 8-12). A charming mantel with what can only be termed a "folk" version of classical pilasters appears in the Stone County J. K. York house (fig. 8-14).

Fig. 8-12. Mantel at Troy Gordon House (1851), Fayetteville Vicinity, Washington County. *Courtesy of the Arkansas Historic Preservation Program* (Exterior shown in fig. 4-63.)

Fig. 8-13. Mantel at Owen Maguire House (c. 1867), Maguiretown, Washington County.

Fig. 8-14. Mantel at J. K. York House (c. 1870), Melrose, Stone County.

Fig. 8-15. Mantel Comprised of Stacked Boards at Hash-Langham House (1878), Goshen Vicinity, Washington County.

Fig. 8-16. Mantel at McBrien-Bellamy House (1896), Old Greersburg Vicinity, Washington County.

Several generalizations about Ozark vernacular interiors can be made on the basis of fieldwork documentation.

(1) Little space for privacy existed, especially by contemporary standards. Most houses were small, three or four rooms, including a kitchen, while many families were large.

(2) Like simple vernacular dwellings all over the world, and like most American houses until the mid-nineteenth century, the interior spaces were unspecialized, performing multiple functions. Living, sleeping, and working areas merged and overlapped. The single exception was that cooking and eating areas were consistently set apart from living and sleeping areas in a separate room or rooms at the rear. In ordinary-sized houses, the kitchen and dining areas were combined in a one-room shed roof addition across the rear, while larger houses (primarily central hall cottages or I-houses) had a separate dining room and kitchen located in a two-room rear ell extension. (Although oral and written histories mention early kitchens in separate outbuildings, most of these have disappeared.) The generalized spaces in Ozark houses contrasted markedly with those in nineteenth-century pattern books, which are replete with specialized rooms and spaces with such labels as "reception hall," "study," "library," "china closet," "back parlor," "dressing room," etc. In good weather, porches also served multiple functions. Family members might play the banjo or guitar or simply sit and visit with neighbors on the front porch. Side or rear porches were likely to be places where women did household chores. Another factor contributing to undifferentiated spaces is that women's chores were often portable. Hand-sewing, shelling peas, snapping beans, spinning, churning, knitting socks, etc., could all be done wherever there was a good breeze in the summertime or a warm, sunny spot in the winter. According to Novelle Blair Baumert, strictly outdoor activities, such as washing or making soap in an iron kettle, were not confined to one place, for the kettle was moved around from season to season. She also recalls that ironing was done outside in summer to avoid the heat of the kitchen stove upon which the irons were heated. Looms were placed in various spots, including living rooms, kitchens, and sometimes outbuildings; one is visible on the porch at the John Avey house (fig. 4-69). Even roofs of houses and barns were utilized as spaces upon which to spread sliced apples and peaches to dry in the sun.

(3) Storage space was limited and closets almost nonexistent, but extra space provided by outbuildings alleviated this problem. Also, possessions were few and wardrobes limited, since most clothing was homemade. The few personal items carried over from season to season could be stored in trunks or boxes under the bed or between the headboard of the bed and the wall. Quilts were sometimes stored between the feather mattress and the straw ticking on the bed itself. Clothes were hung on nails along the wall or on nails in a corner where they were covered with a curtain. Prosperous families might have large wardrobe cabinets as well. Instead of being stored, old clothes were recycled by being torn into strips to make braided, woven, or crocheted rugs. Quilt frames hung from the ceiling. After a meal the dishes were washed and the table was immediately set again, lessening the need for cabinet space.

Many objects were hung on the walls, both in kitchens and other rooms. Food storage seemed to spill over into various rooms in the house as well as in barns and outbuildings. Flour, meal, and kitchen staples were often stored in buckets on the kitchen floor. Many people recall using upstairs lofts and rooms for storage of such foods as flour, meal, dried apples, or peaches. Various items could be kept in hallways or open breezeways as well as in cellars and smokehouses.

The one consistent location for a closet was under the stairway, whether it be located in an open breezeway or in an enclosed central hall. These closet doors were constructed of vertical boards with cross pieces (fig. 8-6).

(4) A time-honored Ozark custom was having a bed in every room, except the kitchen and dining room (and even then there were exceptions). Even the largest house documented, the William Wilson house, had a parlor that eventually was pressed into service as a bedroom (figs. 4-51, 8-20, 8-21). All of the I-houses documented had at least one of the two downstairs front rooms used as a bedroom, while the smaller houses almost always had beds in both front rooms. Even today, country houses of the traditional double pen type often have beds in both front rooms. The practical furniture arrangement required that beds be pushed into corners and that there be space in front of the fireplace for a variable arrangement of rocking chairs and cane-bottom chairs. Such an arrangement is seen in the "living room" (as it is described) of Mrs. Mary Jane Morton Staples, featured on the photo postcard (fig. 8-1). Novelle Blair Baumert, growing up in the Pleasant Grove community in Stone County, said that every house she could remember had a bed, or beds, in every room; even her aunt's house, which was large enough to have a room designated as a parlor, had beds in every room. Another Stone County native, Clarence Jetton, described the first house he lived in and others he could recall, "Now we had two beds. One in the living room and one in the kitchen. I might add that every room in every house we ever lived in was a bedroom regardless of whatever other room it was."[5]

Many houses have upper-story lofts or attics that were left unfinished or only roughly finished; these were generally used only for storage and not as bedroom areas. Clearly, then, a bed downstairs, even in the living room, was preferred over these upper spaces. Undoubtedly, these lofts were uncomfortably cold in winter and hot in summer; perhaps the ever-present fear of fire, too, made family members prefer sleeping close, even sometimes crowded, together. At any rate, this practice indicates that privacy in sleeping areas was not a priority in the allocation of space.

(5) Formal spaces, or spaces reserved for company, were rare. Only the largest houses had a room set aside as a parlor, and even then it often contained a bed. Scholarly writing about high style American interiors associate middle-class parlors with the collecting and displaying of family mementos and possessions, sometimes referring to them as shrines to social respectability and prestige. In the Ozarks, on the contrary, possessions were too few, space too scarce, and life too arduous for this mentality to flourish. Moreover, as previously discussed, social stratification in the Ozarks was and continues to be minimal.

In comparing public with private spaces within a house, the central hallway could be considered a reception area, a public area that visitors would enter first as a kind of middle ground before entering the private areas of the home. For several reasons, this designation of the hallway as a public and receiving space seems only minimally applicable to Ozark houses. Entertaining visitors, other than extended family, was a minor part of Ozark life; as Novelle Baumert recalls, "Company was mostly relatives." (On Sundays, however, neighbors would often informally visit one another.) The lack of desire for a formal receiving space is verified in that, within the overall stock of rural Ozark houses, the central hall house type, with its potentially wasted space in that hall, was the least favored plan. Even some I-houses eschewed this hall in favor of the popular two front doors. When houses did have central halls, a popular arrangement was to have double doors opening at either end of the hall so that in good weather the hall would serve the same function as the open breezeway in a dogtrot house. This arrangement can be seen in the old photograph of an unidentified I-house from the Huntsville area (fig. 8-17). And Rollans and Caswell Wilson recall that the large hallway in their antebellum house was transformed into an all-purpose room in the summer, with the double doors at each end of the hall left open (fig. 4-51).

Fig. 8-17. Unidentified I-house in Huntsville, Madison County. As seen here, most I-houses had double doors at both front and back that could be kept open in warm weather functioning much like the open breezeway of the dogtrot house, but with much more status. *Shiloh Museum of Ozark History (Vivian Lopshire Collection)*

In traditional Ozark houses, it was the front porch instead of the central hall that served as a middle ground or a "public" reception area for the visitor, who, as likely as not, entered a room with a fireplace, an arrangement of chairs at the hearth, and a bed pushed into one corner. Many country houses today still retain these features.

Ozark social events were simple, informal, and often held outside. There were quilting bees, house raisings, banjo and guitar playing and singing, dinner-on-the-grounds at churches, picnics, trips to swimming holes, singing schools, and camp meetings. "Speaking Days," when political candidates met to speak and folks brought picnic lunches, were also popular.

Two entertainments that did take place in the home were square dancing and the closely related "play-party." Since members of fundamentalist churches believed square dancing was sinful, young people convinced their fundamentalist parents that if there were no musical instruments, but simply singing and clapping hands, that square dances would be like "singing games," and hence would be permissible. These were dubbed "play-parties," and special song books were written for them. Both square dances and play-parties were held in various places in the house: in breezeways, on front porches, in living rooms and bedrooms. Jimmie Ford recalled that bedrooms were often favored on such occasions because it was easier to take down beds and remove them than it was to move several pieces of furniture out of a living room.[6]

6) Finally, it seems that Ozark farm families, desirous of attaining a "pride of place," did so simply by building large houses, rather than by having elaborate floor plans or by having interior or exterior decorative architectural details. A two-story house, especially a brick one, was surely a mark of success. Moreover, judging by the popularity of the narrow two-story porticoes embellished with sawnwork that apeared on I-houses, these porches must have added an element of prestige as well. Old photographs show, however, that ornamentation was generally modest. The true luxury surely lay in having rooms without beds in them and hallways spacious enough to accommodate "everything from church to square dances," as Caswell Wilson recalled about his parents' large house. Elaboration and frills went against the grain of Ozark character, after all, and Ozarkers judged people on their farming ability and their characters, not their possessions.[7]

The Economic Function of Ozark Houses

Ozark farms were self-sufficient economic units within which everyone's labor—men's, women's, and children's—was essential for survival. Thus, the farmhouse, in and around which women worked, was as functional as the surrounding fields, barns, and outbuildings. In a 1938 newspaper interview, Mrs. Mahala Rainey of Madison County, on the occasion of her one-hundredth birthday, described Ozark women's responsibilities in the 1850s. Many of these were the "portable" chores noted earlier:

> Girls worked hard in the fifties. They carried almost as much responsibilities as the man, and during the Civil War had it nearly all to tote. . . . The woman in a home had to make most of the clothing for the family. They carded the wool and spun the yarn that went into socks, stockings, gloves and cloth that was woven on the handlooms of those days. They had to make this cloth up into finished clothing, and it was done by hand. They had to make the garden and can the vegetables and fruit. They had to help cure the meat, and if they had any spare time from their work at the house, they worked in the field.[8]

It is important to note that women not only performed housekeeping and maintenance chores but were "producers" of goods that would either be consumed by the family or sold or bartered at the general store. Like other Ozark wives, Daisy Blair not only gathered and preserved the family's food but also made their clothes; she sold chickens she had raised, eggs and special bark she had gathered, and wool she had washed and dried, as well as several varieties of peas for seed that she had grown in her "garden" of thirty acres.

Moreover, as Bonita Musgrave noted in her study of Ozark women's crafts, until the early twentieth century, Ozark women held a flourishing textile industry in their hands. Musgrave documents the impressive extent of this textile making by interviewing Ozark women in the 1920s. They grew flax and cotton for the family's use and raised sheep in what was called "the farm flock." One informant recalled the way cotton was processed at home: "We usually finger-picked the cotton after supper was over and the younger children put to bed. The older members of the family helped and enough could be separated in one night to keep the mother busy carding and spinning the next day, or else to pad a quilt."[9]

Several kinds of cloth were woven, and three yards a day was considered good work. A woolen fabric called "jeans" was often mentioned both by the women interviewed and in old store ledgers as well. Women could either barter jeans at the store for goods or get forty cents a yard credit for it.[10]

In the early 1900s there was usually a woman in each community who still wove on a floor loom and who would weave rag rugs and carpets for others. The housewife would save old clothes, tearing them into strips that she and her daughters would sew together to create large rolls of strips that could then be woven into rugs. Such a rag carpet is visible in the photograph of Mrs. Mary Jane Staples's house (fig. 8-1).

As the twentieth century wore on, fewer Ozark women wove on the large floor looms, but many continued to card, spin, and knit wool sweaters, caps, and socks. For a woman to knit a pair of socks a day after the housework was done was considered a "pretty good day's work." Knitted wool socks could be sold or bartered for twenty cents a pair at the store. Even lamp wicks were commonly knitted at home.[11]

Life in the Blair Log Cabin

Life in the single pen log house of Daisy and Albert Blair in the Pleasant Grove community of Stone County was a microcosm of Ozark domestic life. The Blairs bought the log house in 1910 and lived in it until 1926 when they built a double pen house adjacent to the log cabin, which was then torn down. Their younger daughter, Novelle Blair Baumert, who furnished the information below, still lives in this double pen house. She was born in the log cabin in 1913, and the family activities she recalls took place from around 1920 to 1926.

As seen in the furnishings layout in fig. 8-18, the log pen of the house was eighteen feet square with a stone chimney on the east, two windows at the front, and a full front porch with plain supports. At the rear was a nine-by-eighteen-foot box construction room that served as a combined kitchen and dining room, performing the essential function of separating the eating and dining areas from the living and sleeping areas. All these features are typical.

The front room served as a combined living room, work space, and sleeping area. Here there were three beds, a dresser, a trunk, a sewing machine, a spool cabinet, a corner table (made by Mr. Blair) with a kerosene lamp on it, two cane-bottom chairs, and two rocking chairs in front of the hearth. As is typical of small Ozark houses, there was no heavy, space-consuming upholstered furniture. Instead, all furnishings were pushed into corners and against walls, leaving an open area free for variable arrangements of rocking chairs and the ladder-back, cane-bottom chairs, which are still seen in most Ozark houses. A similar furniture arrangement is visible in the old photograph of Mrs. Mary Jane Staples's house near Prairie Grove (fig. 8-1).

The simple ornamentation in the Blairs' front room consisted of some decorative objects placed on the mantel and, hanging on the wall, an embroidered wall pocket, which was made by the oldest Blair daughter, Opal, that contains dress patterns, a black-and-white inexpensive print of an angel, Mr. Blair's banjo, and Novelle's guitar. There were green shades and lace curtains at the two windows and heavy white counterpanes and embroidered pillow shams on the three beds. Three crocheted rugs lay on the floor and a quilt frame hung from the ceiling.

The walls of the log house had been chinked with wood shingles and mortar on the exterior and lined with sealing boards over the cracks between the logs on the interior. These walls were covered with either newspaper or magazines, which were preferred when they were available. The paper was affixed with a flour and water paste. Mrs. Blair renewed the paper annually.

The wall telephone, hanging in the living room to the right of the front door over "mama's trunk" (in which Sunday clothes were stored), seems an anachronism until one learns that it was the early battery-operated type connecting the two communities of St. James and O'Neill, about twenty miles apart.

Under the crocheted rug at the hearth was a trapdoor leading into a tiny root cellar, the back of which was the chimney wall; in the cellar, shelves were built to hold canned fruits and vegetables and a there was a bin of sand in which to store sweet potatoes, pumpkins, and molasses in the winter. During the coldest weather, eggs were sometimes stored in the cellar as well. Since the kitchen was a rear shed room of flimsy box construction, eggs and even jars of fruit would sometimes freeze if left there.

The Blairs' music making and singing might take place at the hearth or on the front porch in good weather, when the neighbors, who also played, might join them. On Saturday evenings or Sunday afternoons, the family went a short distance to the home of Mr. Blair's parents, where the three younger sons, who all played instruments, joined them in making music.

As indicated in the furnishings plan (fig. 8-18), the kitchen contained a table and two chairs, a pie safe (in which both dishes and leftover food were stored), a firebox, a wood stove, two large wooden buckets on the floor in which flour and meal were stored, a wash shelf near the back door that held two buckets and a stand underneath for the wash pan. Pots, pans, and cooking utensils were hung on the wall, and in the corner was a triangular "closet" consisting of two shelves with cloth tacked over them. The broom hung on a nail near the back door, but the corn-shuck mop hung in the smokehouse. The kitchen, then, served multiple functions as a pantry, as a cooking and food preservation area, and as a dining room. Since hot water was needed for bathing, it also served as a bathroom, as well water was heated on the stove. (In larger houses, people sometimes bathed in bedrooms for greater privacy.) Early irons had to be heated on the stove, too, so ironing was done in the kitchen in cool weather; Mrs. Blair, however, ironed outside in summer, heating the iron on an open fire. In recalling the kitchen, Mrs. Baumert mentioned an Ozark custom that lessened the need for dish storage space: after each meal her mother immediately reset the table with the freshly washed dishes and eating utensils that were then covered with a cloth to keep out dirt and flies. (It was this custom, which, as Jimmie Driftwood recalled, led his father to say after the blessing, "Turn over and take up.") Unlike the front room walls, which were papered, the kitchen walls were bare, unpainted wood.

As both the old photograph and the yard layout show, the Blairs' log smokehouse was located just a few feet away from the rear of the house, and, perhaps because there was no side or rear porch, the little space acted as a breezeway between the house and the smokehouse and became Mrs. Blair's favorite place to sit and snap beans, peel apples, or shell peas. Her cane-bottom chair is visible sitting in that exact spot in the old photograph of the log house (figs. 4-15, 8-19). Stored in the smokehouse were cured meat and sausage, the lard bucket, sorghum molasses (except in the coldest weather when it was moved to the root cellar), bunches of onions, the family's laundry, the soap Mrs. Blair made annually, and an unused side saddle.

The front porch, too, served various functions. Mr. Blair's prized collection of tools sat in a large box right by the front door. Dried apples hung in flour sacks on the exterior wall. In addition to the music making and entertaining mentioned earlier, in mild weather Mr. Blair would sit on the porch and converse with the men who came to see him in his capacity as justice of the peace. Here, too, Mr. Blair practiced his part-time occupation of barbering. Mrs. Blair had a shelf between the corner of the wall and the corner porch post on which sat pots of geraniums and ferns. And growing along strings at the front of the porch were morning glories and balsam cucumbers.

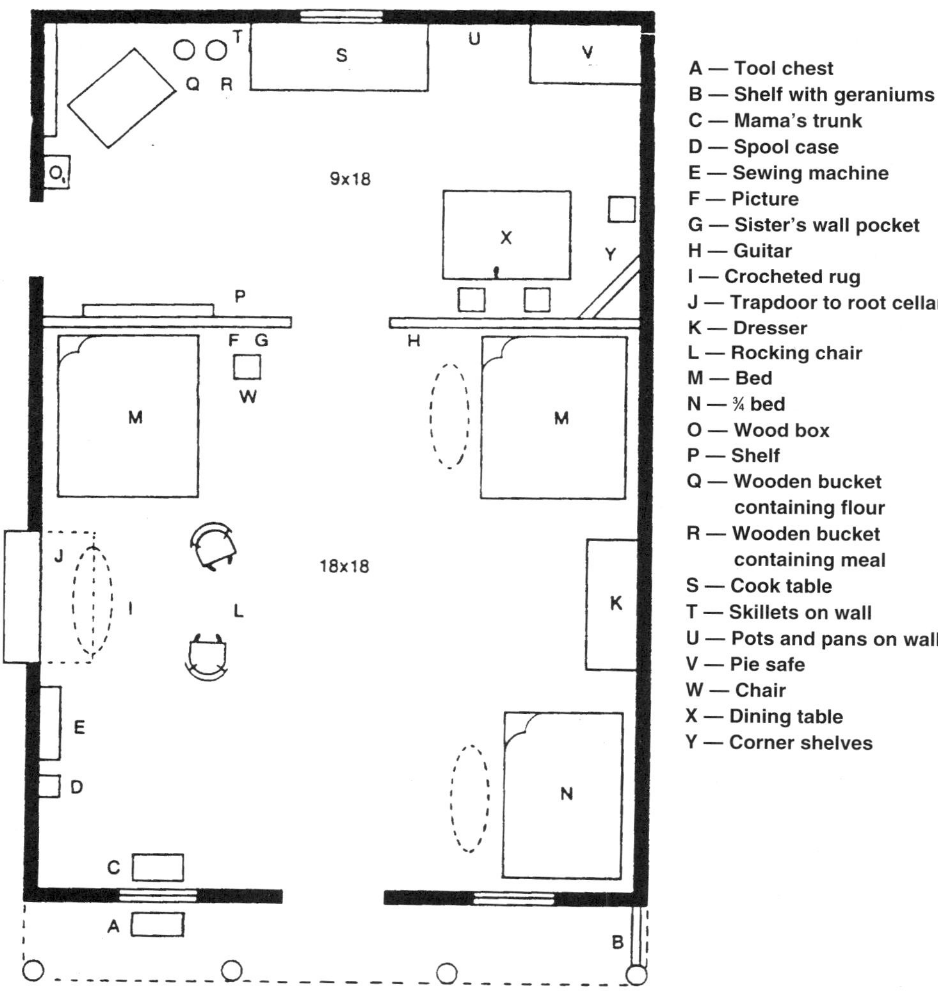

Fig. 8-18. Furnishings Layout for Daisy and Albert Blair Single Pen Log House, Pleasant Grove, Stone County. *Drawn by Dolores Justus*

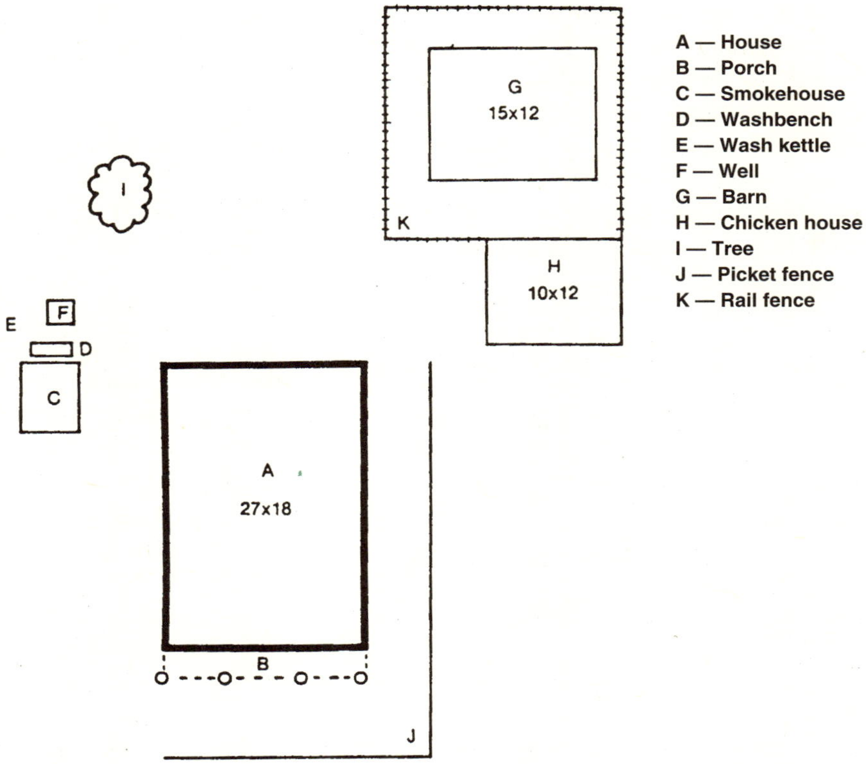

Fig. 8-19. Yard Layout at Daisy and Albert Blair Single Pen Log House, Pleasant Grove, Stone County. *Drawing by Dolores Justus*

Life in the William Wilson I-House

Located in the Rhea's Mill community near Prairie Grove in Washington County, the William Wilson house (fig. 4-51), constructed in 1857–59, is the single largest house and one of the earliest braced frame houses documented in the fieldwork. In 1839 Mr. Wilson and his wife, Eliza McCulloh, immigrated to central Arkansas (Perry and Pulaski counties) from Georgia. Following the deaths of several of their children, the Wilsons moved to the Rhea's Mill area in the mid-1850s. They were attracted by its good farmland and healthful high elevation. Wilson amassed land holdings of 2,400 acres and raised various kinds of stock, including fine saddle horses. The advent of the Frisco Railroad, which ran across the Wilson farm, facilitated marketing, so that in the late nineteenth and early twentieth century, wheat was a major cash crop.

The Wilsons raised five children in this house. The following information was obtained in interviews with Rollans and Caswell Wilson, brothers who are grandsons of William Wilson. (Rollans Wilson is riding the hobbyhorse in the old photograph, fig. 4-51). The period recalled by the Wilson brothers is from about 1910 to 1930. The family members referred to are their father and mother, Andrew Jackson Wilson and Nannie Naomi Cunningham Wilson, and their two brothers, James and Andrew.

Huge by Ozark standards, the Wilson house is an I-house constructed with large oak beams in braced frame construction. Its central hall plan (fig. 4-44) features two front rooms twenty feet square and twelve feet high, separated by a central hall measuring twelve feet in width. It is raised on a high solid-stone foundation. Two exterior brick chimneys were planned, but because of the outbreak of the Civil War, only the east chimney was completed.

As seen in the old photograph of the exterior (fig. 4-51), the focal point of the facade was the two-story narrow portico with a decorative balustrade of sawnwork at the upper level. (This porch has long since vanished.) The double-leaf front doors were surrounded by sidelights and transom. The large nine-over-six light windows had wooden shutters. The rear of the house has a unique configuration: instead of the customary rear ell or rear shed roof addition, there is an extension of the central hall the full length of the house with two full-sized rear rooms (measuring eighteen by twenty feet each) lying on either side. In other words, the first floor arrangement is similar to what is commonly called a Georgian or double pile plan, with four large rooms and a central hall (fig. 4-44). But the Wilson house, although double pile (or two rooms deep) on the first fooor, is single pile on the second story, with its two rooms separated by a central hall, in typical I-house fashion. The side view of the house presents a tall, narrow profile, not unlike that of an I-house with a large rear shed addition, but viewed from the back, the house presents a most unusual arrangement of the two rear rooms having adjoining gable roofs. The interior has the typical horizontal boards covering walls and ceilings, but atypical crown moldings and wallpaper appear in all the rooms except the hallway, which, in contrast, has the customary plain horizontal board paneling painted white. The mantel and most doors have decorative graining, however. The extremely plain stairway (identical to the stairway in the Lawson-Johnson house and in the same location) is placed so that the stair rises from the rear of the hall, so upon entering the front door, one sees the closet beneath the stairs instead of an impressive staircase. When the Wilson brothers were questioned about this odd stairway orientation, they said it was arranged to provide privacy both to the family and to the several hired hands who customarily lived in the upper story. At one time, as many as seven hired hands lived in the house, and, as the furnishings plan indicates (fig. 8-21), their rooms upstairs had several beds in each room, along with trunks, washstands, dressers, tables, and chairs. The Wilson brothers recalled that flour was customarily stored in the northeast bedroom on a table with its legs set in tin cans for protection against mice.

On the first floor, as the furnishings plan indicates (fig. 8-20), the three major rooms (the parlor on the east, the front bedroom on the west, and the master bedroom in the rear southeast corner) all contained beds. Although originally the parlor had been a formal room, as the extended family grew it became Uncle Ab's bedroom as well, with the bed pushed into a corner in typical fashion. Like the Blairs' log house, two rocking chairs sat before the hearth, and quilting frames hung from the ceiling. Caswell Wilson remarked, "They used to say the whole county came here to quilt." Unlike the Blairs' small house, however, the Wilsons' parlor had a round parlor table in the center of the room, over which hung a kerosene lamp with a hobnail glass shade. The parlor also contained a red velvet love seat, a piano, and a large bookcase on the front wall. Generally, the front bedroom and parlor were private rooms for the family. The family room in the front northwest corner had two double beds on the front wall with a dresser between them, a rocking chair, and a "closet" consisting of shelves and space for hanging clothes jutting out from the wall and covered with a curtain. Although the fireplace and chimney for this room were never built, there is an arched walnut mantel on the west wall in front of which sat a stove. The master bedroom in the rear southeast corner contained two beds, a marble-topped dresser, a cherry chest, and a closet similar to the one just described. All the bedrooms had washstands. The Wilson brothers recalled that generally the hired hands bathed in number three washtubs upstairs, while the family members bathed in the kitchen or in one of the downstairs bedrooms.

The kitchen had a door on the east wall leading to a side porch, directly off of which was the well and smokehouse. (A door opened off the front bedroom to this porch as well.) Oddly enough, instead of a separate dining room in a rear ell, which I-houses typically had, a partition ran down the center of the kitchen, separating the food preparation area from the dining area. The dining area had a sideboard, a long dining table, and several chairs. The kitchen was furnished with a cookstove, cook table, cabinet, and sink. After about 1875 the Wilsons had a windmill that pumped water into the kitchen from a cistern.

As in the Blair household, music provided entertainment for the Wilsons. Caswell recalled, "Charlie (a black hired hand) had a mouth organ and played just great; John Butler played the French harp; they'd play in the house in the kitchen. Dad would jig. They'd play right there in the kitchen with Mama cooking."

Depending upon the season, the hallway served a variety of functions. In the winter, the visitor entering the front door would see only a marble-topped round table beside the door on the left and on the opposite side an upholstered "fainting couch." Directly ahead, on the wall opposite the staircase, a tall cherry bookcase stood perpendicular to the wall so that it served as a partial room divider that separated the back from the front of the hall. In the summertime, however, both front and rear double doors would be opened, forming a breezeway similar to that of a dogtrot house. Rocking chairs were moved into the hall for the older people, and the long dining table and chairs were moved here as well. The Wilsons owned a threshing machine, and they did their own harvesting as well as all the other harvesting in the community. As many as twenty men would sit down to eat around the long table during summertime threshing. Additionally, in the summer the women would do kitchen chores, such as cutting cabbage or shelling peas, at the dining table in the hall; they even did the wash here in hot weather. Meanwhile, Caswell Wilson recalled, "The old folks sat in the hall to keep cool."

The Wilsons were congenial and enjoyed sharing their large house. Besides the quilting bees mentioned earlier, "Everything from church to dances were held in that hall, so they told me," Caswell Wilson reported. As hallmarks of their affluence, the Wilsons had not only an unusually large house, but an unusual commitment to education as well. Their furnishings included three large bookcases, which held the extensive library of William Wilson, and when the time came for the Wilson sons to attend high school, the family bought a second house in Prairie Grove and moved there for the school year so the sons could attend school more conveniently.

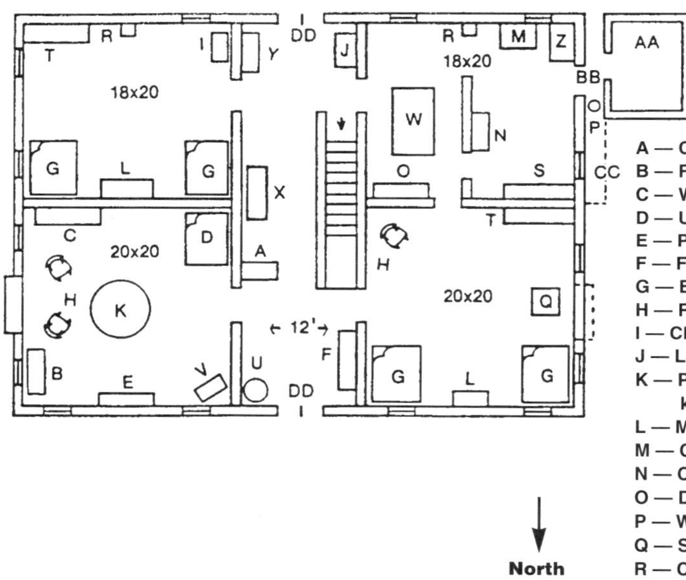

Fig. 8-20. Furnishings Layout for First Floor of Eliza and William Wilson's I-House, Rhea's Mill, Washington County. *Drawing by Dolores Justus*

A — Cherry bookcase 9' tall
B — Red velvet love seat
C — Walnut dresser with marble top
D — Uncle Abe's bed
E — Piano
F — Fainting couch
G — Bed
H — Rocking chair
I — Cherry chest
J — Lavatory
K — Parlor table with hobnail shade, kerosene lamp hanging over it.
L — Marble-top dresser
M — Cookstove
N — Cook table
O — Dining room sideboard
P — Well
Q — Stove
R — Chimney
S — Cabinet
T — Closet
U — Marble-top table
V — Bookcase
W — Dining room table
X — Table
Y — Buffet
Z — Sink
AA — Added room for help, later smokehouse
BB — Breezeway
CC — Side porch
DD — Double doors

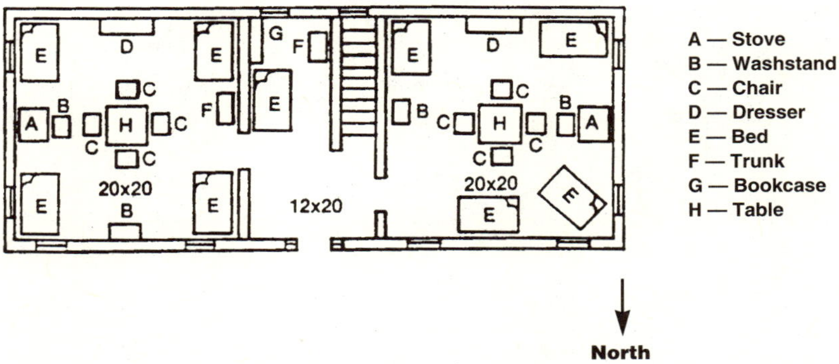

Fig. 8-21. Furnishings Layout for Second Floor of Eliza and William Wilson's I-House, Rhea's Mill, Washington County. *Drawing by Dolores Justus*

Beautifying the House and Yard

Although ornamentation was modest in hard-working homes such as these, decorative architectural components, including mantels, stairways, grained woodwork, and paneled wainscots, have been noted. In addition, several types of decorative accessories, besides furniture, were common. Floor coverings were generally hand woven or crocheted. Rag rugs ranged from small individual rugs (like the one on the Blairs' hearth) to room-size rag carpets (visible in Mrs. Staples's house). The fine central hall house of Thomas M. Hess, however, had stylish straw matting that covered the parlor floor, which may have been imported from New Orleans as many other of their furnishings were. The Hess house also had decorative window shades, as the old photograph shows (fig. 4-59). Judging from old photographs and from people's recollections, lace curtains were quite common, even in one-room houses (fig. 4-18). Other common decorative items included colorful quilts and embroidered and crocheted pieces such as pillow shams, doilies, or wall hangings like the embroidered wall pocket in the Blair house. Inexpensive prints and family photographs hung on the walls alongside utilitarian objects and musical instruments. Patterned wallpaper often lined the walls of frame houses.

Turning now to the spaces immediately outside of the house, a consistent distinction seems to have been made between the front yard and the back (a distinction that hasn't changed much to this day). The front was considered an "ornamental" space, no matter how plain, while the backyard was considered a work space. Thus, wash kettles, wash benches, smokehouses, and other outbuildings rarely obtruded into the front yard. Old photographs indicate that planting shrubs along the foundation of the house, as today's custom dictates, was not done. Instead, small ornamental trees (perhaps fruit trees) were planted in the front yard along with perennial flowers, which might include jonquils,

Fig. 8-22. Unidentified I-House, Washington County. Typical ways of beautifying the yard are seen in this family photograph: there are festoons of ivy along the porch, boards placed between porch columns to hold potted plants and small shrubs growing in containers placed in the yard. Although less dressy than the small decorative portico, the simple two-story full-length porch seen here was a popular choice for rural Ozark I-houses. *Shiloh Museum of Ozark History (Vivian Lopshire Collection)*

peonies, tiger lilies, or rosebushes. Favorite spots for these seem to have been along the front walkway or path or along a stone wall. Vines commonly grew along front porches, and boards were placed between porch columns to hold potted plants. These were described at the Blair house and are visible in the old photograph of an unidentified I-house (fig. 8-22). Small shrubs can also be seen planted in containers in the front yard of this I-house. In keeping with the symmetry of traditional houses, it is common to see two large trees planted on either side of the front yard in old photographs. In Washington County, especially, these trees were often maples.

Modernization

The technological innovations that, as we have seen, changed many aspects of Ozark farms in the early and mid-twentieth century seem to have stopped abruptly at the threshold of farmhouses. By 1930, the cutoff date for this study, scarcely any farms in the Arkansas Ozarks had electricity, running water, or telephones (other than the local battery-operated type).[12] Thus, the farm wife's routine and the organization of various work spaces, especially the kitchen, stayed essentially the same as they were in the nineteenth century. Although some families eventually purchased kerosene refrigerators and gasoline washing machines, these appliances were not common before the 1940s. Even pressure cookers, which made possible canning a wider variety and greater quantity of foods, were not widely used until the mid-1930s.

By 1930 electricity was available only to a few farms in well-populated areas along the main highways. Isolated farms, like Jimmie Ford's near St. James in Stone County, for example, did not receive electricity until the 1950s.

Since 1920 Home Demonstration Agents from the Extension Service in Agriculture and Home Economics had been active in Arkansas in both towns and rural areas. They worked with children's agricultural clubs, encouraged the general cleanup of trash and removal of old buildings, planted trees and shrubs, and presented demonstrations of gardening, cooking, canning, laundry, home conveniences, and kitchen arrangements.[13] By 1938, according to an Extension Service pamphlet entitled "Improving the Kitchen," the U-shaped kitchen was promoted as being the most efficient. Such ideas seem to have had minimal impact upon rural Ozark houses, even after the study period.

In conclusion, the interiors of Ozark dwellings are similar to both the lifestyle of the owners and the exteriors of the houses—simple, straightforward, and hard working like the former, and regular, boxy, and symmetrical like the latter. Kitchens often contained the dining areas, and except for this separation from the rest of the house, spaces for living, working, and sleeping all overlapped, serving multiple functions. "Public" or formal spaces were rare, and luxury was more likely to be conceived of in terms of sheer space (having a sitting room that was not of necessity a bedroom, for example, served as a mark of prosperity) rather than in terms of elaborate floor plans or ornamental architectural details. The William Wilson house is a prime example of the value placed on space. Here the visitor opened the front door, stepped into the spacious hall, and saw, not an elaborate staircase, but a simple closet under the stairs, bare board walls with no crown molding, and newel posts and balustrades of the plainest variety. Although the Wilsons owned one of the largest, most prosperous farms in the entire region as well as the largest house documented in the fieldwork (fig. 4-51), they let function, rather than the desire for display, be their guide; their simple staircase rises from the rear of the hallway to afford privacy for both family members and live-in hired hands.

Chapter 9

Conclusion

Review of Arkansas Ozark Vernacular House Types

A pervasive theme of this study has been that traditional rural culture flourished well into the twentieth century in the Arkansas Ozarks, and that a major aspect of this culture is the persistence of traditional dwelling forms. The region is characterized by its overwhelmingly rural nature, its rough, varied topography, its widespread soil infertility, its geographical insularity, and the homogeneous character of its population, which consists predominantly of Anglo-Saxon Protestants of an Upland South and especially an Appalachian heritage. Especially in the rougher parts of the Ozarks, which remained remote from major transportation links, a frontier quality continued into the 1920s. Of necessity, the people of the Arkansas Ozarks valued and practiced self-sufficiency, yet they also shared close community bonds, not the least of which, as Carl Sauer described it, was "the shared bond of the rigors of making a living in a region blessed with only modest resources."[1] In sum, the dwellings resemble the lifestyles of the inhabitants: both are characterized by simplicity and practicality with a minimum of self-consciousness and class distinction.

In the fieldwork, six traditional house types were identified: the single pen, the double pen, the dogtrot, the one-story central hall cottage, the two-story I-house, and the saddlebag house. These six types correspond to those that Fred Kniffen and Henry Glassie postulated as being typical of the Upland South, emerging originally from the Mid-Atlantic culture source region. This study, then, was partially a test and partially a confirmation of Kniffen's and Glassie's early model of the movement of vernacular house types, a model that has been little examined in the South.[2]

The six traditional types share several important characteristics. They invariably have side-gabled roofs with the entrance in the side that parallels the road. The entrance is never placed in a gable end facing the road; such an orientation is strictly reserved for churches, schools, and stores. The chimneys were generally end chimneys and most often were exterior-end chimneys, instead of internal ones. (Antebellum houses were more likely to have internal-end chimneys.) The number of doors and windows in the facade varies, but they are usually bilaterally symmetrical or at the least balanced. Of paramount importance is the fact that these forms can be viewed as conceptually additive forms arrived at in solving the problem of adding onto a single pen log house, which was often one of the first houses in early settlement. It is also important to note that these same six types remained the preferred and traditional ones long after log construction was obsolete. Thus, the additive quality may have first sprung from necessity, but later became a deliberate aesthetic choice.

As is typical of vernacular architecture, the number of traditional types is small; a few basic ideas underlie the spatial organization of most houses. The open-ended, flexible quality of the additive organization allowed vernacular houses to be modified without destroying the basic character of the design. In typical Ozark recycling fashion, owners often added on to small houses rather than building entirely new ones. The various ways of adding on to single pen houses are discussed in chapter 4 and illustrated in figs. 4-11 to 4-14. These traditional types were viable throughout the 1920s to the end of the study period, 1930. From the 1920s to the 1930s, when Americans everywhere were building the popular bungalow, most Ozarkers were content to remain with the familiar dogtrot house or the double pen, double front door house. These six types are deemed traditional because all appeared in early settlement and all (save one, the central hall cottage) were constructed in log. All are single pile, or one room deep, under the main roof, generally considered to be a characteristic of English folk houses.

It is proposed here that these few simple house types and the modular, additive conception underlying their basic spatial organization formed what cultural geographer Amos Rapoport has termed "the house in the mind's eye," or, in other words, the shared house model that Rapoport has shown is typical of all tradition-bound societies, such as the Ozarks.[3] The vernacular building process is consistent because the knowledge of this shared house model (or models) is shared by everyone, thus there is little need for plans or drawings. Because their spatial organization is so remarkably similar, these six Ozark traditional house types fit well this concept of a shared model. Of these six traditional types, three are singled out for brief discussion here because of their interesting regional aspects: the central hall cottage, the dogtrot house, and the two-story I-house. Until late in the study period when increased road travel apparently motivated owners to enclose the open breezeways of dogtrot houses, the enclosed central hall arrangement appeared only in houses of prosperous families. The one-story central hall cottage was not a popular form. Families who apparently could afford the wasted space of an enclosed central hallway usually inhabited the two-story I-houses. The lack of popularity of the central hall is indicative of the informality of Ozark living. As Kenneth Ames pointed out in his study of the social use of the central hall of the Victorian middle-class house, it served as an important transition space for the visitor to enter before being invited into the more private family rooms.[4] Neighbors dropped by one another's houses, but other than visits by relatives, entertaining in the formal sense was not and still is not a common aspect of Ozark life. Instead, the front porch seemed to serve as the transition area for the visitor, who, as likely as not, walked into a front room containing a bed. In good weather the front porch also served as a space to visit with guests, often with music making as a focus.

The overall arrangements of Ozark traditional houses generally reveal a greater concern for keeping cool in the summer than for keeping warm in the winter. The common one-room-deep arrangement is one such indicator. The popularity of the open central breezeway has already been mentioned. Many central hall houses, whether the one-story cottage or the two-story I-house, imitated the breeze-catching quality of dogtrot houses by having double doors, which could be left open in the summer, at the front and rear of the hallway. These breezeways always functioned as living and working spaces. Of the six traditional Ozark house types, the two-story, one-room-deep I-house is deemed the most common folk house in the eastern United States. As in other rural areas of the Upland South, especially, it is the dominant type that indicates agricultural prosperity, perhaps because in its spatial arrangement—all four rooms are spread across the facade—it presents the most impressive arrangements possible for a house of only four rooms. Such an arrangement provides good ventilation as well.[5]

The late nineteenth- and early twentieth-century repertoire of the Arkansas Ozark vernacular builder was enlarged with three house types that are categorized as nontraditional and popular. Listed in the order in which they begin to appear chronologically they are the following: the bent house, the prow house, and the one-story pyramid roof house. Like the six traditional types, they are generally one-story houses of frame construction, displaying simple, boxy outlines. All eschew the formal central hall plan, retaining instead the traditional spatial organization of two principal rooms lying adjacent to one another across the facade; often they incorporate the familiar two front door arrangement. Unlike the earlier types, however, they appear neither in early settlement nor in log construction. Because their form is influenced by popular culture as well as by tradition-based Ozark building practices, they do appear in many regions of the United States. The two most common popular, nontraditional types, the prow house and the bent house, depart from the usual square or rectangular facade with its side-gabled roof, exhibiting instead an irregularity or a variety of prospects typical of the Victorian picturesque aesthetic displayed in high style houses which spread through middle and late nineteenth-century architectural pattern books.[6] Thus, in the conceptual architectural spectrum discussed earlier, with folk designs at one end and high style architecture at the other, these houses represent a middle ground, exhibiting elements from both traditional and popular sources. Both the prow house and the bent house in the Arkansas Ozarks reflect the typical process by which American vernacular builders absorbed influences from designs from nineteenth-century architectural pattern books. According to Dell Upton, this process was for the vernacular builders simply to extract the novel, picturesque essence of the pattern-book prototype, grafting it onto the traditional house with the least possible change.[7] In the bent house this process simply pulls forward one room of the traditional double pen plan and tops it with a front-gabled roof, thus creating the new look of the juxtaposition of the two perpendicular wings while retaining the familiar two front doors and the large front porch. In the prow house the traditional bilateral symmetry of the old double pen house remains, and the new third room simply forms a perpendicular extension toward the road. Again, the large encircling front porch and the two front doors (one opening into the prow extension) reinforce the traditional look. It is important to note, however, that neither in the case of the prow house nor the bent house is it suggested that the Ozark vernacular builder was literally copying from a particular pattern book. Instead, the pattern books simply served to introduce new forms into the domestic architectural vocabulary, so that by the late nineteenth and early twentieth centuries, when these houses were most popular in the Ozarks, the vernacular builders were simply drawing "from a familiar image, rather than a published source," always in terms of abstraction and simplification.[8]

The third popular house type is also the most recent and the least common during the study period ending in 1930: the one-story pyramid roof house with a square four-room plan. Seemingly most popular after 1915, these houses are clustered primarily in Washington County and in similar Springfield Plain areas rather than in the Boston Mountains. Although they retain the boxy massing of the traditional Ozark houses and often the two front doors as well, the low silhouette, compact plan, and dates of its popularity relate it to the American bungalow rather than to the Victorian architectural pattern-book influences seen in the the bent house and the prow house.

As in most rural areas, change came slowly to the Arkansas Ozarks, whether change took the form of modern farming methods, of the introduction of electricity, or of nontraditional house types. It is important to note that the rate of change is variable in different parts of the Ozarks, and that this change is closely related to the accessibility of an area and ultimately to the fertility of the area. The transition in house types from traditional to newer, nontraditional types correlates with topography to a surprising degree. Like the traditional two-story I-house, which connoted agricultural prosperity, the newer popular types were overwhelmingly associated with the prosperous open areas of the Springfield Plain. It is, of course, in the proximity of the Springfield Plain areas where accessibility to railroads enabled a transition from the old-fashioned subsistence farm to the newer general or specialized types of farming. As we have seen, in the late nineteenth and early twentieth century, improvements in agriculture and transportation coincide with the introduction and popularity of the newer house types.

In the more mountainous areas, however, fewer farms converted from subsistence farming, fewer links with railroads were possible, and fewer Ozark families built houses that departed from the six traditional types. Indeed, geographer W. A. Browne's study shows that in the mountainous sections many farms could still be classified as "frontier-like" as late as 1929.[9]

The Impact of High Style Architecture upon Rural Ozark Houses

One obvious and overarching aspect of high style influence is the pervasive preference for symmetrical forms, both in plan and facade arrangement. As noted in chapter 4 on house types, this symmetry was a result of the tremendous impact of the Georgian style that was fashionable in eastern seaboard urban centers from 1700 to 1800.[10]

Studies of vernacular houses in North Carolina (an area from which many settlers eventually migrated to Arkansas) have shown that by 1850 symmetrical forms had replaced the older asymmetrical folk forms. By the time of the movement westward to Arkansas from North Carolina and especially from Tennessee, symmetry was an integral part of the vernacular sensibility. A second major impact of high style architecture is the I-house form itself, which many architectural historians view as originating in a smaller folk adaptation of the formal, full-sized Georgian house with four rooms arranged symmetrically around a central passageway. The I-house, as has been noted, usually retains the central passage plan, but is only one room deep.

A third major aspect of high style influence on Ozark rural houses has already been discussed, i.e., the addition of three new popular house types (the bent house, the prow house, and the square pyramid roof house) to the older vernacular repertoire of six traditional types.

A fourth major aspect of high style influence remains to be explored, the sometimes subtle, but pervasive influence of the Greek Revival style, which was one of the most enduring in American architectural history. As architectural historian William Pierson described it, "The Greek Revival spread to every civilized part of the country in the years between 1820 and the Civil War. It has been recognized by many, in fact, as America's first truly national style. . . . Indeed, in the hands of the local carpenter it permeated every corner of the land to blossom into one of the most remarkable flowerings of folk art in Western history."[11]

Professor Pierson's comments, first published in 1970, dating the close of the spread of the Greek Revival style to the Civil War, could now readily be modified on the basis of more recent studies of American vernacular houses. In the American hinterlands, and most important for the purposes of this study, in North Carolina, in Tennessee, and especially in the Arkansas Ozarks, the Greek Revival's simple forms, so well suited to frame construction, remained popular long after the Civil War. Indeed, in the study area subtle aspects linger well into the twentieth century, having been absorbed into the vernacular aesthetic.

As is well known, the Greek Revival style was carried west through several carpenters' handbooks long after it was out of fashion in eastern urban centers. The need for these handbooks is self-evident, i.e., the authors judged the elegance and complexity of the decorative moldings, the classical orders, the refined but elaborate doorways, etc., to be beyond the capabilities of the average rural carpenter. It is important to note that all of the architectural details documented in this study that were judged to reflect Greek Revival influence are so simple and diluted in form that they are within the capability of ordinary rural carpenters.

At this point the question might be asked why the early and mid-nineteenth-century Greek Revival elements are so pervasive and persistent when the Arkansas Ozarks generally were settled in a later period when the more romantic, picturesque styles, like the Italianate and the Queen Anne, were current. There may be three reasons for this. (1) To the extent that within the time frame 1830 to 1930 the Arkansas Ozarks had an "aristocracy," they would have been the first families who bought large parcels of the best land in the Springfield Plain areas and managed to establish themselves early on as successful farmers. Insofar as these earliest settlers were aware of architectural styles, it seems to have been the Greek Revival image that they brought with them. Thus, although most of the houses the early settlers built were already out of fashion with regard to the Greek Revival, they nevertheless may have served as models for what prosperous farmhouses should look like. (2) As discussed earlier, parts of Arkansas, notably the Springfield Plain areas of Washington and Benton counties, enjoyed a prosperity in the antebellum period that has hardly been equalled since. This prosperity contributed to the construction of several antebellum houses with varying degrees of consciousness of the Greek Revival style. (3) It is proposed here that many of the neoclassical elements popularized through the spread of the Greek Revival style were so adaptable to the vernacular building aesthetic and its severe, boxy symmetry that these elements were simply absorbed into the vernacular building tradition. Underscoring this supposition is the important fact that three common aspects of earlier high style

Greek Revival houses in the eastern and midwestern areas of the United States were never adopted in the Arkansas Ozarks—the hipped roof, the asymmetrical plan featuring a side hallway, and the gable-front house; it seems that these details were too contrary to the established vernacular building tradition. Moreover, Ozark Greek Revival–influenced vernacular buildings lack the elaborate details so elegant they would have needed a carpenter's handbook to be properly executed.

On the other hand, many smaller details with their roots in the Greek Revival tradition (and perhaps in the earlier Georgian Colonial Revival style as well) seem to have been absorbed into local custom. They include the use of transom and sidelights to illuminate central hallways; lintels of decorative moldings or pedimented lintels; pedimented gables; gable returns; boxed cornices; wide friezeboards at the eaves of both porches and the main block of houses; porch supports in the form of round or square columns; cornerboards that are made to resemble pilasters by having a small, unobtrusive shelf-like "capital" at the top; and moldings as decorative details both on the exterior and interior. The simplest detail, and often the only hint of Greek Revival influence, is the plain wide friezeboard outlining gables and porches that appears in all types of houses as the photographs attest.

It is important to note that builders were content to apply all these Greek Revival related details just discussed to the old traditional types. They appear most frequently on the I-house and the central hall cottage, but their durability is such that they often appear on the plainer types, such as the double pen with two front doors and even on the two new popular types that spring from Queen Anne–style influence, the prow house and the bent house. All such details are readily apparent in the photographs and are generally pointed out in the commentaries as well. Turning now to the influence of the newer, more decorative Queen Anne style, two of the three new popular house types—the prow house and the bent house—have their roots in this style and the Victorian pattern books that helped popularize it across the United States. This has been extensively discussed in chapter 4. The Queen Anne style–inspired decorative elements, such as turned porch columns, spindlework balustrades, "gingerbread" sawnwork, and the decorative shingles that occasionally sheathed gable fronts, are all readily visible in the photographs and are pointed out in the commentaries.

Review of Other Aspects of Ozark Vernacular Houses

The overwhelming choice of material for dwellings was wood. Brick houses were generally two-story emblems of rural prosperity. The field survey of Stone County indicates that not a single rural brick house was constructed there (or if so, none are extant) until after 1930. Despite the excellent stone craftsmanship displayed in many chimneys only one stone dwelling was documented in the study area, constructed by an Irish immigrant in Washington County.

Generally a high degree of log craftsmanship was retained well into the nineteenth century in many sections. In mountainous areas, people homesteading as late as the 1890s apparently built (or had built) their first houses of log, just as people had done two generations previously. Several box constructed houses were documented, and a diagram of this little-understood method is shown in fig. 7-13. Arkansas Ozark farmhouses were originally surrounded by an array of outbuildings necessary for farming. Three diagrams of exceptionally well-preserved farm layouts are presented in figs. 5-1, 5-2, and 5-3. As the traditional Ozark house types are typical of those in the Upland South, so also is the typical Ozark barn type, the transverse crib.

The original cultural landscape, of which the open range was an essential feature, persisted in the Ozarks until the 1950s. In the open range, the landscape seemed like a patchwork of little fenced-in fields and meadows and fenced-in yards of houses. A tripartite division of land existed, much like the division of land during the European medieval period, consisting of woodlands, pastures, and meadows. Since the woodlands were shared in common as pasturage, they represented yet another community bond. Today the little fences are gone and large acreages are instead enclosed with barbed wire, which is invisible from a distance. Many small farms have disappeared and have been replaced by specialized agricultural enterprises like raising cattle or raising chickens for the flourishing chicken processing industry in northwest Arkansas. Many small ramshackle outbuildings have been replaced by huge metal chicken sheds. Many community focal points have disappeared into the countryside as small stores, rural churches, and schools vanish. (It does seem common now, however, for old schoolhouses to be recycled into community churches with no architectural changes necessary.) The absence of old landmarks and fences upon the land exacerbates what European visitors to this country once complained of as an aspect altogether too "wild and formless."[12] As one travels through the countryside today, in all but the most prosperous and populous areas, the sight of a farmhouse is still a welcome one as the wilderness still prevails to a surprising degree, silently engulfing abandoned farmhouses, stone fences, and old farm implements rusting in the fields.

Ozark interiors were generally plain with a series of well-defined square or rectangular rooms with holes cut in the walls for windows and doors. Space set aside for formal use and even for stairways was minimal. Two characteristics remained constant regardless of the size of the house. Space for preparing and eating food was consistently separated from living and working spaces. A kitchen, usually combined with space for dining, was always located at the back of the house apart from the front rooms. Secondly, as is the case with small vernacular houses all over the world, the spaces were multifunctional. In Ozark houses, the combination of sleeping and living spaces was especially prevalent. An important factor in kitchen arrangements was that electricity had barely begun to appear by the close of the study period in 1930, so kitchen and laundry arrangements remained much the same as they were in the nineteenth century.

It is hoped that this study will provide a foundation for future researchers attempting to answer some of the many questions which the fieldwork has raised. Will future study validate the strict geographical distribution of the I-house and the dogtrot house types in which the former is associated with the Springfield Plain areas while dogtrot houses appear to cluster in more remote areas? Will stone houses appear as rarely throughout the Ozarks as they did in the study area? Who was responsible for the excellent log and stone craftsmanship? Were these itinerant craftsmen, or simply specialists within their own communities?

Finally, in much commentary about the Ozarks in general it is common to contrast the "hillmen" with the more affluent farmers of large acreages in fertile areas. This study has stressed topographical differences and their seemingly close relation to the distribution of house types. The two furnishings studies, as we have seen, contrast the small Blair log cabin with the large William Wilson I-house. The Blairs farmed seventy acres in the Boston Mountain area; the Wilsons farmed over two thousand acres in the fertile Springfield Plain. The Blairs depended upon magazines donated by the elder Mrs. Blair, a postmistress, for the annual repapering of their cabin walls; the Wilson family enjoyed William Wilson's substantial library. Is it, then, more accurate to stress that traditionally there were actually "two Ozarks" differentiated by soil fertility, transportation facilities, topography, and differing standards of comfortable living? When one takes the broad view presented by the range of dwelling types in the area, the answer points to a fundamental unity in the Arkansas Ozarks rather than a fundamental divergence. The wealthiest families, like the Wilsons, seemed to live with little class distinction, much like their neighbors. The differences in houses is more that of size than of a desire to be individualistic and to impress one's neighbors. In all areas, ostentation was generally avoided. Moreover, whether in the Springfield Plain or the Boston Mountains, a time lag in building technology and in architectural styles is consistently apparent. The Wilson house with its braced frame construction was obsolete technologically in 1859 just as the log Blair house was obsolete at the end of the nineteenth century. Architects were not called in to design houses, nor were houses copied directly from nineteenth-century architectural plan books. Even the differences delineated here between the traditional house types and the nontraditional popular ones do not extend across the full architectural design spectrum. Rather, all houses were designed either fully within tradition-based building practices or they exhibit merely a grafting-on of selected new aspects to the traditional house types. The dwellings themselves, then, reinforce the idea of a unified, traditional, and conservative society, closely related to the vernacular house types—and undoubtedly to the traditional culture as well—of Tennessee, North Carolina, and Kentucky, the states of origin for most early settlers in the Arkansas Ozarks.

Appendix

Interview with Mrs. Novelle Baumert, Pleasant Grove, Arkansas, June 1985

Life in a One-Room Log House (c. 1920–26)

The House

Novelle Baumert: My father bought the log house in 1910 and I was born in it in 1913. My sister, five years older, was born in another house. Different families had lived in the log house. I guess the one log room was about eighteen by eighteen feet and the lean-to kitchen was about nine by eighteen feet. It was chinked with shingles and white mortar and there were inside sealing boards, too. It was a "saddle notch" log house. The kitchen was box construction. My parents' names were Albert and Daisy Ford Blair. They married in 1906. He was born in 1882 and she was born in 1881.

Inside the House

NB: There was a root cellar that must have been five by six feet that you could only reach from inside the house. You went through a trapdoor that was right in front of the hearth. The chimney formed one wall of the cellar and it had shelves to hold canned fruit, and a bin with sand in it held the sweet potatoes or molasses. We might put the eggs down there if it was real cold; the kitchen was real cold. A jar of peaches left in the kitchen would freeze.

Furnishings

NB: [In the big room] Daddy's bed, Sister's bed, a three-quarter bed, a dresser, two rocking chairs, Mama's trunk, a spoolcase with nine small drawers, and a square table with a shelf below it with books on it and above a kerosene lamp. There were three crocheted rugs, one over the trapdoor in front of the hearth. The [battery-operated, short-range] telephone was right by the front door over Mama's trunk. Mama and I slept together here in the three-quarter bed in the back corner of the room with me up against the wall snuggled against my mother. I felt snug and safe in the world. Sister's bed was in the front corner and Daddy's bed in the other back corner. Daddy would sneak in bed with Mama when he built a fire in the mornings and that would make me mad. Mama was real protective. We couldn't ever get our feet wet. Mama was very clean. We had a shuck mop that Daddy made. It was a board with lots of holes and a handle. You would take the shucks and get them soft in hot water and then poke them through these holes. Here's how we would clean the floors: we would put sandrock [white and soft sand] in the wash pot and we would heat the rock until it made it soft, then we would hammer it out to be smaller on a board, then we would put it in a pan and scatter it on the floor and throw water and homemade soap on it, too. Then we would mop and then rinse with a broom and buckets of water. Mama liked to do this every week. You would really get splinters if you went barefoot on it. This would make the floors all pretty and white. Mama had a rule that after we washed the dishes we would set the table right back again. We would put on four goblets, four plates (all turned over), a molasses pitcher or vinegar, a jar of pickles. We had a cloth to cover the table in between meals. She would send us kids out to get a peach switch to fight flies if we had company. We had an oilcloth tablecloth. It was a big thrill to buy new oilcloth for the table once a year, especially if we were expecting company. Daddy made our walnut table when they first got married.

About the Papered Walls

NB: The kitchen walls were just aged wood, no paint or paper on them. The front room was papered every year with newspapers or, preferably, magazines. *Comfort Magazine* was one. Daddy's mother was the postmistress at Redstripe (her name was Bertie Blair), and so she could afford magazines.

About Beautifying the House

Jean Sizemore: You mentioned the geraniums on the front porch and the morning glories growing up strings; what was inside the house to make it attractive?

NB: There were more plants than geraniums. There were ferns, too. I think Mama must have kept them in the root cellar during winter. There were asparagus ferns and Boston ferns and another fern. You could get them with a subscription to *Comfort Magazine.* She put the ferns on the porch somewhere. In the winter she would bring the ferns and geraniums out every sunny day from the root cellar. Inside, there were green window shades and lace curtains. I remember there was a picture. It was a black-and-white angel print with flowers on the outside of it. The only other thing I remember hanging on the wall was the pretty wall pocket that Sister made around 1922. It was embroidered with a design of a basket of flowers on it. Our neighbor taught her how to embroider. We kept patterns in it. On the mantel were some pretty things. A clock, a tin box decorated with red acorns; the tin box had tobacco in it from great-grandfather's store at St. James and we also kept our receipts from the store account in it. Also a yellow-and-white milky basket and a rose-colored milky vase. We had pretty and heavy white counterpanes on the beds. They were so heavy that Daddy had to wring them out when they were washed every spring cleaning. We had pillow shams that were white with little red cross-stitch designs in a lily pattern; one said "Good Night," the other said "Good Morning." I remember the pretty stand Daddy made; it was thirty-two inches square out of walnut and it had a carved scallop on each corner. It sat in front of the dresser.

JS: Tell me where the kerosene lamps were located; did you sit around the lamps in the evening?

NB: No, the lamps were on either side of the room. There was one on the little stand Daddy made and the other one sat on the dresser. The one on the dresser could be carried into the kitchen, but the one on the stand stayed there all the time.

JS: When did you get electricity?

NB: Not until 1950. To tell you the truth, I think my Dad was afraid of it. But we had a battery radio, and of course the telephone was just a little local battery-operated one and we had a gasoline iron.

In the Kitchen

NB: A dining table which Daddy made, a wood stove, a piesafe, a wood box, two big wooden buckets which held flour and meal, a wash shelf that held two buckets with a stand underneath for the wash pan (the dippers were in the bucket). There was a corner triangular [closet] consisting of two shelves with cloth tacked over it all. Also hanging on the back wall was a piece of oilcloth tacked up and pots and pans hanging beneath it. Mama had a large wooden sifter that would fit in the buckets that held the cornmeal and flour. These buckets sat on the floor in the back wall corner nearest the backdoor.

About Housekeeping and Storage

NB: Mama's trunk had the Sunday clothes in it. We could hang coats in the corner closet. If you weren't using the quilts they could go in the bed between the feather mattress and the straw ticking. The flour and meal were stored in wooden buckets on the floor in the kitchen.

JS: Where were your everyday clothes kept?

NB: I think they hung in the kitchen on a nail under that curtain. I don't think anything hung in the front room. And then we kept them in the dresser drawers. We didn't have many. Or you could store things in boxes. I remember my Grandmother Blair had a "quiltstack"—a big stack of quilts covered with a sheet that was piled up on top of a big storage box higher than your head, and it didn't look bad at all.

JS: Where would people iron?

NB: In the winter in the kitchen, but in the summer we would take it outside and build a little fire with a piece of tin over it to heat the iron on.

JS: Would people use the front porch for chores?

NB: Yes, our neighbors used to comb through cotton they gathered up while sitting on the porch. But, as I told you, my mother seemed to always work sitting in the chair in our side yard.

JS: Where would you sit in the living room to do things like shell peas or make the cloth strips for rugs?

NB: In the chairs in front of the fireplace.

About Food

NB: Every morning we had biscuits. We had light bread once a week. For breakfast usually we would have biscuits, jelly, eggs, bacon, and sometimes ham. For dinner at noon we would have dried peas or beans, potatoes, okra, spinach, sometimes ham and cornbread. We always had cornbread and milk for supper. We didn't have much beef because Daddy couldn't raise much corn on this poor ground to fatten many hogs or beef. So we rarely had beef. But we had chicken on Sunday. We usually had fried chicken because Daddy didn't like chicken and dumplings. Daddy only killed about two hogs. Mama would keep the sausage in muslin down in the center of the lard stand—a large metal container of about forty-eight pounds of lard—bought from the store. A stand in the spring would last through the fall. In spring we would also buy one hundred pounds of sugar. This would get us through the canning season, then we'd just buy a quarter's worth at a time. We sold chickens for twenty cents a pound at the store. We sold eggs, too. We sold eggs regularly, but the chickens only now and then, and some roosters, too.

JS: How did you keep things cold?

NB: We didn't. In back of the smokehouse we had a low place scooped out and stoneware jars with milk in them sitting down in buckets full of water. We would have to keep these buckets full of cool water and sometimes changed the water four or five times a day. In real hot weather, we would set the milk in a larger crock of well water and we would have to refresh it five or six times a day. That's how you kept milk from blinkin' from morning to night. We set the butter in a deep bowl on top of the milk. Mother would churn every other day. After our big cellar was done, Mama could can six hundred quarts a year. In the big drought during the Depression, we had two years worth of canned food. I remember that in the root cellar we kept pumpkins, too, besides the canned vegetables and the sweet potatoes.

Activities after Supper

NB: At night we would read or shell peas or learn our embroidery. We bought the thread. I wrote a poem once about a bushel of peas. I'd like to catch the hulls afire on the hearth. We had all kinds of peas: whippoorwill peas, wild goose peas, polecat peas (they're white with maroon spots), crowder peas, clay peas, red rippers. Dad would repair shoes at night. He was a J. P. [justice of the peace] and a notary public. In the fall he made sorghum; he would set up a mill in the side yard and he'd get every ninth gallon, so he really didn't need to grow any sorghum.

JS: Where would your daddy play the banjo?

NB: In the winter in front of the fireplace; in summertime, out on the front porch. Sometimes his brothers would come over and they would all play together out on the front porch.

JS: Did you ever know anyone when you were growing up who had a parlor just used for that purpose without a bed in it?

NB: No, to tell the truth, I didn't. My Grandmother Blair had a four-room house but there were beds in all the main rooms and in the room she called a parlor. There was an organ in the parlor and a real pretty standtable, about thirty-six inches high with a shelf underneath. It had a white tablecloth trimmed with crochet because she crocheted a lot, and it had a picture or two and maybe a pretty necktie case. Seems like the Bible was on the shelf underneath. Mama kept our Bible in the dresser drawer.

About Company

JS: What about company you might have had?

NB: Men would come for Dad to fill out papers for them at noon and Mama would ask them to stay and eat. Sunday we might have a visitor or two. Most of our visitors were relatives.

JS: Do you remember going to play parties, and if so, where were they held?

NB: I only remember them in the summertime outside.

About Books

JS: What about books?

NB: We didn't have many. A friend had some children's books that we borrowed. I remember reading "Grandaddy Long Legs." My sister would read books over and over. I remember reading *A Christmas Story* for Christmas and Mother Goose rhymes. I don't remember any novels, really. Daddy would buy *Grit* and a newspaper called the *Chicago-American.* He took *Farm and Ranch Magazine* for a year or two.

About Weaving and Quilting

JS: What about weaving and quilting?

NB: The quilt frames hung down from the ceiling. Mama had geese and she also made pillows and beds. I remember Mrs. Copeland had a big loom and she would weave rugs for people who brought their own strings. Mama would tear up strips of material, then we would sew them together and wind them in big balls (about head-size), three or four of them, and she would make a three-by-four- or five-feet rug for about twenty-five cents a yard.

About Wool

NB: We washed and pulled out the burrs and then put it on the barn roof to dry. Then we put it in gunny sacks and shipped it to St. Louis by the mail wagon. Sometimes we would dig up May apples and "red root" and sell that, too. It went to the St. Louis Commission Company. We also dug black haw bark for that company. My mother would reknit socks. My grandmother would knit the wool ones.

In the Yard and around the Exterior of the House

NB: On the front porch there was Daddy's big tool chest and a shelf with geraniums on it. Daddy would barber part time, and he cut people's hair on the front porch. Growing up at one end of the porch Mama had strings of morning glories and balsam cucumbers (with ornamental red balls). The smokehouse was close to the rear of the house, near the back door. The well was to the rear of that, and the wash kettle was a little beyond that. The wash bench would move around. Often it was by the smokehouse; it moved so we could follow the shade; it held two tubs and a washboard. Besides washing in the wash kettle, we also rendered lard to make soap and heated water.

JS: What about the outhouse?

NB: We didn't have one; lots of people didn't. Our first outhouse was built after the Depression when FHA loans were available. With the loan we also bought dishes, bread pans, silverware, cotton mattresses, a sifter. Daddy would go out behind the barn and Mother and Sister and I went out in the weeds to the east. There was no boys' outhouse even at our school. We kept chamberpots under the bed at night, but not in the daytime. There was no side porch. There was a big rock step at the backdoor. In the little space between the smokehouse and the side of the house, there was a chair usually where Mama sat to peel apples, or shell peas, or snap beans. Mama dried a lot of peaches and apples. On the front porch Daddy had a long toolbox made out of planks. There were also dried apples on nails on the front porch.

JS: What about the smokehouse?

NB: Onions hung on the smokehouse in bunches. The broom may have hung in the kitchen under the curtain, but I know the mop hung in the smokehouse. There was a ceiling over part of it and hooks to hang things from the rafters.

About the Yard

NB: The yard would grow up in those yellow bitterweeds and we kids would have to pull them. Big jimpson weeds would grow, too; Dad would mow them down with a mower.

JS: Were there a lot of snakes around?

NB: I think the hogs killed them. You know, I think they are worse now.

The Barn and the Arrangement of the Whole Acreage

[See layout of location of barn and pastures, fig. 8-19.]

NB: In the pasture we kept three mules and three or four cows, but the cows could go all over the place; so could the pigs. In the orchard we grew apples, peaches, and pears. We would dry them on top of the barn. After they were dried they'd be put in a sack. It was hard to keep the worms out. Sassafrass would help to keep the worms out. Sometimes we would have to carry the sacks out to sit in the sun or heat in the oven to kill all the worms. We had a chicken house maybe twenty feet long; it had two compartments, one with a roost, the other with nests. The owls were bad, but the foxes and coyotes were kept down by hunting. Now the coyotes will get all the chickens. We owned seventy acres total. One year we raised tobacco near the barn. The ground was too poor for corn, but we raised some. We raised cotton, but we had to fertilize for it. We took it to the gin at Pleasant Grove and then to Batesville. We always grew something for hay, maize, and sudan grass. Every hill of corn we grew had peas also. The crowder peas would pull the corn down. The acreage was in two places; there was the forty acres near the house then there was Dad's other thirty acres separated from the house by Smith's land. In the forty acres near the house we switched crops and pasture. In the back thirty acres we grew vegetables: Irish potatoes, dried beans, squash, tomatoes, okra, cucumbers, beets, spinach, and turnip greens. We could ride the old mules out to the garden in the back thirty acres. We could put the vegetables we picked in sacks on the mule's back. Mama tended this garden. She would get so busy that she would get Sister to fix supper.

About the Barn

NB: This barn was built when I was small; the first one blew away. It held mule stables, pea bin, cotton seedbin, corn crib; it had a door to scoop corn from the wagon into the barn in the barn drive. We used to hang Irish potatoes on the side of the barn or keep them on the ground near the edge of the corn crib and then bring them in the root cellar. The barn loft was for corn tops for fodder. In the barn we kept the corn and all Mama's peas in a bin in one corner. There was a big wooden box and also gunny sacks full of peas. We'd shell peas about January and get ready to sell them. We'd put them in a fifty-pound flour sack and then when it was full, we'd take it to the Pleasant Grove store to sell for seed. Sister and I would get a batch to shell and get to keep the money. And we each had a hen's nest to get money from.

About the 1926 House

[This is the house Mrs. Baumert presently lives in; it is a one-story, double pen plan with two front doors; it was constructed immediately adjacent to the site of the small log house in which she was raised. See fig. 4-24.]

NB: This house had an ell porch on the rear and the side. Dad built it with the help of a carpenter. He got the lumber from the back thirty. He took it to Grandad's sawmill. He planed the original weatherboard, every bit. The front weatherboard on the house was replaced in the 1940s.

About Mrs. Baumert's Later Life

NB: I went to DeShay High School for two years, but I didn't finish. Mother died and Dad wanted me to stay here. Daddy always lived here in this house with us (her own later family). He said it was just like having his family here all over again. I moved to Hanford, Washington, in the winter of 1943 to work. I lived in the Ladies' Barracks. That was where I met my husband; he was from Austin, Texas. After the war we moved in here with Daddy.

Notes

Notes to Chapter 1

1. Diane Tebbetts, "Traditional Houses of Independence County, Arkansas," *Pioneer America* 10 (June 1978): 37–55. Dr. Tebbetts' informative study is the only article on rural Arkansas Ozark houses to be published in a scholarly journal. It defines only traditional house types, however, and is limited to Independence County.
2. Dell Upton and John Michael Vlach, *Common Places: Readings in American Vernacular Architecture* (Athens and London: University of Georgia Press, 1986), xv.
3. Ibid., xvi.
4. Ibid.
5. Ibid.
6. Ibid.
7. Henry Glassie, *Pattern in the Material Folk Culture of the Eastern United States* (Philadelphia: University of Pennsylvania Press, 1968), 5.
8. Allen G. Noble, *Wood, Brick and Stone: The North American Settlement Landscape*, vol. 1, *Houses* (Amherst: University of Massachusetts Press, 1984), 107.
9. Glassie, *Pattern,* 4.
10. Noble, 107.
11. Glassie, *Pattern,* 33.

Notes to Chapter 2

1. N. M. Fenneman, *Physiography of Eastern United States* (New York: McGraw-Hill, 1938), 631. As geographer Milton Rafferty has noted, the exact boundaries of the Ozarks are subject to interpretation and disagreement among the experts. Some, for example, expand the Ozark boundaries to include the Arkansas River Valley and the Ouachita Ridge. Some also include the Shawneetown Hills, which stretch across southern Illinois. Rafferty himself delineates the boundaries as follows: "The boundaries of the Ozarks are marked in a general way by major rivers. On the east is the Mississippi . . . . On the north the Ozarks extend just beyond the Missouri River. . . . The Black River parallels the southeastern boundary of the Ozarks. . . . The southern boundary follows along the low hills that parallel the north side of the Arkansas River valley. The western boundary is not as well defined. In the southwest the Neosho River (sometimes Grand River) and its tributary, Spring River, form a visible boundary. The remainder of the western boundary . . . follows the seam where Pennsylvanian-age rocks . . . overlap

older Mississippian-age rocks." Milton Rafferty, *The Ozarks: Land and Life* (Norman: University of Oklahoma Press, 1980), 3.

2. Rafferty, 3–4.

3. John Solomon Otto and Ben Wayne Banks, "The Banks Family of Yell County, Arkansas: A 'Plain Folk' Family of the Highlands South," *Arkansas Historical Quarterly* 61 (1982): 153. "Trees living in ultisols possess deep, complex networks of roots to collect leaching minerals; consequently, most of the nutrients are locked up in living forest vegetation and not in the soils."

4. C. F. Marbut, *Soil Reconnaissance of the Ozark Region of Missouri and Arkansas* (Washington, D.C.: Government Printing Office, 1914), 1840.

5. Robert Walz, "Migration into Arkansas 1834–1880" (Ph.D. diss., University of Texas, 1958), 38.

6. Rafferty, 7.

7. O. O. Maxfield, "The Geography of the Boston Mountains" (Ph.D. diss., Ohio State University, 1963), 2. The greatest width of the Boston Mountains is forty-five miles along a north-south line extended through Green Forest, Arkansas, according to Maxfield. They are surrounded by the Springfield Plain, the Gulf Coastal Plain, the Arkansas Valley, and the Osage Plain to the north, east, south, and west, respectively.

8. Rafferty, 18.

9. Marbut, 1781.

10. Maxfield, 117.

11. Rafferty, 19.

12. Ibid., 14.

13. Maxfield, 131–42. Maxfield makes a detailed comparison of agriculture within the Boston Mountains and other areas within Arkansas using data from Virgil B. Fielder, *Type of Farming Areas in Arkansas,* Agricultural Experiment Station Bulletin 555 (Fayetteville: University of Arkansas, 1955).

14. E. Joan Wilson Miller, "The Ozark Culture Region as Revealed by Traditional Materials," *Annals of Association of American Geographers* 58 (March 1968): 51–71.

15. The culmination of interest in the rich folk material of the Arkansas Ozarks was the establishment in 1971 of the Ozark Folk Center in Mountain View, Arkansas (Stone County), as a state park dedicated to the documentation and preservation of Ozark traditional culture. A professional folklorist is on the staff; an archives has been established, and ongoing demonstrations of traditional Ozark crafts and concerts of folk music are held throughout most of the year. In addition, another Ozark archives, the Regional Culture Center, was recently established at Arkansas College in Batesville (Independence County).

16. Interview with Truman Davis, Pleasant Grove vicinity, Stone County, October 15, 1984.

17. Miller, 55.

18. Walz, 115.

19. Maxfield, 109.

20. John Solomon Otto and Augustus Marion Burns III, "Traditional Agricultural Practices in the Arkansas Highlands," *Journal of American Folklore* 94, no. 372 (1981): 166–87.

21. Ibid., 1. Otto and Burns assert that the forest fallowing practiced in the Southern Highlands originated with the Scotch-Irish who adapted the bush fallowing they had practiced in Ireland to the more heavily forested New World by adopting Delaware Indian techniques of forest fallowing and slash-and-burn cultivation. For a detailed history of these methods, the reader is referred to this excellent study, 177–81.

22. In the mid-1830s Albert Pike described a typical Arkansas farmstead: "It was like most other settlements in this country. A field of about forty acres was under cultivation, filled with huge blackened trunks, gigantic skeletons of trees, throwing their bare, withered sapless branches forth, as though a whirlwind had been among them with its crashing destruction." Albert Pike, "Letters from Arkansas," in *Travels in the Old South: Selected from Periodicals of the Times,* Eugene Schwaab and Jacqueline Bull, eds. (Lexington: University of Kentucky Press, 1973), 216–17.
23. Otto and Burns, 185–86.
24. Ibid., 183.
25. Rafferty, 149.
26. Otto and Burns, 172.
27. Ibid., 177.
28. Otto and Banks, 163.
29. Rafferty, 4.
30. Carl O. Sauer, *The Geography of the Ozark Highland of Missouri (*University of Chicago, 1920; reprint, New York: AMS Press, 1971), 4–5.
31. Ibid., 6.

Notes to Chapter 3

1. Malcolm Rohrbaugh, *The Trans-Appalachian Frontier* (New York: Oxford University Press, 1978), 272–73.
2. Leland DuVall, *Arkansas: Colony and State* (Little Rock: Rose Publishing Co. 1973), 1.
3. David Tucker, *Arkansas: A People and Their Reputation* (Memphis: Memphis State University Press, 1985), 62.
4. For example, the illiteracy rates among whites were higher in the Ozarks than in more populous and centrally located counties in Arkansas in 1910, according to the U.S. Census. The three populous counties had the following rates of illiteracy: Jefferson County, 2.3 percent; Pulaski County (where the capital is located), 2.7 percent; Sebastian County, 4.2 percent. Four typical Ozark counties had the following rates of illiteracy: Stone County, 12 percent; Newton County, 13 percent; Madison County, 11.4 percent; and Izard County, 11.3 percent. *U.S. Bureau of Census, Thirteenth Census of the United States* 2, *Population 1910,* Table of Composition and Characteristics of Population for States and for Counties, Arkansas, Table 1 (Washington, D.C.: Government Printing Office, 1913), 118–31. The family income was not listed on the U.S. Census until 1959. According to the 1959 U.S. Census, the median family incomes in the three previously cited populous counties were the following: Jefferson County, $3,671; Pulaski County, $4,935; Sebastian County, $4,241. Median family incomes in four typical Ozark counties were the following: Stone County, $1,740; Newton County, $1,666; Madison County, $1,928; Izard County, $2,953. U.S. Bureau of Census, *Eighteenth Census of Population* 1, *Characteristics of Population*: *Part V, Arkansas* (Washington, D.C.: Government Printing Office, 1960), 5-214, 5-219. (The figures in Washington County prove, once again, that it was atypical of the Ozarks as a whole. Washington County's rate of illiteracy in 1910 was 4.3 percent and the median family income in 1959 was $3,683.)
5. Harry Ashmore, *Arkansas: A Bicentennial History* (New York: W. W. Norton and Co., 1978), xvii.

6. *Arkansas Gazette*, May 23, 1832.

7. Before steamboats began ascending the rivers of Arkansas in 1822, and somewhat later on the White River, immigrants depended upon the flatboat, the dugout, and the keelboat. The flatboat was unwieldy for poling up the rivers of Arkansas, all of which flow generally southeasterly. The dugout was more maneuverable but could carry only limited cargo. Immigrants seem to have favored the keelboat because it combined the best features, having considerable capacity as well as maneuverability. See Walz, 316.

8. Walter Moffatt, "Transportation in Arkansas, 1819–1840," *Arkansas Historical Quarterly* 15 (Autumn 1956): 191. Moffatt's article is full of horror stories of early travel in Arkansas gleaned from journals of hardy travelers and from accounts in the *Arkansas Gazette* of poor travel conditions. These nineteenth-century accounts form only the beginning of a long legacy of anecdotes and jokes about poor transportation in Arkansas, culminating, perhaps, in a best-selling twenty-five-cent joke book published in 1903 called *On a Slow Train through Arkansas*.

9. As late as 1835, mail service between Little Rock and Memphis (which traveled over one of the earliest and best roads in the territory) was so bad that a public meeting of protest was held. *Arkansas Gazette*, January 31, 1835.

10. Walz, 19.

11. The revisionist view of Arkansas's bid for statehood is best expressed in David M. Tucker's *Arkansas: A People and Their Reputation:* "The movement for statehood began in 1833 when the Territory of Michigan applied for admission to the union . . . as a free state without human slavery and this, of course, threatened to upset the congressional custom of balancing the number of free and slave states. Arkansas planters and representatives claimed that Southern patriotism required pushing Arkansas forward as a candidate for statehood to prevent Michigan from tipping the balance of power against slavery. . . . Banking to be sure, was not then made the leading issue in the debate but it was later charged that the planters' desire for banking had been the central reason for pushing Arkansas prematurely into the Union at a time when her population of 52,000 was only half that of Michigan." Tucker, 20.

12. Walz, 295.

13. Rohrbaugh, 282.

14. Ibid., 272, 292.

15. Ibid., 286.

16. *Batesville News*, November 22, 1938.

17. Kent R. Brown, *Fayetteville: A Pictorial History* (Norfolk and Virginia Beach: Donning Co. Publishers, 1982), 14.

18. Bruce Francis Pilcher, "The Settlement Geography of Prairie Township, Washington County, Arkansas" (M.A. thesis, University of Arkansas, 1975), 33.

19. Arkansas Historic Preservation Program, "Historic Resources of Stone County, Arkansas," Nomination to the National Register of Historic Places (Little Rock: 1985), 2.

20. Pilcher, 57–58.

21. Bernice Karnes, "Early Days at West Fork," *Flashback* (November 1956): 14.

22. "Early Store Ledgers in Washington County," *Flashback* (August 1957): 5.

23. Ashmore, 68.

24. Tucker, 7.

25. C. Fred Williams, et al., *A Documentary History of Arkansas* (Fayetteville: University of Arkansas Press, 1984), 50. The informative discussion about the plantation system in Arkansas in this recent book asserts: "Economically the plantation was the more important (in comparison to the self-sufficient farm) and specialized in cash crops, often to the point that food had to be purchased from outside. These large-scale

enterprises varied in size, but generally they contained at least two hundred acres of land actually under cultivation. Unless the planter had this much, plus more acres to put into operation after the older land had played out, it was simply not feasible for him to emphasize a single crop. The census does not provide a clear indication of the number of plantations, but of 33,190 farms in Arkansas in 1860, only 4,607 possessed more than one hundred acres."

26. Rafferty, 48.

27. James Doolin, "Conditions of Slavery in Washington County," *Flashback* (February 1980): 5–7.

28. Sauer, 141.

29. W. J. Lemke and Ted R. Worley, *The Butterfield Overland Mail in Arkansas* (Little Rock: Arkansas History Commission, 1957), 3–5. Lemke and Worley explain: "From Fayetteville southward over the Boston Mountains to Van Buren, the Butterfield's engineers had selected the old Boston Mountain Road which was rougher but more direct than the Cane Hill Road. This Boston Mountain section of the route soon earned a reputation as 'the roughest ten miles between St. Louis and San Francisco.'"

30. Tucker, 26.

31. Pilcher, 42.

32. Arkansas Historic Preservation Program, "Historic Resources of Stone County," 3.

33. Sandra Luther, "A Brief History of Stone County," *Heritage of Stone* 1, no. 1 (June 1972): 8.

34. Sauer, 116.

35. Williams, et al., 100–101. The most striking testimony to Unionist support among Arkansas was the enlistment of some fifteen thousand white and black men in the Union army.

36. Pilcher, 43.

37. W. Stockard, *The History of Lawrence, Jackson, Independence and Stone Counties Arkansas: Counties of the 3rd Judicial District* (Little Rock: Arkansas Democrat Co., 1904), 69.

38. Ashmore, 97.

39. Tucker, 38.

40. Kent R. Brown, 22.

41. Robert Besom, "The Golden Age of Brick in Washington County," *Flashback* (August 1981): 13–23.

42. Miller, 55.

43. Ashmore, 116.

44. Ibid., 119.

45. DuVall, 2.

46. Williams, et al., 123.

47. Ashmore, 121.

48. Karnes, 18.

49. "Washington County's Great Cultivated Acreage," *The Republic* (St. Louis: April 5, 1897), 9.

50. Kent R. Brown, 40.

51. Zella Carr and Eugene Gibson, "A History of Summers Community," vertical file, Washington County Historical Society.

52. C. Allen Brown, "The Benjamin F. Johnson Residence, Middle Fork Valley," *Flashback* (November 1980): 12.

53. Kent R. Brown, 40.

54. Luther, 11.

55. Rafferty, 185–86.
56. Tucker, 82.
57. Ibid.
58. Rafferty, 176.
59. Ibid., 173.
60. Tucker, 64.
61. Clarence Jetton, "Twelve Years on Cajun Creek," *Heritage of Stone* 10(1) (1986): 4.
62. Rafferty, 185.
63. Ibid.
64. Ibid., 150.
65. Ibid.
66. Pilcher, 40.
67. Carl L. Schiefer, Jr., "Washington County, Arkansas: A Geography of Population Change, 1840–1970" (M.A. thesis, University of Arkansas, 1976), 52.
68. U.S. Department of Agriculture, Bureau of Census, *Census of Agriculture 1930* 11, Part 2, Table 1 (Washington, D.C.: Government Printing Office, 1931), 784.
69. W. A. Browne, "Some Frontier Conditions in the Hilly Portions of the Ozarks," *Journal of Geography* 28(5) (May 1929): 181–87.
70. Ruth Holt Payne, "Living Off the Land," *Flashback* (November 1975): 20.
71. Stacey Kocher, "The Kochers' Wheat Threshing," *Heritage of Stone* 9(2) (1985): 12–13.
72. According to Bernice Karnes's reminiscences of early days in Washington County, the singing schools often continued for eight weeks, meeting on Saturday and Sunday for all-day sessions, with one dollar paid for the entire instruction. The pupils learned to sing by note. "On the last Sunday of the term everyone in the neighborhood assembled for an all-day affair to hear the pupils demonstrate what they had learned." Karnes, 13.
73. Kent R. Brown, 25.
74. Ibid., 10.
75. Conrad Q. Russell, "Lincoln's Apple Heritage," *Flashback* (February 1979): 28.
76. Ibid., 26–27.
77. Verna Williams, "Early History of Herpel," *Heritage of Stone* 1(2) (1983): 2.
78. Melissa Loy Massey, "History of School District No. 54," *Heritage of Stone* 1(54) (June 1972): 24.
79. Interview with Renzo Hurst, Cove Creek, Arkansas, June 15, 1984.
80. Interview with W. A. Lower, Fayetteville, Arkansas, June 1, 1984.
81. Interview with Agnes Pierce, Cove Creek, Arkansas, June 30, 1984.
82. Ashmore, 121.

Notes to Chapter 4

1. Fred Kniffen, "Folk Housing: Key to Diffusion," *Annals of the Association of American Geographers* 55(4) (December 1965): 553.
2. Tebbetts, 45–46.
3. Kniffen, "Folk Housing," 549–77.
4. Glassie, *Pattern* 35–37. Glassie differs from Kniffen only in that he cites four cultural hearth source areas, instead of three, by differentiating the southernmost culture hearth into two spheres: the area of the Chesapeake Bay and the Atlantic coast from southern North Carolina through Georgia.

5. Robert Bastian, "Indiana Folk Architecture: A Lower Midwestern Index," *Pioneer America* (December 1977): 116.
6. Kniffen, "Folk Housing," 558.
7. Glassie, *Pattern,* 39.
8. Kniffen, "Folk Housing," 561.
9. Ibid.
10. Martin Wright, "Log Culture in Hill Louisiana," (Ph.D. diss., Louisiana State University, 1956), 35.
11. Pierce Lewis, "The Geography of Old Houses," *Earth and Mineral Sciences* 39(5) (February 1970): 33.
12. Henry Glassie, *Folk Housing in Middle Virginia* (Knoxville: University of Tennessee Press, 1975), 163.
13. Amos Rapoport, *House Form and Culture* (Englewood Cliffs, N.J.: Prentice-Hall Co., 1969), 5.
14. Upton and Vlach, xxi.
15. Rapoport, 4.
16. Glassie, *Middle Virginia*, 166.
17. Ibid.
18. Rapoport, 5.
19. Henry Glassie, "The Types of the Southern Mountain Cabin," in J. H. Brunvand, ed., *The Study of American Folklore* (New York: W. W. Norton & Co., 1968), 340.
20. Many scholars have noted the persistence of the sixteen-by-sixteen-foot dimension in single pen houses with varying explanations. Eugene Wilson states that the distance between a pair of crucks in old English building tradition was one bay, or about sixteen feet. Wilson also cites the frequent answer that the length of the bay was originally determined by the space required to house four oxen. (See Eugene Wilson, *Alabama Folk Houses* [Montgomery: Alabama Historical Commission, 1975], 54. Another reason often cited is that sixteen by sixteen feet represents the room size most comfortably warmed by a single fireplace. Henry Glassie has this to say on the subject, "In England, this square house or room was generally sixteen feet on a side. The usual reason offered to explain these dimensions is that this was the amount of space comfortable for oxen, but whether or not a byre or (as is more likely) some system of folk measurement lies at its origin, its persistence would seem to owe a debt to the comfort a carrier of Anglo-American culture feels within a square space about sixteen feet on a side." (See Glassie, *Middle Virginia*, 118.)
21. Presumably, the Tidewater-influenced floor plan in the study area corresponds with the floor plans of Texas log buildings, according to Terry Jordan's extensive study. (See Terry Jordan, *Texas Log Buildings: A Folk Architecture* [Austin: University of Texas Press, 1978], 108.) Conversely, Diane Tebbetts' study of traditional houses in Independence County, Arkansas (a county adjacent to Stone County on the east), found that the single pen houses were almost evenly divided between square and rectangular. It is not clear, however, whether Dr. Tebbetts was using the strictest definition of a rectangular floor plan, i.e., one in which the sides exceed the length of the facade by at least five feet. (See Tebbetts, 44.)
22. In his study of folk houses of the Little Dixie area of Missouri, Howard Wight Marshall found that two-story single pen houses were common enough to be considered a major type, appearing in both log and balloon frame construction and in both towns and the countryside. See Howard Wight Marshall, *Folk Architecture in Little Dixie: A Regional Culture in Missouri* (Columbia: University of Missouri Press, 1981), 57–62.
23. Doug Swaim, "North Carolina Folk Housing," in Doug Swaim, ed., *Carolina*

Dwelling: Toward Preservation of Place; In Celebration of the Vernacular Landscape. Student Publication of the School of Design, 26. (Raleigh: North Carolina State University, 1978), 32.

24. Tebbetts, 45.
25. Ibid., 46.
26. Jordan, *Texas Log Buildings,* 115.
27. Ibid., 117–18.
28. Glassie, *Pattern,* 89, 98. As Glassie notes, the term "dogtrot" is used promiscuously and confusingly. The key element is not simply the open hallway, for this can be created when a wing is added to the rear or end with a breezeway left between, but rather the key distinguishing feature is an open hall separating units of equal size and symmetrical relationship.
29. Jordan, *Texas Log Buildings,* 119.
30. Glassie, *Pattern,* 112.
31. Jordan, *Texas Log Buildings,* 119.
32. Ibid., 123.
33. In her survey of Independence County, Arkansas, traditional houses, Diane Tebbetts estimated that dogtrot houses comprised 22 percent of the total. (See Tebbetts, 47.) Independence County, as noted earlier, adjoins Stone County on the east, but is not nearly as mountainous and isolated.
34. Mr. Noah McCarn's fine, unremodeled dogtrot house of 1920 in Stone County is an exception. Located on Highway 5, a heavily traveled tourist route into Mountain View (site of the Ozark Folk Center), the house is a great attraction for amateur photographers who frequently stop and ask permission to photograph it. The taciturn Mr. McCarn finds this bothersome, rues the day the road was paved, and wishes he could afford to close up his breezeway.
35. Swaim, 38. See also Bastian, 123.
36. Kniffen, "Folk Housing," 555.
37. Ibid.
38. Glassie, *Pattern,* 66. The two studies Glassie cites as being "the most recent and finest works on English domestic architecture" are M. W. Barley, *The English Farmhouse and Cottage* (London: 1961) and Raymond B. Wood-Jones, *Traditional Domestic Architecture in the Banbury Region* (Manchester: 1963).
39. Kniffen, "Folk Housing," 555.
40. Fred Kniffen, "Louisiana House Types," *Annals of the Association of American Geographers* 26(4) (December 1936): 190. In his later study, "Folk Housing: Key to Diffusion," Kniffen gives a more detailed account of his growing awareness of the importance of the I-house, relating that he first recognized the type in 1930 in Indiana as constituting a link with the Middle Atlantic source area. Besides its significance in Louisiana, which was recognized in the middle thirties, "a generally like structure showed up in North Carolina . . . and suggestively similar houses appeared throughout the Upland South and its extension north of the Ohio River and abundantly and old in the Middle Atlantic states and the northern Tidewater South." Kniffen, "Folk Housing," 555.
41. Michael Southern, "The I-House as a Carrier of Style in Three Counties of the Northeastern Piedmont," in Doug Swaim, ed., *Carolina Dwelling,* 71.
42. Ibid.
43. Several recent regional studies have described I-houses typical of a given region. A few of these sources are Bastian, 123; William Montell and Lynn Morse, *Kentucky Folk Architecture* (Lexington: University Press of Kentucky, 1976), 31–40; Tebbetts, 46. See also my book, *Alleghany Architecture: A Pictorial Survey* (Sparta, N.C.: Alleghany County Historic Properties Commission, 1984).

44. Bastian, 121.

45. Southern, 71. In illustrating I-house floor plans, Richard Pillsbury differentiates between "pre-classical" and "classical" versions. See Richard Pillsbury, "Patterns in the Folk and Vernacular House Forms of the Pennsylvania Culture Region," *Pioneer America* 9 (July 1977): 17.

46. Swaim, 38–39.

47. Southern, 70–83. Studies of high style architecture in various locales will sometimes group I-houses in high style categories based upon their architectural details and ornamentation. Kniffen, for example, notes I-houses grouped as Greek Revival houses in W. D. Peat's *Indiana Houses of the Nineteenth Century* (Indianapolis: Indiana Historical Society, 1962). Margaret Keyes features I-houses "with Italianate Characteristics Applied to a Basic Rectangular Form" in figs. 38 to 42 in her book, *Nineteenth-Century Home Architecture of Iowa City* (Iowa City: University of Iowa Press, 1966).

48. Tebbetts, 49.

49. Brown, 8–19.

50. Swaim, 38.

51. Glassie, *Middle Virginia*, 171.

52. Ibid., 170.

53. In Arkansas sometimes the term "central hall cottage" may refer to a one-story, two-room-deep (double pile) plan, also called a "half-Georgian plan" by Glassie, Swaim, and others. This central hall cottage with a two-room-deep plan is associated in Arkansas with Greek Revival–influenced houses in central and southern Arkansas. Several are located in Old Washington in Hempstead County. It is not a common type in Arkansas, however; the two-room-deep central hall house is cited as a prosperous farm dwelling in the Deep South, comparable (according to Henry Glassie) to the I-house as a prosperous rural dwelling in the Upland South and the Midwest. (See Glassie, *Pattern*, 109.)

54. John J. G. Blumenson, *Identifying American Architecture: A Pictorial Guide to Style and Terms, 1600–1945* (Nashville: American Association for State and Local History, 1977), 26–27.

55. Bastian, 123.

56. Howard Wight Marshall cites four other terms for this house type, which he calls the "T" house: upright and wing house, temple form house, cross-wing house, and "L" house. See Marshall, 123. The term "T" or "L" house, although a common one, is not used here because it describes more than one type of house. For example, I-houses can have both "T" and "L" shaped plans.

57. Dell Upton specifically disavows the bent house's connections with Greek Revival and other neoclassical houses with large gable-end blocks and smaller side wings. This disavowal includes the house Pierce Lewis calls the "upright-and-wing house," and, by implication, Henry Glassie's "temple form house" cited in the note above. Upton argues that the bent house and the neoclassical houses are not directly related: "Pierce Lewis has seen these buildings as part of a tradition that he calls 'upright and wing' houses and that stretches back to the early nineteenth century. This would connect the bent houses with Greek Revival and other neoclassical houses with a large gable-end block and smaller side wings. Despite the superficial resemblance, I argue that the two are significantly different. In the bent houses, the principal spaces were distributed throughout both wings, which were normally given approximately equal visual weight. Bent houses cloaked integrated spaces behind a single overall image. The upright-and-wing house was originally a way of joining secondary spaces to a main block while preserving the temple image of the large block. The latter was clearly dominant and it usually contained all the principal rooms. I am suggesting, therefore, that the Gothic and Italianate

houses of the 1840s and 1850s were probably more significant for subsequent American domestic vernacular architecture than the neoclassical ones of 1800–1850." See Dell Upton, "Pattern Books and Professionalism: Aspects of Domestic Architecture in America, 1800–1860," *Winterthur Portfolio* 19(2–3) (Summer–Fall 1984): 145.

58. William H. Pierson, Jr., *American Buildings and Their Architects: Technology and the Picturesque* (Garden City, N.Y.: Doubleday and Company, 1978), 307.

59. Ibid.

60. Ibid.

61. Ibid.

62. Upton, 144.

63. Ibid.

64. Ibid., 141.

65. Ibid., 149.

66. Ibid., 142.

67. Ibid., 144.

68. Amos J. Bicknell and William T. Comstock, *Modern Architectural Designs and Details* (New York, 1881) Plates 50, 52.

69. Lewis, 109.

Notes to Chapter 5

1. B. J. Wilhelm, Jr., "Folk Settlement in the Blue Ridge Mountains," *Keystone Folklore Quarterly* 12–13 (1967–68): 163.

2. Wright, 91.

3. I am indebted to Jimmy Driftwood of Timbo (in Stone County) for a detailed discussion of the use of and the importance of smokehouses. Pork was the Ozarker's staple meat; beef was rarely eaten. Chicken (either fried or in chicken and dumplings) was served usually on Sundays only. Hog killing time took place in November, but if one had an especially large family, butchering might be done a second time in February. (Interview with Jimmy Driftwood, Timbo, Arkansas, May 1985.)

4. Ruth Holt Payne, "Memorabilia of Early Mills," *Flashback* (February 1963): 11.

5. Kniffen, "Folk Housing," 564.

6. Henry Glassie, "Barns Across Southern England: A Note on Transatlantic Comparison and Architectural Meanings," *Pioneer America* 7 (1975): 14.

7. Perhaps because of the complications of preserving fresh fruit, most people in the Ozarks used dried fruit rather than fresh fruit. Indeed, in all parts of Arkansas, older residents recall drying both peaches and apples (in slices or in quarters) in trays on the roofs of their houses. Drying fruit on one's roof required several days of sunshine, rather than the twenty-four hours needed for the specially constructed apple dryer.

8. Interview with Mrs. Novelle Baumert, Pleasant Grove, Arkansas, June 15, 1984.

Notes to Chapter 6

1. Douglas Crary, "A Geographer Looks at the Landscape," *Landscape* 9(1) (1959): 23.

2. John B. Jackson, *Discovering the Vernacular Landscape* (New Haven: Yale University Press, 1984), 150.

3. Ibid., 15.

4. Ibid., 151.
5. Sauer, 8–26.
6. Ibid., 41.
7. Ibid., 45.
8. Miller, 69–70.
9. Sauer, 177.
10. Miller, 70.
11. This predilection for building isolated homesteads was not characteristic of the French, who were the earliest settlers on the northern border of the Missouri Ozarks along the Mississippi River. St. Genevieve was founded around 1731. Except when they were engaged in hunting, trapping, or mining activities, French settlers consistently gravitated toward villages. According to Carl Sauer, "The most likely explanation rests on the social instincts of the French and on the character of their cultivation. They cared a great deal for the social amenities, and could supply these only by living together in villages. Moreover, the French produced the food needed to supply their small wants from garden patches, which did not necessitate the detached farms on which the Americans, producers of extensive crops, lived." Sauer, 91. The villages were regularly laid out in squares with the houses standing toward the streets, and the interior of the area was composed of gardens and orchards.
12. Maxfield, 163–70.
13. Maxfield, 168.
14. John Mason Peck, *A Guide for Emigrants, Containing Sketches of Illinois, Missouri and the Adjacent Parts* (Boston: Lincoln and Edmonds, 1831; reprint, New York: Arno Press, Inc., 1975), 181.
15. Earl Berry, *Pioneer Life and Pioneer Families of the Ozarks* (Cassville, Mo.: Litho Printers, 1980), 17.
16. Miller, 68.
17. Sally Ann McMurry, *Families and Farmhouses in Nineteenth Century America: Vernacular Design and Social Change* (New York: Oxford University Press), 64.
18. The orientation of houses varies, of course, from culture to culture. The orientation may be based on symbolism, or on a rational orientation to climatic conditions, or, as in the case of much modern domestic architecture, on an aesthetic orientation as the house relates to its site. Several studies of American vernacular architecture have concluded that it is a commonplace that nineteenth-century houses are of this social orientation, i.e., they face the road. However, eighteenth-century houses are more likely to be related to the cardinal points in an orientation to climate. In my study of Iowa farmhouses, extensive literature about wise construction of farmhouses was found to be directed at Iowa farmers, and this advice always urged siting the dwelling in relation to the prevailing winds. Perhaps this is another point that only further study can clarify, but at this stage of research, no farm literature aimed at Ozark farmers was found to have been circulated in the study area. Glassie, *Middle Virginia,* 121; Jean Sizemore, "The Iowa Farmhouse (1857–1950): A Literature Survey," Preliminary Structure Report Prepared for the Iowa State Historical Department, Division of Historic Preservation, Iowa City, 1979, 51.
19. Jackson, *Vernacular Landscape,* 151.
20. An interesting chronology of American wood fences is given by John Fraser Hart and Eugene Cotton Mather in "The American Fence." The angled rail fence (known as "snake" or "worm" or "zig-zag" fence) was the dominant type until the late nineteenth century in most parts of the country. Its disadvantages were that it consumed much timber to build and removed from cultivation a strip of land about ten-feet wide. As timber

resources became depleted, it was replaced by the straight-rail type, sometimes called "post and rail." Barbed-wire fence, which was invented in 1873, and the somewhat later woven wire fences replaced all the previous types. John Fraser Hart and Eugene Cotton Mather, "The American Fence," *Landscape* 6 (Spring 1957): 4–9.

21. The stone fences scattered throughout the Ozarks are picturesque remnants of the traditional landscape. (These are discussed in chapter 7.) Sometimes they are rather roughly and unevenly piled up, but sometimes they exhibit more careful craftsmanship. They seem to be rather unpredictable in layout, sometimes fencing off a steep drop-off, sometimes fencing an entire pasture, and sometimes fencing just portions of a pasture. Wilbur Zelinsky theorizes that stone fences, in whatever region of the country in which they were built, appeared only later, after people had tossed rocks in heaps along the edges of fields in the process of farming. The very first fences were brush, stump, or rail. Wilbur Zelinsky, "Walls and Fences," *Landscape* 8 (Spring 1959): 31.

22. Jackson, *Vernacular Landscape,* 44.

23. Ibid., 47.

24. W. A. Browne, 184.

25. David Lowenthal, "The American Scene," *The Geographical Review* 58 (1968): 62.

26. Reyner Banham, "Urbanism: USA," *Architectural Review* 130 (1964): 305.

27. Lowenthal, 69.

Notes to Chapter 7

1. Paul E. Sprague, "The Origin of Balloon Framing," *Journal of the Society of Architectural Historians* 40(4) (December 1981): 311–19. There has been much interest in the balloon frame's origin since Siegfried Gideon identified its inventor as George Snow of Chicago in the building of St. Mary's Church there in 1833. Gideon published this finding in his well-known book, *Space, Time, and Architecture* (Cambridge, Mass.: Harvard University Press, 1941), 281–88. A short time later, Walker Field corrected Gideon's assertion, citing instead a carpenter named Augustine Taylor, who also helped build St. Mary's Church. Most recently, Paul E. Sprague has verified that the inventor was indeed George Snow, but that the correct date is 1832 and the correct site a warehouse in Chicago, and not St. Mary's Church. (See Walker Field, "A Re-examination into the Invention of the Balloon Frame," *Journal of Society of Architectural Historians* 2 [1942]: 3–29. And Paul E. Sprague, 311–19.) By far the most comprehensive discussion of the history and technology of ballon frame construction is in the recent book by Fred W. Peterson, *Homes in the Heartland: Balloon Frame Farmhouses of the Upper Midwest* (Lawrence: University Press of Kansas, 1992), which was published too late for me to draw upon in this study.

2. Leland Roth, ed., *America Builds: Source Documents in American Architecture and Planning* (New York: Harper & Row, 1983), 53.

3. The full titles and dates for these two books are: Gervase Wheeler, *Homes for the People in Suburb and Country; the Villa, the Mansion and the Cottage, Adapted to American Climate and Wants* (New York: 1855), 1–2. And William E. Bell, *Carpentry Made Easy; or, The Science and Art of Framing on a New and Improved System with Specific Instructions for Building Balloon Frames* (Philadelphia: 1858), Plate 6.

4. Marshall, 93.

5. The most comprehensive study of log construction of a particular locale is Terry Jordan, *Texas Log Buildings,* 108. Two other good regional studies are: Zelinsky, "The

Log House in Georgia," and Sarah Brown, "Log Buildings in Southwest Arkansas," Department of American Studies, George Washington, 1986. Three classic studies are: Fred Kniffen and Henry Glassie, "Building in Wood in the Eastern United States: A Time-Place Perspective" in Upton and Vlach's *Common Places,* 159–81; Henry Glassie, "Southern Mountain Cabin"; Fred Kniffen, "On Corner Timbering," *Pioneer America* 1(1) (January 1969): 1–8. A broad new study is Terry Jordan, *American Log Buildings: An Old World Tradition* (Chapel Hill and London: University of North Carolina Press, 1985). For an extensive bibliography of sources dealing with log construction, see Jordan, *Texas Log Buildings,* 212–14.

6. Warren E. Roberts, "The Tools Used in Building Log Houses in Indiana," in Dell Upton and John Michael Vlach, eds., *Common Places: Readings in American Vernacular Architecture* (Athens and London: University of Georgia Press, 1986), 182–203.

7. According to Terry Jordan, these areas were "Finland, most of European Russia, Poland, Czechoslovakia, the Alpine Lands, the Black Forest of Germany, the mountainous spine of Yugoslavia, and the Carpathians," Jordan, *Texas Log Buildings,* 21.

8. Again, Jordan is specific about which areas of Germany were the source areas for log construction. Pointing out that the group which brought this log working technique was erroneously called "Pennsylvania Dutch" (a corruption of Deutsche, or German) he states, "By no means were all the Pennsylvania Germans familiar with log construction in their European homeland. In fact, the largest contingent came from Rhenish Germany, particularly the Palatinate, where log buildings were unknown. But some others came from Canton Bern in Switzerland, from the Black Forest of Wurttemberg, from the German-inhabited western and northern hill fringe of present Czechoslovakia, and from adjacent portions of Silesia and Saxony—in every case, districts where log construction was known." Jordan, *Texas Log Buildings,* 24.

9. Terry Jordan, in his newest book, *American Log Buildings,* retreats from his earlier position which was part of the consensus that American log construction stemmed from the Pennsylvania Germans. Jordan gives the credit to the Scandinavians, in particular the Finns. Jordan, *American Log Buildings,* 146–51.

10. Jordan, *Texas Log Buildings,* 24.

11. Richard Pillsbury and Andrew Kardos, *A Field Guide to the Folk Architecture of the Northeastern United States,* Geography Publications at Dartmouth, ed. Robert E. Huke and John W. Sommer, no. 8 (Hanover, N.H.: Dartmouth College, 1970), 47.

12. Kniffen and Glassie, 173.

13. Jordan, *Texas Log Buildings,* 15, 49–81.

14. Kniffen and Glassie, 58.

15. Jordan, *Texas Log Buildings,* 36.

16. In the county adjacent to Stone County on the east, Independence County, Diane Tebbetts found the half-dovetail notch prevalent only in the township that had been settled longest. Elsewhere in the county, the square notch dominated. Tebbetts, 42.

17. Kniffen and Glassie, 176.

18. Jordan, *Texas Log Buildings,* 65.

19. Roberts, 182–203.

20. Paul Faris, *Ozark Log Cabin Folks: The Way They Were* (Little Rock: Rose Publishing Co., 1983), 83–84. Parson Wilson's log cabin had a rear shed room which was attached at the time of the original construction. In 1918 two more rooms were added on laterally to help accommodate many children. The house was never covered with weatherboard.

21. Ibid., 87, 90.

22. Zelinsky, 180.
23. Interview with Jimmie Ford, St. James vicinity, Stone County, Arkansas, December 1986.
24. Arkansas Historic Preservation Program, "Historic Resources of Stone County, Arkansas," Nomination to the National Register of Historic Places (Little Rock: 1985), 3–4, 7–8.
25. Faris, 79–91.
26. Ibid., 50.
27. Mr. John Callahan of Turkey Creek in Stone County told of having built a one-room log house (sixteen feet by eighteen feet) for his bride and himself in the early 1930s with "a good old-fashioned house-raising" to erect it. He later tore down the house and recycled the logs in other uses. (Interview with John Callahan, Turkey Creek, Arkansas, March 1, 1983.)
28. Tebbetts, 43. In the study area, balloon frame houses always have exteriors of horizontal weatherboard; therefore, a board-and-batten exterior is a good sign one should look closely for evidence of box construction.
29. John B. Jackson, "The Movable Dwelling," in *Discovering the Vernacular Landscape* (New Haven and London: Yale University Press, 1984), 99. Besides being small and economical to build, box houses were cold. According to Remmel Lawson, of Drake's Creek in Madison County, the box house in which he grew up was so cold that in the winter "my mom would put eggs in the middle of the bed in a quilt and even then they'd freeze sometimes." (Interview with Remmel Lawson, Drake's Creek, Arkansas, July 1984.)
30. Ibid., 99.
31. Ibid., 98.
32. Ibid., 99.
33. The description of braced frame construction was taken from Carl Condit's *American Building: Materials and Techniques from the First Colonial Settlements to the Present* (Chicago: University of Chicago Press, 1968), 6–8. Dell Upton provides a comprehensive view of the various regional characteristics of timber construction in an article entitled "Traditional Timber Framing," in *Material Culture of the Wooden Age*, ed. Brooke Hindle (Tarrytown, N.Y.: Sleepy Hollow Press, Sleepy Hollow Restorations, Inc. 1981), 35–93.
34. Besom, 16. In this excellent article Besom describes the brickmaking method that was universally practiced until the introduction of machine-made bricks in the latter third of the nineteenth century. In this method the clay was placed into molds by hand, allowed to dry on a pallet, and then burned in clamps, which were green bricks carefully arranged to form their own kiln. With coal or wood as the heat source, the clamps were plastered over with mud and fired for weeks. Besom, 13–14.
35. Ibid., 17.
36. Ibid., 22.
37. Glassie, *Pattern,* 100.
38. Works Progress Administration, *Arkansas: A Guide to the State* (New York: Hastings House Publishers, 1941), 142.
39. A well-known guidebook to architectural styles cites the popular dates for the Greek Revival as being from 1820 to 1860; however, many architectural historians believe the style was outmoded by 1845 in eastern urban areas. Blumenson, 26–27.

Notes to Chapter 8

1. Jean E. Hess, "Domestic Interiors in Northern New Mexico," *Heresies* (Spring 1981): 30.

2. John B. Jackson, "Essential Architecture," *Landscape* (Spring 1961): 27.

3. Interview with Mrs. Novelle Blair Baumert, Pleasant Grove, Arkansas, June 5 and 6, 1985 and June 18, 1986. Interview with Rollans Wilson, Prairie Grove, Arkansas, August 10, 1987. Interview with Caswell Wilson, Prairie Grove, Arkansas, August 11 and December 12, 1987.

4. Interview with Jimmy and Cleda Driftwood, Timbo, Arkansas, June 12, 1987, November 25, 1990.

5. Jetton, 7.

6. Interview with Jimmy Ford, St. James vicinity, Stone County, Arkansas, December 1986.

7. Faris, 27.

8. "Aunt Mahala Rainey Recalls Her Girlhood in the Fifties," *Arkansas Gazette,* March 20, 1938, 11.

9. Bonita Musgrave, "A Study of the Home and Local Crafts of the Pioneers of Washington County, Arkansas" (Master's thesis, Arkansas State Teachers' College, 1929), 27.

10. Ibid., 38.

11. Ibid., 30.

12. The progress report of the Rural Electrification Program published in 1945 states, ". . . Rural electrification in Arkansas was not emphasized prior to 1935 . . . With the advent of rural electrification co-operatives in this state in 1937 and with the design of new, low-cost line materials and methods, added impetus was created in 1937." Based on a county-by-county comparison published in this same report, we learn that Stone County prior to 1945 had only 24 miles of electrical line in the county, and this was along the main highways only. The projected total for 1946 was a total of 117 miles of line. Newton County, a mountainous county comparable to Stone County in population and topography, had 137 miles of line by 1945, with a projected total of 190 miles of line by 1946. Interestingly, Washington County is once again surprisingly progressive. Prior to 1945 there were 587 miles of electrical line in Washington County, slightly more than Pulaski County's total of 578 by the end of 1946. Washington County was projected to have a total of 1,109 miles of line, the most of any county in the state, by the end of 1946. Arkansas Public Service Commission, *Rural Electrification Progress Report,* Table II: "Miles of Pole Line Constructed," (Little Rock: 1945), 4.

13. Home Demonstration agents from the Extension Service in Agriculture and Home Economics had been active in rural areas in Arkansas since 1920. They gave demonstrations on gardening, cooking, canning, laundry, home conveniences, and kitchen arrangement. Without the conveniences, it is doubtful that much kitchen rearrangement took place in the study area. *Annual Report of Extension Service in Agriculture and Home Economics in Arkansas for 1920* (Little Rock: 1920), 5.

Notes to Chapter 9

1. Sauer, 6.

2. Bastian, 116.

3. Rapoport, 5–6.
4. Kenneth L. Ames, "Meaning in Artifacts: Hall Furnishings in Victorian America," in *Common Places: Readings in American Vernacular Architecture,* Dell Upton and John Michael Vlach, eds. (Athens and London: University of Georgia Press, 1986), 244, 255.
5. Southern, 71.
6. Upton, 149.
7. Ibid., 141.
8. Ibid., 142.
9. W. A. Browne, 184.
10. Blumenson, 19.
11. William H. Pierson, Jr., *American Buildings and Their Architects: The Colonial and Neo-Classical Styles* (Garden City, N.Y.: Anchor Press, Doubleday and Company, 1976), 210, 214.
12. Lowenthal, 62.

Selected Bibliography

Articles

Besom, Robert D. "The Golden Age of Brick in Washington County." *Flashback* (August 1981): 10–16.

Brown, C. Allen. "The Benjamin F. Johnson Residence, Middle Fork Valley." *Flashback* (November 1980): 8–19.

Brown, Sarah. "Folk Architecture in Arkansas." In *An Arkansas Folklore Sourcebook*, W. K. McNeil and William Clements, eds. Fayetteville: University of Arkansas Press, 1992.

Browne, W. A. "Some Frontier Conditions in the Hilly Portions of the Ozarks." *Journal of Geography* 28(5) (May 1929): 184–88.

Dew, Lee A. "The Negative Image of Arkansas in the Early Twentieth Century." *Arkansas Historical Quarterly* 39 (Summer 1980): 125–35.

Doolin, James. "Conditions of Slavery in Washington County." *Flashback* (February 1980): 5–8, 30–35.

"Early Store Ledgers in Washington County." *Flashback* (August 1957): 5–9.

Glassie, Henry. "The Appalachian Log Cabin." *Mountain Life and Work* 39(4) (Winter 1963): 12.

____. "The Types of the Southern Mountain Cabin." In *The Study of American Folklore: An Introduction*, Jan Harold Brunvand, ed., 391–420. New York: W. W. Norton and Co., 1978.

Jackson, John Brinckerhoff. "Essential Architecture." *Landscape* 10(30) (Spring 1961): 27–30.

Jetton, Clarence. "Twelve Years on Cajun Creek." *Heritage of Stone* 10(1) (Summer 1986): 1–38.

Jordan, Terry G. "Alpine, Alemannic and American Log Architecture." *Annals of the Association of American Geographers* 70 (June 1980): 154–80.

Karnes, Bernice. "Early Days at West Fork." *Flashback* (November 1956): 10–15.

Kniffen, Fred B. "Folk Housing: Key to Diffusion." *Annals of the Association of American Geographers* 55 (December 1965): 549–77.

Kniffen, Fred B., and Henry Glassie. "Building in Wood in the Eastern United States: A Time-Place Perspective." *The Geographical Review* 56 (1966): 38–66.

Kocher, Stacey. "The Kochers' Wheat Threshing." *Heritage of Stone* 9(2) (1985): 12–13.

Lemke, W. J. "Early Tax Records of Washington County." *Flashback* (September 1962): 3–7.

Lowenthal, David. "The American Scene." *The Geographical Review* 58(5) (1968): 61–88.

Luther, Sandra. "A Brief History of Stone County." *Heritage of Stone* 1(1) (June 1972): 3–19.

Lynch, Bobbie Byars. "Early Mills of Washington County." *Flashback* (February 1975): 1–5.

Massey, Melissa Loy. "History of School District No. 54." *Heritage of Stone* 1(54) (June 1972): 24.

Miller, E. Joan Wilson. "The Ozark Region as Revealed by Traditional Materials." *Annals of the Association of American Geographers* 58 (March 1968): 51–71.

Moffatt, Walter. "Transportation in Arkansas, 1819–1840." *Arkansas Historical Quarterly* 15 (Autumn 1956): 180–97.

Otto, John Solomon. "Slavery in the Mountains." *Arkansas Historical Quarterly* 39 (1980): 35–52.

Otto, John Solomon, and Ben Wayne Banks. "The Banks Family of Yell County, Arkansas: A 'Plain Folk' Family of the Highlands South." *Arkansas Historical Quarterly* 41 (Summer 1982): 146–67.

Otto, John Solomon, and Augustus M. Burns III. "Traditional Agricultural Practices in the Arkansas Highlands." *Journal of American Folklore* 94 (372) (1981): 166–87.

Payne, Ruth Holt. "Living Off the Land." *Flashback* (November 1975): 12–20.

____. "Memorabilia of Early Mills." *Flashback* (February 1963): 11.

Pitcaithley, Dwight. "Settlement of the Arkansas Ozarks: The Buffalo River Valley." *Arkansas Historical Quarterly* 37 (Autumn 1978): 203–22.

Russell, Conrad Q. "Lincoln's Apple Heritage." *Flashback* (February 1979): 24–28.

Southern, Michael. "The I-House as a Carrier of Style in Three Counties of the Northeastern Piedmont." In Doug Swaim, ed., *Carolina Dwelling: Toward Preservation of Place; In Celebration of the Vernacular Landscape* Student Publication of the School of Design, vol. 26. Raleigh: North Carolina State University, 1978.

Sprague, Paul E. "The Origin of Balloon Framing." *Journal of the Society of Architectural Historians* 40(4) (December 1981): 311–19.

Swaim, Doug. "North Carolina Folk Housing." In Doug Swaim, ed., *Carolina Dwelling: Toward Preservation of Place; In Celebration of the Vernacular Landscape.* Student Publication of the School of Design, vol. 26. Raleigh: North Carolina State University, 1978.

Tebbetts, Diane. "Traditional Houses of Independence County, Arkansas." *Pioneer America* 10 (June 1978): 37–55.

Upton, Dell. "Pattern Books and Professionalism: Aspects of the Transformation of Domestic Architecture in America 1800–1860." *Winterthur Portfolio* 19 (Summer–Fall 1984): 107–50.

Walz, Robert Bradshaw. "Migration Into Arkansas 1820–1880: Incentives and Means of Travel." *Arkansas Historical Quarterly* 17 (Winter 1958): 310–24.

Williams, Verna. "Early History of Herpel." *Heritage of Stone* 1(2) (1983): 2.

Books

Ashmore, Harry. *Arkansas: A Bicentennial History.* New York: W. W. Norton and Co., 1978.

Berry, Earl. *Pioneer Life and Pioneer Families of the Ozarks.* Cassville, Mo.: Litho Printers, 1980.

Brown, Kent R. *Fayetteville: A Pictorial History*. Norfork and Virginia Beach: Donning Company Publishers, 1982.

Campbell, William S. *One Hundred Years of Fayetteville,* 1828–1928. Jefferson City, Mo., 1928.

Condit, Carl W. *American Building: Materials and Techniques from the First Colonial Settlements to the Present*. Chicago: University of Chicago Press, 1968.

DuVall, Leland. *Arkansas: Colony and State*. Little Rock: Rose Publishing Co., 1973.

Faris, Paul. *Ozark Log Cabin Folks: The Way They Were*. Little Rock: Rose Publishing Co., 1983.

Glassie, Henry. *Folk Housing in Middle Virginia: A Structural Analysis of Historic Artifacts*. Knoxville: University of Tennessee Press, 1975.

____. *Pattern in the Material Folk Culture of the Eastern United States*. Philadelphia: University of Pennsylvania Press, 1968.

Goodspeed's History of Benton, Washington, Carroll, Madison, Crawford, Franklin and Sebastian Counties Arkansas. Chicago: Goodspeed Publishing Co., 1889.

Herndon, Dallas T., ed. *Annals of Arkansas*, 4 vols. Hopkinsville, Ky., and Little Rock, Ark.: Historical Record Association, 1947.

____. *Centennial History of Arkansas*, 3 vols. Chicago: S. J. Clarke Publishing Co., 1922.

Jackson, John Brinckerhoff. *Discovering the Vernacular Landscape*. New Haven and London: Yale University Press, 1984.

Jordan, Terry G. *American Log Buildings: An Old World Tradition*. Chapel Hill and London: University of North Carolina Press, 1985.

____. *Texas Log Buildings: A Folk Architecture*. Austin: University of Texas Press, 1978.

Lemke, W. J., and Ted R. Worley. *The Butterfield Overland Mail in Arkansas*. Little Rock: Arkansas History Commission, 1957.

____. *Historic Washington County, Arkansas*. Fayetteville: Washington County Historical Society, n.d.

____. *The William Wilson Records*. Fayetteville: Washington County Historical Society, 1960.

Marshall, Howard Wight. *Folk Architecture in Little Dixie: A Regional Culture in Missouri*. Columbia and London: University of Missouri Press, 1981.

McMurray, Sally Ann. *Families and Farmhouses in Nineteenth Century America: Vernacular Design and Social Change*. New York: Oxford University Press, 1988.

McNeil, W. K., and William K. Clements, eds. *An Arkansas Folklore Sourcebook*. Fayetteville: University of Arkansas Press, 1992.

Noble, Allen G. *Wood, Brick and Stone: The North American Settlement Landscape*. Vol. 1, Houses. Amherst: University of Massachusetts Press, 1984.

Page, Tate C. *Voices of Moccasin Creek*. Point Lookout, Mo.: School of the Ozarks Press, 1972.

Peck, J. M. *A Guide for Emigrants, Containing Sketches of Illinois, Missouri and the Adjacent Parts*. Boston: Lincoln and Edmonds, 1831; reprint, New York: Arno Press, 1975.

Pierson, William H., Jr. *American Buildings and Their Architects: The Colonial and Neo-Classical Styles*. Garden City, N.Y.: Anchor Press, Doubleday and Company, 1976.

____. *American Buildings and Their Architects: Technology and the Picturesque*. Garden City, N.Y.: Anchor Press, Doubleday and Company, 1978.

Rafferty, Milton. *The Ozarks: Land and Life*. Norman: University of Oklahoma Press, 1980.

Rapoport, Amos. *House Form and Culture*. Foundations of Cultural Geography Series. Englewood Cliffs, N.J.: Prentice Hall, 1969.

Rhea, Rev. J. H. *Thirty Years in Arkansaw*. Cedar Rapids, Iowa: Republican Printing Co., 1896.
Rohrbaugh, Malcolm. *The Trans-Appalachian Frontier: People, Societies and Institutions, 1775–1850*. New York: Oxford University Press, 1978.
Sauer, Carl O. *The Geography of the Ozark Highland of Missouri*. Chicago: University of Chicago Press, 1920; reprint, New York: AMS Press, 1971.
Shiloh Museum. *History of Washington County, Arkansas*. Springdale, Ark.: Shiloh Museum, 1989.
Shinn, Josiah H. *Pioneers and Makers of Arkansas*. Baltimore: Genealogical Publishing Co., 1967.
Sizemore, Jean. *Alleghany Architecture: A Pictorial Survey*. Sparta, North Carolina: Alleghany County Historic Properties Commission, 1984.
Skelton, G. V. *Atlas of Washington County, Arkansas, Compiled from Official Records, Personal Surveys*. Fayetteville, 1894.
Stockard, W. *The History of Lawrence, Jackson, Independence, and Stone Counties Arkansas: Counties of the Third Judicial District*. Little Rock: Arkansas Democrat Co., 1904.
Stroud, Hubert B., and Gerald T. Hanson. *Arkansas Geography: The Physical Landscape and the Historical-Cultural Setting*. Little Rock: Rose Publishing Co., 1981.
Swaim, Doug, ed. *Carolina Dwelling: Toward Preservation of Place; In Celebration of the Vernacular Landscape*. Student Publication of the School of Design, vol. 26. Raleigh: North Carolina State University, 1978.
Tucker, David M. *Arkansas: A People and Their Reputation*. Memphis: Memphis State University Press, 1985.
Upton, Dell, and John Michael Vlach. *Common Places: Readings in American Vernacular Architecture*. Athens and London: University of Georgia Press, 1986.
Williams, C. Fred, S. Charles Bolton, Carl H. Moneyhon, and LeRoy T. Williams, eds. *A Documentary History of Arkansas*. Fayetteville: University of Arkansas Press, 1984.
Works Progress Administration. *Arkansas: A Guide to the State*. New York: Hastings House Publishers, 1941.

Unpublished Manuscripts

Arkansas History Commission, Little Rock, Arkansas. Works Progress Administration Collection for Stone County.
____. Works Progress Administration Collection for Washington County.
Arkansas Historic Preservation Program. "Historic Resources of Stone County, Arkansas." Multiple Resource Nomination to the National Register of Historic Places. Little Rock: 1985.
Courtney, Stephen. "The McGarrah-Reed House." School of Architecture paper, University of Arkansas, Fayetteville, 1976.
Maxfield, O. O. "The Geography of the Boston Mountains." Ph.D. diss., Ohio State University, 1963.
Mitchell, Steve, Donald Brown, and Michael Swanda. "Board Shanty: Box Construction in White County, Arkansas." Little Rock: Arkansas Historic Preservation Program, 1986.

Musgrave, Bonita. "A Study of the Home and Local Crafts of the Pioneers of Washington County, Arkansas." M.S. thesis, Arkansas State Teachers College, 1929.

Pilcher, Bruce Francis. "The Settlement Geography of Prairie Township, Washington County, Arkansas." M.A. thesis, University of Arkansas, Fayetteville, 1975.

Schiefer, Carl L., Jr. "Washington County, Arkansas: A Geography of Population Change 1840–1970." M.A. thesis, University of Arkansas, Fayetteville, 1976.

Schmidt, James. "The Antiquities of Route 74." School of Architecture paper, University of Arkansas, Fayetteville, 1976.

Sizemore, Jean. "The Iowa Farmhouse (1857–1950): A Literature Survey." Iowa State Historical Department, Division of Historic Preservation, 1979.

Stahle, David William. "Tree Ring Dating of Selected Arkansas Log Buildings," M.A. thesis, University of Arkansas, Fayetteville, 1978.

Walz, Robert B. "Migration Into Arkansas, 1834–1880." Ph.D. diss., University of Texas, 1958.

Other Materials

Annual Report of Extension Service in Agriculture and Home Economics in Arkansas for 1920. Little Rock: 1920.

Arkansas Public Service Commission. *Rural Electrification Progress Report*. Little Rock: 1945.

Atlas of Washington County, Arkansas. Fayetteville, Arkansas: 1894.

Plat Book of Washington County. Fayetteville, Arkansas.

United States Bureau of Census. *Thirteenth Census of the United States*. Vol. 2, *Population 1910*. "Table of Composition and Characteristics of Population for States and for Counties, Arkansas, Table I." Washington, D.C.: U. S. Government Printing Office, 1913: 118–31.

____. *Eighteenth Census of Population*. Vol. 1, "Characteristics of Population" Part V: Arkansas. Washington, D.C.: U. S. Government Printing Office, 1960: 214–19.

Index